i

MARS ON TRIAL

José PorrúaTuranzas, S.A.

EDICIONES

Director General:
JOSÉ PORRÚA VENERO

Sub-Director General:
ENRIQUE PORRÚA VENERO

Director:
CONSTANTINO GARCÍA GARVÍA

Executive Director: American Division: BRUNO M. DAMIANI

stuóia humanitatis

DIRECTED BY

BRUNO M. DAMIANI

The Catholic University of America

ADVISORY BOARD

MARS ON TRIAL

War as Seen
by French Writers of the
Twentieth Century

BY
CHESTER W. OBUCHOWSKI

studia humanitatis

PUBLISHER, PRINTER AND DISTRIBUTOR
José Porrúa Turanzas, S. A.
Cea Bermúdez, 10 - Madrid-3
España

Dep. legal M. 38.935.-1978

I. S. B. N. 84-7317-077-6

IMPRESO EN ESPAÑA
PRINTED IN SPAIN

Ediciones José Porrúa Turanzas, S. A.
Cea Bermúdez, 10 - Madrid-3

TALLERES GRÁFICOS PORRÚA, S. A.
JOSÉ, 10 - MADRID-29

This book is dedicated
to the memory of
my parents,
CASIMIR AND STEFANIA OBUCHOWSKI

TABLE OF CONTENTS

PAGE

ACKNOWLEDGEMENTS   XI

PREFACE   XIII

CHAPTER I

THE IMPACT OF WAR ON EIGHT FRENCH
WRITERS   1

Introductory Note   1
Aesthete in Wartime: Marcel Proust   2
Gide Dares to Be Himself   7
The Case of Conscience of Anatole France ...   12
The Grand Illusion of Drieu la Rochelle   18
Apollinaire: War, the Supreme Novelty   22
Jean Giraudoux: The Impressionistic Vision...   26
Montherlant and the Survival of the Fittest...   31
Charles Péguy, Passionate Patriot   36

CHAPTER II

PACIFISM IN THE FRENCH NOVEL BETWEEN
THE WORLD WARS   43

Introduction   43
Alain: War, a Crime of Passion   48
Roland Dorgelès, Short-Term Pacifist   51
Jules Romains, Man of Good Will   52
Romain Rolland above and in the Mêlée   57

The Radical Pacifism of Henri Barbusse 79
*Roger Martin du Gard and the Collapse of
    Socialist Pacifism* 94
Jean Giono, Champion of Peasant Pacifism... 107
André Chamson and Religious Pacifism 117
The Sentimental Pacifism of Georges Duhamel. 127

CHAPTER III

IN OCCUPIED AND LIBERATED FRANCE WITH
JEAN-LOUIS CURTIS 137

CHAPTER IV

THE CONCENTRATIONARY WORLD OF
PIERRE GASCAR 193

CHAPTER V

WINGED WARRIORS 215

Jules Roy and the Exupérian Heritage 215
The Almost Incredible Pierre Clostermann ... 231

CHAPTER VI

FRENCH WRITERS LOOK AT «THE DIRTY
WAR» 247

CHAPTER VII

ALGERIA: THE TORTURED CONSCIENCE... ... 267

SELECTED BIBLIOGRAPHY 297

INDEX 299

ACKNOWLEDGEMENTS

It is a pleasure for me to record my indebtedness and express my profound gratitude to the following:

My wife, Wanda, and my children, Lorraine, Janice, and Edward, who rendered me moral support far beyond the call of familial duty and who were ever fruitful of salutary suggestion. I owe further thanks to Lorraine for her flawless typing of my manuscript.

Professor Henri Peyre, whose intellectual guidance and numerous bibliographical leads were invaluable in the early stages of my research and writing and whose personal inspiration has sustained me at every stage.

Monsieur Michel Mohrt, from whose vast knowledge of French war literature I benefited considerably in the course of a single restaurant breakfast sitting.

Professor Herbert S. Weil, Jr. for the penetrating critique he gave me upon reading three chapters of my manuscript in their original version.

Mr. David Johnson for his aid in procuring books for my use from the Firestone Library of Princeton University.

The Service de Presse et d'Information of the Ambassade de France for kindly supplying me with data related to my research that was unavailable from other sources.

The staff of the Wilbur L. Cross Library of the University of Connecticut for their unfailingly cheerful service.

The University of Connecticut Research Foundation for its generous financial support of this publishing effort.

Professor Richard P. Kinkade for sparking my interest in the STUDIA HUMANITATIS series.

Professor Bruno M. Damiani for handling all the editorial matters leading to the publication of my book with exemplary efficiency and dispatch.

PREFACE

The present work primarily examines the positions assumed by a large body of French writers on the four wars that their nation has fought in our century and on issues related to them. A rather substantial amount of background material on these wars has been included in order to give perspective and relief to their thinking. To a lesser extent it studies the pacifism of six prominent personalities of their number. The period under study began in early August, 1914, with the not very tearful «adieux à la Gare de l'Est,» with high-spirited soldiers backed by a solidly united nation leaving for «the war to end all wars,» convinced that they would get the nasty business over within a fortnight or two. It ended in March 1962 with a lost war in Algeria (even if the French army had not suffered a military defeat), with seditious high-ranking officers being hauled off to prison and with defiant paratroopers of the French Foreign Legion, some of whom had badly compromised their soldierly honor, chanting refrains of Edith Piaf's «Non, je ne regrette rien.» For better than half of those years France was either at war or under enemy occupation. Victory had been won in 1918, but at a terrible cost. The glorious chapters in French histories on the First Battle of the Marne, on Verdun, and on lesser known victories would, before many years went by, be followed by accounts of a second disaster at Sedan, of a swift, crushing defeat, and of two massively frustrating, unpopular wars against guerrilla forces culminating in France's loss of Indochina and Algeria. Add to this all the humiliations and divisions born of enemy occupation and the further discord provoked by the Algerian War. All in all, the period was marked by far more humiliating defeats and retreats than heady victories, by much more exasperation than exhilaration. Manifestly these were years that tried the souls of Frenchmen. It would seem fitting, then, that we see how, for their part, French writers of our age, in and out of uniform, combatant and non-combatant, *engagés* and *non engagés*, professional and other, saw the wars that they lived and some of the issues bound up with them.

Chapters I and II of this book draw heavily on an unpublished thesis by the writer submitted to Yale University in 1950 for the degree of doctor of philosophy. Chapter II also incorporates material from an article by him which appeared in the *Modern Language Quarterly*: September, 1954. In their previous form, chapters IV, VI, and VII appeared, respectively, as articles in the February 1961, May 1967, and October 1968 issues of *The French Review*. Chapter V is essentially made up of material I used for articles published in *The French Review*, December, 1954, and in *Symposium*, Fall, 1956. Chapter III is entirely of recent composition. No part of it has heretofore been submitted for publication.

Unless otherwise indicated, all of the French-to-English translations are my own.

CHAPTER I

THE IMPACT OF WAR ON EIGHT FRENCH WRITERS

Introductory Note

In his aptly titled *Jours sanglants: La guerre de 1914-1918* (1964), Academician Jacques Chastenet reminds us that of the 7,948,000 Frenchmen—20 per cent of the population— mobilized during those years, 16.5 per cent died in uniform; that, furthermore, 27 per cent of the dead were men 18 to 27 years of age, truly the flower of French youth. He lists the total for wounded as 2,800,000, and the cost of material damage at 35,000,000,000 gold francs (1). Is it any wonder, then, that however much the French suffered during the Second World War, it is the First which remains for them «La Grande Guerre»? Surely the *vin de la victoire* they drank on November 11, 1918, must have tasted rather sour.

The best know of the French men of letters to perish in the shipwreck were Alain-Fournier, Guillaume Apollinaire, Jean-Marc Bernard, Guy de Cassagnac, Émile Clermont, Paul Drouot, André Lafon, Charles Muller, Charles Péguy, Louis Pergaud, Ernest Psichari, and Albert Thierry. The present

---

(1) Jacques Chastenet, *Jours sanglants: La guerre de 1914-1918* (Paris: Hachette, 1964), pp. 189-93.

1

chapter will focus on the thoughts on war and reactions to war of eight writers, mainly against the background of World War I. Included among them are two of the casualties of the war, Apollinaire and Péguy, and three authors who saw no service in 1914-18, Anatole France, André Gide, and Marcel Proust. All eight of them provide particularly interesting case histories.

Aesthete in Wartime: Marcel Proust

Marcel Proust (1871-1922), author of the epoch-making *A la recherche du temps perdu,* saw no service in the First World War, having been exempted on account of the asthmatic condition from which he had been suffering since the age of nine. Shaken by the outbreak of hostilities, he suspended work on his great novel. But, realizing that his years were numbered, he soon took up his pen again, stubbornly bent on completing it before death overtook him. To the extent that his health and his punishing work schedule permitted, he attended concerts and dined at such of his old haunts as the Ritz and Ciro's in the company of his aristocratic friends, or entertained them at his Boulevard Haussmann apartment. Commiserating with those of his friends and domestics who were now in the trenches, Proust kept up a steady eastward flow of packages of chocolate and tobacco for them. He carefully followed the progress of the war on a huge map while indulging the passion for military strategy that he had acquired at the age of eighteen, when, in spite of his delicate health and distaste for physical activity, he completed a year of military service with no ill effects and with manifest enjoyment (2). And not for anything would

---

(2) André Maurois points out that Proust «was not exactly a brilliant soldier,» since seventy-three out of the seventy-four men

he have sought shelter while dazzling aerial battles were being fought in the skies above Paris, one of which he watched with rapt attention from a balcony of the Ritz. His artist's conscience was too strict for that: his storehouse could never be overfull. In the early spring of 1918, with the capital under bombardment by «Big Berthas,» naval-type guns of unprecedented range, he would serenely continue work on his novelistic symphony while the rest of the household huddled in the cellar.

Those tragic war years were bound to have severe emotional repercussions on the hypersensitive Proust. Never had he been as lonely; his surgeon brother's war-debilitated condition and constant exposure to danger in the combat zone nagged him; and war was claiming the lives of dear friends —of whom Bertrand de Fénelon was the dearest—as well as of their sons. The «immenses angoisses,» «serrements de coeur,» and «crises d'âme» punctuating his 1914-18 correspondence bespeak a dejection sometimes bordering on despair. Nor was the insensitivity to human suffering of the social aristocrats amongst whom he moved calculated to raise his spirits. His conscience dictated that he should do something about it, and the artist in him recognized in it a rich lode for exploitation. So, the social historian that he had once become in order to portray the deportment of Parisian high society at the time of the Dreyfus Affair again fused with the social satirist that he had never ceased being—this time to bring into view their deportment during the European holocaust. This he did in the book-length chapter, «M. de Charlus pendant la guerre,» of volume I of his *Le Temps retrouvé*. As always, Marcel is the narrator.

of his instructional platoon rated above him. *Proust: Portrait of a Genius*, trans. Gerard Hopkins (New York: Harper & Bros., 1950), p. 40.

The Verdurin salon was now situated in a luxury hotel, because the shortage of coal and electricity had made entertaining at their mansion difficult. The women of Mme. Verdurin's circle now wore cylindrical turbans, Egyptian tunics, brief skirts, leggings, and whatever other accoutrements they thought would please the eyes of the «dear combatants.» They too wished to do their bit for the war effort, so they gave charitable teas at which they played bridge and avidly discussed the latest news from the «front.» Since the hostess was well connected with officials in the government and at supreme army headquarters, she quite naturally fell into the habit of substituting «we» for «France» in disseminating the news to which she was privy. With her drawing room now a veritable message center, it was a simple matter for her to entice her news-hungry sisters to it with the words «Come at five to talk about the war.»—«as,» the novelist adds, «she would have said in other times: 'Come and talk about the [Dreyfus] Affair...'» (3). That was not the case with males, however. Inasmuch as their numbers were steadily dwindling on the Paris social scene, Mme. Verdurin often had to pull strings with high-ranking political and military officials to guarantee the presence of a respectable number of men of distinction at her dinners and *soirées*. Indeed, all was not peaceful these many miles from the front. The capital's *haut monde* was at war also. Social lions and lionesses had to be captured by the rival salons and their loyalty secured. Hence, behind the façade of froth and frivolity, major battles were being waged. And any weapons served—cajolery, flattery, lies, and defamation of character—to mention only some of them. At this sort of warfare Mme. Verdurin was pretty much in a class by herself, but

(3) Marcel Proust, *A la recherche du temps perdu*, in *Oeuvres complètes*, vol. 7 (Paris: NFR, 1932), p. 54.

the stress was showing. Not so much, though, that the news of the sinking of the *Lusitania,* headlined in a newspaper she was reading one fine morning, should have upset her unduly. «How horrible!...That is more horrible than the most frightful stage tragedy,» she exclaimed, while, however, her face mirrored her pleasure at savoring the first *croissant* that she had been able to procure in a long time (4).

Where patriotism is concerned, Proust's sympathies are not on the side of the *député* Bontemps, a *jusqu'auboutiste* who will have no part of peace until the Kaiser is brought before a firing squad and Germany broken up into minuscule states. And certainly they are not with the Baron de Charlus; the German blood which the baron's mother had given him was now somehow causing him to speak like a defeatist, one harboring the secret hope that the Germans would make a very good showing in the war. Rather, Proust's sentiments are patently those of the very blue-blooded Saint-Loup. Although covering himself with glory as a danger-courting infantry officer—he is a Croix de guerre winner—Saint-Loup dwells only on the bravery of others, mainly that of «the lower classes, working men, and small shopkeepers» (5). He would no more call attention to his own heroism than he would wear his love of France on his sleeve. It is in the logic of his attitude that he has no stomach for anything even mildly smelling of an excessive patriotism. Saint-Loup likewise praises the valor of the German soldier, prides himself on the absence of «Boche» from his vocabulary, and makes a point of referring to the Kaiser as «l'Empereur Guillaume.» He deplores the ban on Wagnerian music, hums Schumann airs, and publicly quotes lines from the writings of Romain Rolland and even of Nietzsche. Ultimately, while covering

---

(4) *Ibid.,* p. 107.
(5) *Ibid.,* p. 79.

the retreat of his men, he falls at the hands of the enemy he does not hate. His conduct in the war contrasts sharply with that of Marcel's onetime schoolmate, Bloch. A loud-mouthed superpatriot as long as he is confident that his myopia will disqualify him from active duty, Bloch becomes a coward and a rabid antimilitarist as soon as a medical board declares him fit.

It is easy to imagine how much the Proustian genius recoiled before the turgid nonsense of war propaganda. No-where in Proust's chapter on the 1914-18 years does his satire have a sharper sting than when he concerns himself with it. Proust's Sorbonne professor, Brichot, and the dip-lomat Norpois were now busily dispensing chauvinistic eye-wash to the reading public. Masters in the art of the cliché, they stuff their columns with such gems as «General Winter,» «the die is cast,» «the Beast at bay, reduced to impotence,» and «the dawn of victory.» Naturally, Schiller is made by them to shudder in his grave at what his living compatriots are doing, and we are assured that «the Germans will no longer be able to look Beethoven's statue in the face.» A battle raging at Vauquois takes on an importance that shrinks the dimensions of Thermopylae and of Austerlitz. Accounts of a succession of defeats are made to read so much like those of victories that a skeptical Marcel remarks, «I, however, was startled at the speed with which the scene of these victories was approaching Paris» (6). His servant Françoise also states the case well. Having herself grown skeptical about the fidelity of wartime reporting, she observes, «When the war began, we were told that the Germans were mur-derers, brigands, real bandits, BBBoches» (7).

Whereas Proust mercilessly held up to ridicule the social

_____
(6) *Ibid.*, p. 76.
(7) *Ibid.*, p. 202.

élite of the faubourg Saint-Germain for their continuing pursuit of pleasure during the holocaust, he was not, to be sure, himself innocent of such behavior. Nor did his poor health of itself account for his failure to make himself available, even on a part-time basis, for any work related to the war effort or to the alleviation of human suffering. Rather, it is apparent that Proust, like that other literary giant of his age, Paul Valéry, was of the view that not only is the aesthetic way of life the best one, but that an artist best serves his country in time of war, or at any time, by the production of great art. Hence, Proust left it to others to dedicate themselves to the tasks of war, whether with their hands or with their minds. As he surely saw it, wars would be won or lost, and nations would prosper, decline, or die, but great art, which has no boundaries, would endure forever. Accordingly, it is quite easy to concur with the view of Léon Pierre-Quint that «For Proust...the important dates of the Revolution or the Empire doubtless imply a certain number of historical consequences, but they are of a far lesser significance than the song of a bird or a breeze which inspired Chateaubriand to write some of the pages of his *Mémoires d'outre-tombe*» (8).

Gide Dares to Be Himself

Forty-five in 1914, André Gide was exempted from military duty because of his age and health. Wanting very much to be of aid to his country in its hour of trial, he signed up with the Paris branch of the Red Cross. After a few weeks he resigned, exasperated by the confusion that reigned there and accounting the work of the organization as little more

---

(8) Léon Pierre-Quint, *Marcel Proust, sa vie, son oeuvre*, new ed., rev. and enl. (Paris: Éditions du Sagittaire, 1935), p. 380.

than a duplication of that being done by hospitals. For the next year and a half he immersed himself in volunteer duty at the capital's Foyer Franco-Belge, a center established to assist Belgians fleeing before the invading Germans. Gide comforted the refugees, helped administer the center, presided over committee meetings, kept books, and performed sundry other tasks for which neither his training nor his nature had prepared him. This painfully shy artistic introvert, who had never felt at home in a crowd, was now being daily inundated by fresh waves of human beings. He who had always been self-absorbed, who had liked to work out his own problems in the minds of the characters of his books, was now wholly absorbed by the problems of people he had never even seen before. The strain told. Sympathetic as he was with the plight of the refugees, he confessed: «How many times, at the Foyer, caring for, consoling, sustaining those poor rags, capable only of moaning, infirm, unsmiling, without an ideal, without beauty, I felt rising within me the terrible question: Do they deserve to be saved?» (9). Consequently, it was with a feeling of immense relief that Gide, in February 1916, terminated his philanthropic career. He was now free to revert to the only mode of life that could please him—one of voracious reading, silent meditation, and writing. However, having made a vow in 1914 to preserve a complete silence for the duration of the war, he made no attempt to get anything published until after the Armistice. For him these were likewise years of intense personal and religious crises.

On August 1, 1914, with everything pointing to the inevitability of the conflict, Gide thus describes his mood: «In lieu of a heart I feel only a wet rag in my breast; the

_____

(9) André Gide, *Journal (1913-1922)* (Rio de Janeiro: Americ, n.d.), Oct. 26, 1915, p. 161.

obsessive thought of war stands between my eyes like a frightful rod against which all my other thoughts strike» (10). The expression of such emotion was not, however, typical of him. Before long he avowed, «... Nothing is less natural to me than anything which upsets my intellectual equilibrium. If it were not for *public opinion,* I feel that I could enjoy an ode of Horace even under enemy fire» (11). In point of fact, for the remainder of the war Gide maintained a dispassion worthy of his literary idol, Goethe. By and large, whether in regard to individuals, groups, or nations affected by the war, he spoke in remarkably unemotional accents. Some of the entries that he made in his *Journal* are little short of shocking in their concision, all the more so that, as often as not, he immediately switches his attention to matters which by comparison can only be viewed as trivial. On August 5, 1914, he records the German invasion of Belgium in five words, then recounts his own day in detail. For September 18, 1914, his entire entry reads: «This morning, before eight o'clock, a telegram brought by the great-nephew of the post-mistress: «Charles Péguy fell before the enemy in the Argonne sector.» Théo sent it to me» (12). By the same token, he does not even mention the deaths, in the early autumn of 1914, of well-known writers Ernest Psichari, Alain-Fournier, and Émile Clermont. The names of such wartime personalities as Joffre, Foch, Galliéni, Pétain, and Clemenceau appear nowhere. No mention is made of Russia's military collapse after its 1917 Revolution, while the Revolution itself is scanted by a very

---

(10) *Ibid.,* Aug. 1, 1914, p. 85.

(11) *Ibid.,* Aug. 14, 1914, p. 98. A December 11, 1942 diary entry made by Gide at Tunis, where he was then living, reads: «Finished *Le Rouge et le Noir* during the night, while a rather heavy [Allied] bombing was in progress.» *Journal (1942-1949)* (Paris: Gallimard, 1950), p. 51.

(12) Gide, *Journal (1913-1922),* Sept. 18, 1914, p. 132.

brief and oblique reference. The five-day First Battle of the Marne on whose outcome the fate of the nation hung is at no time alluded to, nor is the titanic nine-month Battle of Verdun—nor the Armistice for that matter. Even as a diarist, therefore, the Gide who preached the doctrine of «daring to be oneself» put his teaching into practice.

Toward Germany and the Germans Gide maintained a posture of scrupulous objectivity. Having witnessed the raiding of a German-owned dairy store by an angry mob on the day after the outbreak of war, he could readily gauge the spirit of the hour. He for his part would make no concession to it, then or later. He saw no reason why he should not go on reading the works of the great German writers and philosophers who had long claimed his attention. Chauvinism had always been an obscenity with him, so why should it have ceased being that simply because his nation was at war? And had he not long emphasized that the closer France and Germany drew together, the better would their individual interests be served? He lent no credence to widely circulated rumors apropos the mutilation of children by enemy soldiers, insistently demanding scientific proof thereof. He found «nauseating» the tone employed by French journalists in speaking of the Germans, each vying with all the others in venom and in the rhetoric that he abominated. He denounced as «absurd and criminal» their news-inflating headlines, and in numerous entries of his diary he demonstrated how cleverly they went about manufacturing their lies by understatement, omission, or the nimble ordering of words. «This atmosphere of falsehood is stifling, poisonous, deadly,» (13) he complained.

In the earliest days of the war Gide had imparted a number of comments to his diary reflecting his pleasure with

_____

(13) *Ibid.*, a Sunday in Sept., 1916, p. 215.

the unity and spirit of the French population and his interest in the events. However, as the months and years dragged on, and as his personal problems mounted, his enthusiasm for the national cause waned perceptibly. Certainly it was at a very low ebb when, on June 2, 1918, with a violent battle raging at Château-Thierry, he objected, «At times it seems as if there were something impious and desperate about our resistance...» (14).

It is in a similar defeatist spirit that Gide welcomed the 1940 Armistice. More than a week before it was signed he wrote: «Unquestionably there is no shame in being vanquished when the forces of the enemy are so superior» (15). A few months later he reasoned: «Coming to terms with yesterday's enemy and accepting the inevitable is not cowardice, it is wisdom...He who balks at fate is trapped; what's the use of bruising oneself against the bars of one's cage? To suffer less from the tight confines of one's jail, one has only to stay in the middle of it» (16).

Ironically, while in the wake of the defeat Gide was being assailed in some quarters as a spreader of libertarian poisons and demoralizer of youth who had greatly contributed toward the sapping of the nation's foundations, he in turn was dotting the pages of his *Journal* with such standard items from the Vichy phrasebook as «indiscipline,» «moral and spiritual decline,» «deep decay,» «a nation benumbed by comfort,» and «a worm-eaten edifice.» At first he placed his trust in Pétain. But it did not take him many months to reach the conclusion that Vichy's National Revolution could only lead France farther down the road to ruin. For all that,

---

(14) *Ibid.*, June 2, 1918, p. 336.
(15) Gide, *Pages de journal, 1939-1942* (New York: Pantheon Books, 1944), June 14, 1940, p. 34.
(16) *Ibid.*, Sept. 5, 1940, p. 74.

his thinking was hardly that of a *Résistant*. On May 6, 1941, he could still write, «We are now at the mercy of a power that knows no mercy. And nothing seems to me more vain than an unavailing revolt» (17).

On May 4, 1942, Gide left the South of France, where he had been living since late 1939, and sailed for Tunis. There he experienced German occupation firsthand, and later observed the liberation of the city with utmost fascination. At the invitation of General de Gaulle, Gide had dinner with him in Algiers on June 26, 1943. Had his *Pages de journal, 1939-1942* already been in print, there is no chance that France's leading *Résistant* would have cared to break bread with him.

The Case of Conscience of Anatole France

Anatole France (1844-1924), *né* Jacques Anatole Thibault, had fought somewhat unenthusiastically in the Franco-Prussian War and had emerged from it less shaken by the national *débâcle* than most of his fellow combatants. In those years he had no pronounced likes or dislikes vis-à-vis the army. However, an affection for it grew on him by degrees as he pursued readings in Vigny and in French history, until it reached its high point with the Boulanger craze. By that time he had become an avowed partisan of *revanche*.

Inasmuch as he was later converted to pacifism and internationalism, not a few of the opinions he voiced in the eighties and early nineties were to remain a source of embarrassment to him. These were years when the army, its prestige already severely undermined by the 1870-71 defeats, was being subjected to virulent attacks that were further

_____
(17) *Ibid.*, May 6, 1941, p. 111.

eroding the public's faith in it. Zola, in his collection of short stories *Les Soirées de Médan* (1880), painted the soldier as petty, coarse, and wanting in genuine bravery, whereas in his *La Débâcle* (1892) he redeemed the humble soldier and reviled his leaders while portraying the army as the victim rather than the cause of the rout. In his travel journal «Sur l'eau,» Maupassant, a veteran of the Franco-Prussian War, inveighed against militarists as «the scourge of the earth» and condemned war in the bitterest accents imaginable (18). Pierre Loti's *Le Roman d'un spahi* (1881) presented the colonial soldier as little more than a drunken brawler. To Paul Bonnetain (*Autour de la caserne*) (1890), Lucien Descaves (*Sous-offs*) (1890), and Abel Hermant (*Le Cavalier Miserey*) (1887), everything about the army was sordid. Hermant's book particularly incensed Anatole France. A colonel's order that all copies of the book confiscated in his unit be burned on a dunghill and his warning that any soldier caught with the book in his possession would be thrown into the brig evoked France's generous praise. With sweeping unrestraint he paid homage to the military establishment, affirming, «... If in human society there is by the consent of all a sacred thing, it is the army» (19). And he contended that the men of the Middle Ages had prepared the modern world for our enjoyment thanks to the exaltation of the military virtues, «the basic virtues upon which every human order reposes, even today» (20).

Be that as it may, across the span of his young and middle years nothing was further from his thoughts than *engagement*. Egoist, epicure, sensualist, aesthete, he was

---

(18) See Maupassant, «Sur l'eau,» in *Oeuvres complètes,* vol. 13 (Paris: H. Piazza, 1971), pp. 182-86.
(19) Anatole France, «Le Cavalier Miserey,» *La Vie littéraire,* vol. 1 (Paris: Calmann-Lévy, 1888), p. 80.
(20) *Ibid.*, «M. Leconte de Lisle à l'Académie Française,» p. 97.

serenely detached from the affairs of the world at large. Little by little, though, events were throwing him off his individualistic guard, until finally the succession of the Boulanger, Panama, and Dreyfus scandals pulled him into the lists. From the moment he stepped forward to defend the victimized Jewish captain, overcoming his innate aversion for speechmaking and for congress with the common herd, he was never again wholly to withdraw himself from them. He was a socialist from 1895 to 1919 and a communist *sympathisant* for a few years thereafter; a skeptical humanist he had always been. During the last three decades of his life this former devotee of art for art's sake raised his voice on every major political and social issue of the day, with the large majority of his works from 1897 onward bearing the distinct impress of a reformatory intent.

No longer was he the nationalist he had been from 1886 to 1889, the years of the Boulanger adventure. He had looked for great things from the general, who had also become his personal friend, but Boulanger let him down badly. A pacifist of record as of 1892, with the publication of his *Les Opinions de M. Jérôme Coignard,* he subsequently stigmatized all wars: international, colonial, and civil. Appearing but a half-year before the outbreak of World War I, his *La Révolte des anges* had the utter futility of war as its thesis. In it Lucifer gives up his plan to subjugate heaven in the belief that, as a conqueror subject to all the vices which come of conquest, he could only provoke further strife. «Comrades,» he pleaded, «... let us not conquer heaven. It is enough to be able to do so. War only breeds war, and victory, defeat» (21). Scoffingly France sought to prove the fallacy of military genius, and heaped scorn upon «birdbrained

---

(21) France, *La Révolte des anges* (Paris: Calmann-Lévy, 1914), p. 409.

generals,» recipients of palms for master strokes when, he was convinced, the play of kismetic forces or the application of puerile principles accounted for them. Military science was therefore a myth, an idle fancy. Other of these pages are suffused with commentary on the grossness of military justice and on the barbarity of courts-martial which had no qualms about inflicting capital punishment for soldiers' unauthorized visits to family deathbeds.

To those who spoke of the grandeur and the glory of a career in uniform, as France himself had once done, his abbé Coignard retorted that military service was «the most frightful plague of civilized nations» (22). The abbé preferred to harp on what he reckoned the servitude, the empty glory, and the cruelty bound up with it. Others could, if they wished, puff up war as affording the supreme test of a man's courage. As for himself, he was persuaded that war required less courage than a peasant had to summon up in his never-ending struggle against nature. He set no store by arguments in favor of war waged in defense of a just cause, for the preservation of national honor, and the like, regarding the sacrifices entailed as totally out of scale with a war's real objectives, always adroitly screened from the unsuspecting. Caustically he acknowledged a single imperious *casus belli,* man's need to give periodic release to his evil instincts. «With very few exceptions, of which I am one, man may be defined as an animal with a musket» (23), he declared.

In the years immediately preceding the First World War France made enough antiwar speeches to convince observers that guarding the peace had become his foremost objective. In true socialist fashion he did battle with capitalism and

---

(22) France, *Les Opinions de M. Jérôme Coignard* (Paris: Calmann-Lévy, 1893), p. 158.
(23) *Ibid.,* p. 158.

clamored for the abolition of the three-year service law and the reduction of armaments. And if, in addition, he considered it worthwhile to wage spectacular compaigns against the buying of toy pistols and sailor suits for little boys, this was not because he thought that he had the answer to the war riddle. The best that he dared hope for was that the unremitting growth of armies and spread of armaments would cause the monster to «croak from obesity» (24).

Came the war and came a radical change of front on the part of the aging Anatole France. Having raised a tempest by his letter of September 22, 1914, in the review *Guerre Sociale,* wherein he closed a scorching philippic against the Germans with a promise of amicable reconciliation with them in the postwar, the septuagenarian writer volunteered to shoulder a gun for the fatherland. Perhaps he told himself that if in 1870 Victor Hugo could offer his services to the army at sixty-eight, there was no valid reason why a man who was only a few years older should not do so in 1914. France was, of course, rejected for active duty. Not to be denied, the erstwhile pacifist stepped up the pace of his propagandizing. While Romain Rolland firmly stood his ground, France, false to his ideal, conventionally cried havoc upon the «barbarians,» demanded the extinction of the German «hydra,» sang the praises of *poilu* and colonel alike, and tossed about patriotic slogans and catchwords *à la* Barrès, Maurras, and Léon Daudet. Thundering against the diabolic enemy's martial methods, he wrote, «They killed the peace, they are killing war. They are making it a monster that cannot live: it is too ugly. On your feet for the last of wars!» (25). The metamorphosis from pacifist to militarist, from socialist to militarist, was, it seemed to all, complete.

(24) *Ibid.,* p. 180.
(25) France, *Sur la voie glorieuse* (Paris: Champion, 1915), p. 90.

The European fire raged on and on, but in 1916 France had all but ceased feeding it his fuel. Had he therefore had a change of heart? His wartime correspondents and intimates knew better; to them he had long been showing his hand (26). However, it was not until the publication of Marcel Le Goff's *Anatole France à la Béchellerie* (1924) that public light was shed upon the thoughts behind his retreat from propagandistic action. Privy to France's off-the-cuff utterances in his frequent visits to his country home in Touraine during the war, Le Goff was well placed to know his true sentiments on the holocaust. His book, which confirms and expands the revelations made by Anatole France in his wartime correspondence, presents more than enough evidence to convince the reader that a shocking discrepancy had existed between his subject's publicly and privately aired views of wartime and that his drift off the pacifist course was wholly simulated. According to Le Goff, he had wanted to see the olive branch held out to the enemy as early as the morrow of the Marne (27). The terms hardly seemed to matter. He eagerly welcomed any signs, however embryonic, of peace feelers. The mass homicide of Verdun could not be justified—or even the war itself. Capitalists were all but laughing over spilt blood and bribing the press to keep afloat the great lie about the war's sacred character. The arrival of American troops in 1917 distressed him since it could only prolong the useless slaughter.

Why, then, had he not spoken his mind? Because, Le Goff gathered, he succumbed under the weight of generalized public pressure; because, too, Le Goff emphasizes, ever since

---

(26) Marie-Claire Bancquart gives a detailed account of his revelations to them in her book *Anatole France Polémiste* (Paris: A. G. Nizet, 1962).

(27) Marcel Le Goff, *Anatole France à la Béchellerie* (Paris: Delteil, 1924), p. 169.

2

Jaurès' eve-of-war death at the hand of an assassin, France had been living in the fear that a like fate would befall him, had been receiving stacks of threatening letters, and was certain that he was being shadowed by hostile parties. That he yielded out of cowardice France conceded; that he did so not entirely against his better judgment, he insisted, «Yes, I spoke and wrote like my concierge. I am ashamed of it, but it was necessary» (28).

The Grand Illusion of Drieu la Rochelle

To a greater degree than any French literary figure of the age, Pierre Drieu la Rochelle (1893-1945) mirrored the disenchantments of the generation that went directly from lecture halls into trenches, issuing from them reeling, bewildered, lost. The decadent world that they reentered was being shaped by others for others less weary than they. Manifestly it was no place for a Drieu suffering more from weakness of character than from war-born neuroses. An inveterate preacher of spiritual regeneration, he was notably unsuccessful at self-regeneration. In his desperate striving to find his way out of the labyrinth, to give direction and purpose to his life, Drieu swam with every current. At one time or another, he embraced, in whole or in part, Dadaism, Surrealism, materialism, asceticism, athleticism, mysticism, pacifism, Maurrasism, European federalism, socialism, and fascism, German-style. And destiny always seemed to be waiting around the bend to waylay him whenever his own weakness did not trip him up. Vacillating between short-lived disciplines and protracted debauches, he ended a suicide in March 1945, after enthusiastically bowing submission to the Germans

---

(28) *Ibid.*, p. 47.

whose strength he had long admired and after editing at their bidding the *Nouvelle Revue Française.* Drugs and alcohol had afforded him no escape; the political action to which he had given himself in the belief that it could test his strength like war had tested it only brought him monumental frustration; and eroticism had proven to be no adequate substitute for the profound emotional experience of armed combat in revealing his true nature to himself, always a primary objective with him.

Twenty-one in 1914, Drieu had hardly completed his compulsory military training when the war broke out. Off he went to meet the enemy, with a copy of Nietzsche's *Zarathustra* in his haversack. He served for the duration, and was thrice wounded in the course of the five brief stints he did at the front. He fought with distinction as an infantryman at Charleroi, in the Champagne sector, in the Dardanelles, and at Verdun before being attached to the American army as an interpreter in 1918.

Drieu entered on the literary scene in 1917 with the publication of his *Interrogation,* a collection of highly lyric poems in free verse that he had written two years earlier. In the beginning, as the book shows, war was the answer to his prayer. As a young boy he could not exorcise the ghosts of even such distant national disasters as those of Crécy, Poitiers, and Agincourt, and he dreamt of fighting in glittering campaigns just as his great-grandfather, a sergeant in the army of Napoleon, had done. Nourishing these dreams were his readings in Barrès, Péguy, Maurras, Paul Adam, D'Annunzio, and Kipling. But there were additional reasons for his welcoming war's embrace:—His delight that the hour for atonement was at hand and that the young men of his generation were being called upon to blot out the stigma of Sedan, to avenge the crime which, he thought, had weighed much too lightly on the graybeards who had witnessed yet managed to forget them.—His consuming appetite for ever deeper emotional experience, with the war offering an unparalleled opportunity for pairing dreams with action. —His Nietzschean aspiration to challenge fate, to rise to the occasion, to outdo himself, to meet the supreme test while measuring his strength when brought face to face with danger and death.—The mystical ecstasy he experienced during the few bayonet charges in which he participated. —The communion beyond compare of men whose lives hung on a thread.—The blessed solemnity that war had introduced into his random life.—The personal conviction—here he antedates Elie Faure—that wars are necessary to incite the will to create, to inflame the imagination, to dynamize the inner self. Why, then, shed tears over bomb damage to the cathedral of Reims inasmuch as youth inspired will have its day, will build yet more magnificent cathedrals? War, itself dependent on progress, will bring progress in every sphere— «War, revolution of the blood, state of flux of the brain, war, progress, necessity of our day» (29).

However, not for long was Drieu to go on extolling war or, for that matter, enjoying it. As early as 1920, with the publication of his second collection of poems, *Fond de cantine,* it was apparent that he was looking at war through very different eyes, and in 1934 a more mature Drieu would confess that already in 1915 he had been bitterly cursing it (30). Modern war, he had discovered, was a far cry from the glorious contest hallowed by a Joinville or a Montluc in which an individual's skill and muscles counted for something. How now was a soldier to set himself apart from

---

(29) Pierre Drieu la Rochelle, «Caserne haïe,» *Interrogation* (Paris: Gallimard, 1917), p. 62.
(30) See Drieu la Rochelle, *La Comédie de Charleroi* (Paris: Gallimard, 1934), p. 27.

his fellows while for the most part fighting a remote enemy upon whom untold numbers of increasingly deadly shells were impersonally rained? How often could he charge the enemy, bayonet gleaming in the sun, if the spray of machine-gun fire greeted him as soon as he took a step forward? How was he to protect himself from asphyxiating gasses and the brutal contrivances of chemists and engineers? Drieu had dreamt of becoming a leader of men in battle and a hero fighting in «an arena of glory,» but the reality of the trenches had relegated him to the condition of «a calf marked for death like ten million calves and steers...in the stockyards of Chicago» (31). And if modern war still had any glamor attached to it, the omnipresent mud and squalor, combined with the terrible boredom and monotony of life at the front between attacks, sufficed to kill it. Besides, as he emphasized in his political essay *Mesure de la France* (1922), he could take no satisfaction in a victory gained, to his mind, by sheer force of numbers. So he pointed an accusatory finger at his compatriots for having failed to best the Germans without the aid of numerous allies, snapping, «We didn't sleep alone with Victory» (32). Although Drieu himself was never to father any children, he proceeded to tongue-lash his country-men for committing race suicide through birth control, thus inviting attack by their much more fecund neighbors to the east.

It may justly be affirmed that Drieu, who had always glorified force and martial valor, and who had prized virility as much as he prized anything, had never been truly virile except as a courageous and efficient fighter in the trenches. Never again was he to demonstrate such strength of will and

(31) *Ibid.*, p. 57.
(32) Drieu la Rochelle, «Le retour du soldat,» *Mesure de la France* (Paris: Grasset, 1922), p. 8.

stoutness of heart. The ordeal by fire that he lived so admirably had marked him forever, as it had marked stronger men than he. No lover of losers and a constant reprimander of them, Drieu was, save for some thrilling hours in the smoke of battle, the eternal loser.

Apollinaire: War, the Supreme Novelty

Guillaume Apollinaire (1880-1918), baptized Wilhelm-Apollinaris Kostrowitsky, had been under no obligation to serve in the French army. He had been born in Italy of a Polish mother and an Italian father and was not to become a naturalized citizen of his adopted country until 1916. It was because of his citizenship status that he was turned down when he volunteered for military service in August 1914. Successful in his second attempt in December, he was assigned for training to an artillery regiment at Nîmes.

Nobody could have been more astounded than the Montmartre and Montparnasse friends of Apollinaire, *enfant terrible* of the cubists, at how completely he adapted to military life. This free spirit, this hard-drinking bohemian, was in more ways than one a latter-day François Villon, but was subject to none of the bouts of remorse for which the medieval poet was famous. Nonetheless, knowing as they did Apollinaire's idiosyncrasies and power to surprise, they should have been less surprised. At Nîmes he plunged into his new life with zest, finding it enormously fulfilling. He loved to play the *grand seigneur,* strutting down the avenues of the city, cane in hand, shimmering pistol in holster, regretting only that his uniform was wanting in the dash and color of those of bygone days. Far from suffering from an artist's aversion to the noise and promiscuity of garrison life, the gregarious Apollinaire took delight in them and quickly made friends with peasants and lords indiscriminately. He cheerfully accepted the chains of discipline and performed menial tasks without complaint. He worked hard at the business of becoming a soldier and took pride in his progress. Having set his sights on becoming an officer, a decorated hero, and a leader of men, he thirsted for promotions and fidgeted impatiently between them. Were it not that his correspondents had never had occasion to question his sincerity, they very likely would have rejected as counterfeit the unabashed patriotism that now shone through his letters. And not for a moment did Apollinaire doubt that he would prove to be a most worthy defender of the Republic.

The opportunity to do so soon presented itself. He enthusiastically welcomed it. After a while garrison life in Nîmes had become a bit humdrum, and he had always needed novelty like his lifeblood. When, in early April, 1915, artillery gunner Apollinaire arrived at the front, in Champagne, he was beside himself with joy. Where but on a battlefield might the adventurer that he was find more adventure and live more intensely? Certainly of rats, flies, and mud there was no lack, yet living conditions were quite tolerable, and the enemy shells exploding all around him did not frighten him overmuch. «We enjoy everything, even our sufferings,» (33) he wrote.

Whatever dejection he felt was soon dissipated in the contemplation of war's gala pageant. Gratifying his insatiate imagination in a vast debauch—he was a poet first, last, and always—Apollinaire discovered undreamt of beauty in the rumbling earth and polychromatic heavens (34). In the flush

---

(33) Guillaume Apollinaire, «À l'Italie,» in «Calligrammes,» *Oeuvres poétiques*, eds. Marcel Adéma and Michel Décaudin, with a Preface by André Billy (Paris: Gallimard, 1956), p. 275.
(34) In his book *The Warriors: Reflections on Men in Battle* (New York: Harcourt, Brace, 1959), J. Glenn Gray attaches much importance to the «lust of the eye» in making war attractive to

of his discovery, he poured out one poem after another, wishing to share his impressions with his absent friends and the two women in his life at that time, Madeleine Pagès and Louise de Coligny-Châtillon. These poems would later be assembled to constitute the bulk of his *Calligrammes* collection.

«Oh God! how pretty war is!» (35)—he exclaimed. In his mind's eye shells are bottles of frothing champagne or soaring cats, meowing as they spin through the atmosphere before bursting into dazzling sprays of flowers. Crashing into the earth, they remind him of dogs scattering sand upward upon relieving nature. Flares are night-blooming flowers or dancing women. The airplanes whirling above do not drop bombs, they lay eggs. He compares the vividness of his remembrance of Madeleine with that of the spotlight used for aiming artillery guns at night. And what better way to describe his love-agitated being than by likening it to the churned earth of the battle zone? While the poet does from time to time inject a tender note of pity for the suffering and the dead, his exuberance rapidly gains the upper hand. He much prefers to joke about Germans disturbing his meditations with their noise, or about his being no respecter of reputations, since he has directed the fire of heavy guns on a communication trench named after Goethe.

However, for Apollinaire life as an artilleryman had one distinct drawback. He still itched to be an officer, and there were no signs that he was about to receive a commission in spite of his quick rise through the noncom ranks. Hence,

---

men. A similar view was held by Alain, who wrote: «If it were more commonly understood that war is a spectacle, the idea—a good one—of abolishing this variety of pleasure in the name of the public weal and of morality...would find acceptance.» *Sentiments, Passions et Signes* (Paris: Gallimard, 1935), p. 13.

(35) Apollinaire, «L'Adieu du cavalier,» in *Calligrammes*, p. 253.

in late November, 1915, he applied for transfer to the infantry and was commissioned a second lieutenant.

For Apollinaire it was still the same Champagne but a radically different world. Gone were war's beauty and romance. Gone were the relative comforts he had enjoyed as an artilleryman. He was horrified. His new comrades were worried, sullen warriors, not the jovial types that manned artillery pieces. He saw himself as a troglodyte dwelling in foul, vermin-infested holes inundated with mud, whose chalky walls were sometimes reinforced with cadavers. The fighting was fierce, the fatigue inhuman. The trenches were constantly under heavy bombardment. Death enveloped him. In less than three months 2,800 men and 90 officers of his regiment had been killed. His letters now reflected his weariness and despair, as did the handful of poems that he somehow managed to write. «Did, then, Christ come into the world of men in vain?» (36)—he asked.

In happier days when, as an artilleryman, he was never at a loss for a pun, he had written Madame Jane Mortier, «Ici, amie, c'est la guerre...Obus-Roi» (37). In the end it was that monarch that claimed him. In a wooded area near Berry-au-Bac, on March 17, 1916, while he was reading the latest issue of the *Mercure de France,* shell fragments tore a hole into his head above the right temple. Debilitated by his wound and the two operations it necessitated, the second a trepanation which was performed two months later, Apollinaire succumbed to influenza just two days before the Armistice—as truly a victim of war as one fallen on a battlefield.

---

(36) «Chant de l'honneur,» in *Calligrammes,* p. 305.
(37) «Lettres de Guillaume Apollinaire,» *Les Marges,* no. 17 (1920), April 26, 1915, p. 87. Apollinaire here plays on the title of Alfred Jarry's burlesque drama, *Ubu Roi* (1896).

Jean Giraudoux: The Impressionistic Vision

> «Forgive me, oh war, for having caressed
> you on every occasion that I could» (38).

Such was the epigraph that Jean Giraudoux (1882-1944) chose for his *Adorable Clio* (1920), a book of sketches based on his war experiences. These are not the words of a former soldier who had led a life of ease and comfort in the safety of a rear echelon headquarters but rather those of one who saw service in the infantry both as an enlisted man and as an officer, in Alsace, on the Marne, and in the Dardanelles. Moreover, he earned three citations and the cross of the Légion d'honneur, becoming the war's first soldier-writer to win the cross for valorous conduct. When in 1916 the second of the injuries he suffered permanently sidelined him, he went to Portugal as a member of a French military mission, then to the United States, where he trained officer candidates at Harvard. Upon his return to France in late 1917, he was promoted to captain and assigned to liaison duty at the headquarters of the U.S. Army.

Should we not, nevertheless, be tempted to dismiss as vainglorious nonsense Giraudoux's claim that he actually sought and enjoyed the caresses of the war monster? Even recognizing his well-known love of mystification, the answer would have to be emphatically in the negative. To begin with, few men's natures and philosophies have been as ideally suited for enduring, even enjoying, war. Like the characters in his books, he was endowed with a wide-eyed, universal curiosity and with an exceptional receptivity to the infinite multiplicity of experience that life affords. Like them too, he was hardly addicted to the introspection and

---

(38) Jean Giraudoux, *Adorable Clio* (Paris: Émile-Paul, 1918), n. pag.

self-analysis which can so easily devastate a person's morale. His captivation with the freshness of youth and of springtime was never to quit him; these would continue to occupy an enormous place in his works. Nor would he ever lose the enthusiasm for life and the fondness for fun of the young, taking the fun where he found it and creating it where it was absent. Like the youthful heroine of his novel *Suzanne et le Pacifique* (1921), he effervesced with gaiety and laughter, allowing nothing to frighten or wound him for long. Yet, because life subjects every human being to unhappiness and suffering, he braced his even temper and native optimism with a studied serenity and a stoic resignation.

It should not, therefore, amaze us that Giraudoux could assure his intimate friend and correspondent, Paul Morand, that he would have been capable of living happily even in prison (39). For his part, Morand, writing of Giraudoux's participation in the failed British-French Dardanelles expedition of 1915, assures us that «He went through that hell in the same fashion as he would have gone through Switzerland» (40). As a matter of fact, what Giraudoux's narratives on his campaigns, in his *Lectures pour une ombre* (1918) and in *Adorable Clio* (1920), best reveal is that he fought them with genuine relish and a smiling good humor. Despite his wounds, illnesses, and protracted hospitalizations, at no time did he ever so much as intimate that they weighed heavily upon his spirit.

Death takes no holiday from Giraudoux's war, nor does his army sleep on feather beds, but the comic, the playful, invariably triumph. Advancing into battle for the first time,

---

(39) See Donald Inskip, *Jean Giraudoux: The Making of a Dramatist* (London: Oxford University Press, 1958), p. 13.

(40) Paul Morand, *Adieu à Giraudoux* (Parrentruy, Switzerland: Éditions des Portes de France, 1944), p. 27.

the thirty-two-year-old recruit recalls examination jitters of quieter years. He is able to invoke «Vive la classe!» as a battle cry during a bayonet charge. An attack over, his thoughts focus more sharply on the aroma of wine released from the smashed flasks of his comrades than on anything else. The capture of Mulhouse does not excite him as much as an eau de Cologne skirmish with replacements coming into the line or verbal duels with the enemy troops across the way. In trenches newly taken by the French, he is not so nauseated by the sight of dead Germans that he cannot quip that they «could not live without breathing.» The thought of dying oppresses him about as much as would the prospect of having to «carry a bird in one's hand for five years.» He might even be suggesting that his comrades in arms were similarly inclined to shrink death's dimensions. They are heard conversing thus:

— And what about Jalicot?
— He's all right, but Vergniaud has been killed.
— And Pupion?
— He's fine, but Bereire is dead (41).

True to his custom, he paints his picture of the great First Battle of the Marne in which he fought with a nonchalance, wit, and preoccupation with trivia which the sensitive might view as unseemly at best. In no way can a reader know from his bizarre account that he is treating of one of the war's most crucial battles. The courage, the tenacity, the serious commentary, the sacrifices, the slaughter—these he leaves to reporters and historians. Only his impressionistic vision of it matters to him. When the Armistice

---

(41) Giraudoux, *Lectures pour une ombre* (Paris: Émile-Paul, 1918), p. 248.

finally arrives, he feels no exhilaration. He simply records, together with other trifles, his satisfaction that he will no longer be obliged to idolize women or to endure living in heavily overpopulated trenches.

That, apart from the matchless subjective experience it afforded him, Giraudoux regarded war as the scourge of civilized man is borne out by his earnest probings of the causes of Franco-German tensions in the *entre-deux-guerres* period. A Germanophile from his early school days, he remained perplexed, until Hitlerism showed its face, by the fact that the French and German neighbors had for so long found it so difficult to occupy the same continent. Siegfried von Kleist, protagonist of his novel *Siegfried et le Limousin* (1922), and of *Siegfried* (1928), the dramatic version of it, put it this way: «It would be beyond reason if in a human soul in which the most contrary vices and virtues live together, only the words «German» and «French» could not come to terms. As for me, I refuse to dig trenches within myself» (42).

With the 1935 publication of his play *La Guerre de Troie n'aura pas lieu*, Giraudoux made plain his conviction that Siegfried's hopes for the reconciliation of the ancient enemies would be dashed. A work of patent topicality, since in that year Hitler was tearing up the disarmament clauses of the Treaty of Versailles and reintroducing conscription, it betrayed the playwright's belief in the ineluctability of war in general and of another European war in particular. In it the kidnapped Hélène will be returned to the Greeks, yet Hector's determination to close the gates of war and to keep them «bolted and padlocked» will go for naught: a mysterious fatality bound up with man's nature and with complex

---

(42) Giraudoux, *Siegfried*, in *Théâtre complet*, vol. 1 (Neuchâtel: Ides et Calendes, 1945), act 4, sc. 3, p. 119.

economic and social forces will again open them. And it is not hard to see whose opinion Giraudoux shares when, in a war hymn that the drumbeating Trojan poet Demokos is composing, he compares the face of war to that of Hélène, while Hécube, for her part, prefers to compare it to «a monkey's backside» (43).

Demokos, around whose person Giraudoux builds a powerful satire of war propaganda, emerges as a thoroughly unlovable type. This petty man of letters places no mean premium on the role of intellectual dispensers of propaganda. Addressing his associates, he declares, «In wartime it is not enough for us to polish weapons for our soldiers. It is indispensable that they be raised to the pinnacle of enthusiasm. The physical intoxication which their leaders will induce at the hour of attack by generously distributing resin wine will have little effect against the Greeks unless it is reinforced with the moral intoxication which we poets shall infuse» (44).

Ironically, Giraudoux himself would before long be performing the function of a Demokos. On July 29, 1939, he accepted a bid from the Daladier government to assume the newly created post of Minister of Information. After September 3 he continued as head of his ministry while also radiobroadcasting propaganda to French troops. This deeply sincere man of kindly disposition, with an incurable bent for discovering poetry in even the grimmest reality, now had as his opposite number the ruthless Joseph Goebbels. Giraudoux had entered a valley of shadows. Harried on all sides, he ruled or tried to rule a band of disputatious intellectual prima donnas who were often at cross-purposes;

---

(43) Giraudoux, *La Guerre de Troie n'aura pas lieu*, in *Théâtre complet*, vol. 6 (Neuchâtel: Ides et Calendes, 1946), act 2, scenes 4-5, p. 88.
(44) *Ibid.*, act 2, sc. 4, p. 70.

confusion reigned; and to cap all, he proved to be a hopelessly inept administrator and propagandist. There can be no doubt that he had been happier fighting against Germans during the Great War.

Montherlant and the Survival of the Fittest

> In the war, I well knew that, from one minute to the next, I could be killed or disfigured, or be paralyzed or go crazy. Nevertheless, on the whole I enjoyed war (45).

It is in these plain terms that Henry de Montherlant (1896-1972) described what was in fact the capital experience of his life. Indeed, he would have felt badly cheated had the portals of war not opened to him. As a boy, not content to play soldier, he devoured bulky tomes on ancient Rome, drunk on the descriptions of its iron-sinewed warriors, disciplined legions, and engarlanded heroes. At the age of ten he was already the author of a life of Scipio Africanus, conqueror of the mighty Hannibal. But the ancients were ably seconded in the task of inculcating in the lad the cult of energy and of heroism by such moderns as Barrès, D'Annunzio, and Nietzsche, whom he soon took to his bosom. Many years later, in 1923, he would shed far more tears over the death of Barrès than he had shed over that of either of his parents.

It was, therefore, very much in the natural order of things that Montherlant, eighteen in 1914, should have wanted to enlist. Besides, he wished to accompany his best friend, who was enlisting. However, since his gravely ill mother firmly opposed the idea—his father had been deceased for

---

(45) Henry de Montherlant, *Les Lépreuses* (Paris: Grasset, 1939), p. 183.

some months—he did not enter the service until after her death in 1916. Significantly, the youth's 1914 play *L'Exil*, which was not to be published until 1929, clearly attested to his inability to forgive his mother for keeping him out of uniform for two years. His fight was not yet won, though. Found to be suffering from hypertrophy of the heart, he was placed in the auxiliary services and assigned to a headquarters unit for secretarial duties. In 1917, at his urging, influential friends intervened in his behalf and got him transferred to an infantry regiment at the front. Winner of three citations, he steadfastly declined invitations to attend officer candidate school. After suffering a serious injury in combat, he finished his soldierly career as an interpreter attached to the American army. By then, however, he had fulfilled himself in the shadow of death to a degree that he would never again attain. This had been life *in extremis,* and he had relished it. He too had «thought the bargain was both good and just» (46). He too had discovered on the field of strife what P.-J. Proudhon exalted as «the communion and paradise of the brave» (47).

Montherlant invariably poured much of himself into the mold in which he fashioned the male characters of his books. Alban de Bricoule, the youthful hero of his war novel *Le Songe* (1922), is no exception. Once this volunteer has liberated himself from rear echelon secretarial chores, he is a happy warrior. Not only is he again at the side of his truest

---

(46) The reference is to an unnamed poem by Seamus Haughey, a Royal Canadian Air Force pilot killed during the Second World War. Cited by Jules Roy, *L'Homme à l'épée* (Paris: Gallimard, 1957), p. 32. The verses cited are:

Mention my name in passing if you must,
As one knew the terms, slay or be slain,
And thought the bargain was both good and just.

(47) P.-J. Proudhon, *La Guerre et la paix*, tome 1, in *Oeuvres complètes*, vol. 13 (Paris: Librairie Internationale, 1869), p. 282.

friend, Stanislas Prinet, but he is also consumed with the desire to avail himself of the multiple pleasures which war can tender him. Foremost among these is the opportunity beyond compare of demonstrating his superiority over the ordinary run of men. Preeminence he must have at any price. He more than accepts war's hazards; he hunts them out, flirts with them. Whereas Henry Fleming, hero of Stephen Crane's *The Red Badge of Courage,* must fight a great uphill battle with himself to gain a measure of respectability after initially panicking before the enemy and running for cover, Alban is in full command of himself from the outset. He remains, up to the time of Prinet's death in action, the cocksure, vainglorious soldier who, upon being warned that life in the line might not be a joyride, disdainfully asks, «Would you have me put to mediocre tests?» (48). Death holds no terrors for him so long as he can die on his own terms: in mortal combat and at the side of the best of real men, those of the exclusive fraternity of arms. But first he must capture trophies and know the supreme rapture of murdering one of the species «homo sapiens.» When at last he drives a German to bay, he fires point-blank into his face, disregarding his unmistakable gesture of surrender. He then finishes him off in some of the most savage ways known to fighting man, shouting, «Joy! Joy! Joy!» Having passed this test, Alban sees himself on the threshold of supermanhood. He is now filled with «a sense of progress, of a higher virility, of renewed self-confidence,» for he has been delivered of the «malaise which had been tormenting him since his arrival at the front, analogous to the fermentation of nature in a still virginal young boy» (49). He has partaken of the

---

(48) Montherlant, *Le Songe* (Paris: Grasset, 1922), p. 45.
(49) *Ibid.,* pp. 125-26.

3

Dionysian ecstasy toward which Nietzsche had been directing him.

Alban must push aside any block on his road to glory. With softness of heart he can have no truck. Thus, he cold-bloodedly slays Prinet's dog lest his bark betray their position to the enemy. Thus, he brutally terminates his close friendship with the nurse-athlete Dominique Soubrier when by falling deeply in love with him she dares trespass on the sacrosanct domain of the male sex, threatening to diminish his virility with her poisonous sentimentality.

Alban revels in the simplicity and the liberty of life at the front, away from the stifling totalitarianisms of the civilian community. For him war is a period when everything goes, «as during the carnival season in old Venice.» One need only trouble his head with staying alive long enough to gather in war's lush emotional harvest. Hence, the unleashing of his instincts, his refusal to be subject to the orders of superiors, his arming himself with a pistol even though he is a private, and his solo expeditions over whichever areas of the battlefield beckon. A superman must be sufficient unto himself.

Alban serves not his country but himself. Patriotism has no place in his scheme of things. He is blind to and unconcerned with the meaning of the momentous events of which he is part, declaring, «I am ignorant of any useful purpose that my sacrifice may have, and at bottom I believe that I am sacrificing myself to something that amounts to nothing...» (50).

Albeit rarely, Montherlant does open war's ugliest sights to the reader's view. At the same time, he does on occasion

---

(50) *Ibid.*, p. 171. Cf. «Any man who, on the eve of combat, questions himself, like Cassius, about the value of the cause, can only be gripped with despair if he is an intelligent man. ... It

open Alban's heart to the suffering of its victims. He is, for example, seen comforting wounded Germans. If, however, Prinet's death crushes him—the bonds of virile friendship count for very much in the Montherlantian universe—he cannot afford the luxury of sustained compassion where the misfortunes of persons less close to him are concerned. For a strong man that sort of behavior can never be in season.

As for Montherlant himself, upon his demobilization in 1919, he embraced sport as the new object of his affection, not as a spectator but as a performer. On the cinder track, on the soccer field, and in the bullring he sought the thrills, the intoxication, and the challenges with which armed combat had generously supplied him. Here, short of war, was the ideal proving ground. Here too, if in a lesser way, it was a question of the survival of the fittest, and in the bullring at least, you could slay an adversary without pity and without hate—the way any right-minded Frenchman should have killed Germans in the war.

The resurgence of German militarism in the thirties did not take Montherlant by surprise: he had publicly predicted its coming in the very wake of the 1918 Armistice. As the storm clouds again gathered over Europe, he regularly took his compatriots to task for neglecting to prepare to meet force with force, justifying the sulfurous language to which he often resorted by reminding them that indignation too could be a manifestation of love. In the essays of *L'Équinoxe de septembre* (1938), he bitterly denounced his government's sellout to the Nazis at Munich as well as the widespread pacifist mentality that had led to it.

At the outbreak of World War II Montherlant volunteered

---

is a matter of knowing if, under its banner, indifferent in itself, one will realize oneself.» Montherlant, *L'Équinoxe de septembre* (Paris: Grasset, 1938), p. 191.

for active duty, but failed to pass the physical examination. Some might have seen as a logical corollary to this and to his aggressive antipacifist stance of a score of years his joining the Resistance as soon as the opportunity presented itself. He did quite the contrary. In the essays of his *Solstice de juin* (1941), he berated the French for permitting themselves to be bested on the battlefield, and advocated acceptance of the German victory and obedience to the Vichy government in language that could not but shock: «... It is *before* and *during* that one must make trouble for the adversary, not *after*... For once let us be good sports.» (51)— he wrote. Nor did he make any secret of his enormous admiration for the legions of Hitler that had speedily overwhelmed his countrymen. He had, after all, made a religion of force, and this was force at its upper limit. All the same, there were times when Montherlant was publicly critical not only of Vichy but even of the Germans, and he was surely unafraid of standing up to the latter whenever he felt that they were intent upon exploiting his writings or his personal prestige for political ends.

Charles Péguy, Passionate Patriot

> Le plus beau pays d'avant le jugement...
> Ce monument unique au monde: la France (52).

—Such was the tribute paid his homeland by Charles Péguy (1873-1914). If France has had other sons who have loved her as dearly, none has so persistently and so eloquently testified to his love for her. This son of humble artisans

---

(51) Montherlant, *Le Solstice de juin* (Paris: Grasset, 1941), p. 311.

(52) Charles Péguy, «De la situation faite au parti intellectuel devant les accidents de la gloire temporelle,» *Oeuvres en prose 1898-1908* (Paris: Gallimard, 1959), p. 1181.

and descendant of winegrowers loved her soil and her cities, her peasants and her kings, her sinners and her saints. He loved her warriors and he loved no less the Joinvilles and the Michelets who had radiated her glory across the ages and throughout the world. He loved her as the guarantor of liberty, as the illuminator of thought, and believed that the Almighty had assigned her a mission of awesome responsibility among nations. The «Gesta Dei per Francos» was for him a self-evident truth. In his personal bible the French were the chosen people. So great was Péguy's love for his country that in an age of travel he never once set foot outside its narrow boundaries.

His spiritual sister he recognized in Joan of Arc, deliverer of his native Orléans. So great was Péguy's reverence for the Soldier-Maid that he exalted her on hundreds of pages. Next on his list of heroes was Saint Louis, wager of «just wars,» who, like the «Pucelle,» fought hard and prayed hard. Other of his saintly idols were the soldier Martin, Bernard, preacher of the second crusade, and Geneviève, Aignan, and Loup, defenders of the *patrie* against the pagan hordes.

His imagination fired by readings in Corneille and Hugo, as well as in French history, the young Péguy's dreams were being disturbed because of heaven's slowness in placing him at the head of battle-avid columns. The fear gnawed at his heart that he would die before winning his «inscription historique,» before living in an «epoch,» an earthshaking term of French history such as were 1789-1815, 1830, and 1848, when heroes are made, as contrasted with a «period,» a time of inaction, of stolidity, and sterility.

For a brief day, with the Dreyfus Affair, Péguy thought that he had entered upon an epoch. He hurled all his native energy and pugnacity into the fray, since he could not tolerate having France go on living in disgrace before God and men.

But as soon as the «mystique» of the Affair degenerated into «politique;» as soon, that is to say, as the upholding of an individual's rights and of national honor had become subservient to bitter factional dispute and wild political exploitation, he felt that justice, France, and he himself had been cheated.

Péguy first tasted military life in 1892, when he enlisted after failing in his first attempt to pass the stiff entrance examination of the École Normale Supérieure. It at once captivated him and infused in him a spirit of heroic elevation. He took an extraordinary fancy to the stringent discipline, Spartan exertions, and robust male camaraderie of camp and bivouac. He liked to receive and especially to give orders, and he prided himself as much on the nattiness of his uniform as on his proficiency with the bayonet. When in later years he went back for summer training as a reserve officer, he had further cause for jubilation; not only did he welcome a periodic check on the corporal and spiritual erosions born of his endless trials and tribulations, but he was also convinced that the hour of national retribution was soon to strike. All of this is hardly what might have been expected of a socialist, and he had been one since the age of twenty. But Péguy was never capable of orthodoxy in anything.

Consequently, the landing of Kaiser Wilhelm II at Tangiers on March 31, 1905, followed by his sword-rattling speech at the German legation there, was not for Péguy as much of an eye-opener as it was for millions of his compatriots. He had sensed for some time that the Germans were once more girding for battle. While outwardly he railed against the perfidy of the enemy, secretly he was elated, for he saw this event as finally bringing his drowsy countrymen to their patriotic senses. He further saw his own course marked out clearly; he immediately proceeded to the Bon Marché department store to buy supplementary clothing and diverse other articles that could stand him in good stead on the battlefield. Himself mentally mobilized, he now urged others to meet the gravity of the hour by maintaining a constant alert and by working without pause to advance the nation's preparedness for war.

From 1905 to 1914 he waged an unabating campaign against pacifists, antimilitarists, and internationalists, pillorying them at every turn as obstructionists of national union. In his essays «L'Argent» and «L'Argent suite» (both 1913), he disallowed the validity of pet socialist antiwar doctrines, and denounced as stuff and nonsense («sornettes») such of their catch phrases as «peace at any price,» «war resolves nothing,» and «war only breeds war.» He who had always been of the belief that one of the cardinal duties of the French intellectuals of the age should have been the laying of the foundation stones of *revanche,* who from his youngest years hated the Germany that had humiliated his father's generation probably as much as the young Hannibal hated Rome, could not find words strong enough with which to brand the likes of Jaurès, Herr, and Hervé. They and their socialist brethren were all «traitors» and «Pan-Germanists» diabolically bent on leading their country down the path of destruction. Ever the absolutist, Péguy had an absolutist prescription for dealing with dissidents once hostilities were underway. He wrote: «... In time of war there can be room for only one policy, that of the National Convention. But we must not deceive ourselves: the policy of the National Convention means Jaurès in a tumbril and the rolling of a drum to drown that loud voice» (53). Here, then, was the Christian Péguy practically inviting—as the atheist Maurras, whom he detested, would later do—the murder of his former friend, the man who had earned his unqualified

_____
(53) Péguy, «L'Argent suite,» *Oeuvres en prose 1909-1914,* ed. Marcel Péguy (Paris: Gallimard, 1957), p. 1184.

admiration amidst the tumult of the Dreyfus days. Worshipper of saints, Péguy had always been too unforgiving a soul, too passionate a hater, to have himself been a saint.

In «Notre Patrie» (1905), Péguy impugned the motives of those who degraded the flag and the army while taking secret delight in military parades and ceremonial. He was, however, sooner disposed to excuse their transgressions than those of Victor Hugo, whom he had so many reasons for idolizing, considering it sickening that the giant of French Romanticism should at times have wooed public favor by singing hymns to peace and at other times have drawn inspiration for his verse from war and warriors, depending on how the winds of change were blowing.

Zero hour found him ready. Hungry for action, for glory, and even for martyrdom, infantry lieutenant Péguy, now forty-one, volunteered for combat and promptly left for the front with his regiment. This impassioned Orléannais was, he was satisfied, at last living in an «epoch.» And this was a just war, the only kind he believed in. Saint Louis could scarcely have departed on a crusade to the Holy Land with more joy in his heart. Like that other doomed soldier-poet, Rupert Brooke, he too could have written, «Now God be thanked Who has matched us with His hour...» (54). In an August 8 letter to his dear friend, Mme. Geneviève Favre, he wrote, «... If I should not return, remember me without mourning. Thirty years of living would not be worth what we are going to do in a few weeks» (55).

As fate would have it, and as he himself would have had it, he was straightway to earn his «inscription historique.»

---

(54) Rupert Brooke, «Peace.» *The Poetical Works of Rupert Brooke*, ed. Geoffrey Keynes (London: Faber & Faber, 1946), p. 19.
(55) Péguy, *Lettres et entretiens* (Paris: L'Artisan du Livre, 1927), Aug. 8, 1914, p. 36.

He fell leading his platoon in a charge at Villeroy, near Meaux, on September 5, on the eve of the First Battle of the Marne. With his death was born the legend of a noble patriotic life nobly sacrificed.   In the minds of many his most fitting epitaph would have been his own quatrain:

> Heureux ceux qui sont morts pour la terre charnelle
> Mais pourvu que ce fût dans une juste guerre.
> Heureux ceux qui sont morts pour quatre coins de terre.
> Heureux ceux qui sont morts d'une mort solennelle (56).

(56) Péguy, «Ève,» *Oeuvres poétiques complètes*, eds. Marcel Péguy, with an Introduction by François Porché (Paris: Gallimard, 1957), p. 1028.

CHAPTER II

PACIFISM IN THE FRENCH NOVEL BETWEEN THE
WORLD WARS

Introduction

It is not necessary to subscribe to Pierre-Joseph Proudhon's
thesis that «war is the deepest, the most sublime phenomenon of our moral life» (1) to concede that the problem of
war eradication is one of the thorniest ever to have tried
the wits of man.   In an ancient variation on the «make
love not war» theme, Aristophanes' Lysistrata could bring
an end to the fighting between the Athenians and the Spartans
by uniting their women in a campaign to withhold their
favors from their men.   But the solutions of the comic stage
are inoperative in the world of reality.   For his part, Gaston
Bouthoul, an astute student of the relationships between armed
conflict and the demographic structures of nations, is not
being facetious in maintaining that «the 'Club Méditerranée'
... has done more for the European concept [and therefore
for peace] than all political propaganda» (2).   This is well

_____

(1) Pierre-Joseph Proudhon, *La Guerre et la paix*, tome 2, in
Oeuvres complètes, vol. 14 (Paris: Librairie Internationale, 1869),
p. 302.
(2) Gaston Bouthoul, *L'Infanticide différé* (Paris: Hachette,
1970), p. 237.

and good, but it takes more than the Club Méditerranée concept to convert swords to plowshares so long as economic imbalances between nations exist, their populations explode, and the politicians that govern them think in terms of the balance of power. Moral disarmament can readily be preached by those who overlook man's native aggressiveness and, as Kant, De Maistre, and Proudhon all have emphasized, his strange fascination with war-begotten glory. Alfred de Vigny doubtless laid bare many a boy's mind and heart in describing how his classmates and he himself felt about being in school while the Napoleonic wars were still in progress. «War,» he wrote, «was very much present in the *lycée,* the drums were muffling the voices of the teachers, and the mysterious voice of books spoke only a cold and pedantic language to us. In our eyes logarithms and tropes were but steps to climb to the star of the Legion of Honor, the most beautiful star in the sky for children» (3). Few generals weep upon examining the casualty lists of their battles, as the victorious Wellington wept when he saw those of Waterloo. Writers of obituaries would assure us that the Pattons and the Rommels will join the Napoleons and the Alexanders in Valhalla's top gallery, and the incomparable panegyrist Pericles saw to it that the Athenians who fell in the Peloponnesian War received proper funerals. But peace crusaders have always met with formidable opposition. With the deeply disgruntled Germans of the early depression years pacifist Erich Maria Remarque's all-time best selling war novel, *All Quiet on the Western Front* (1929), proved no match for Adolf Hitler's *Mein Kampf,* and we are reminded that «Aristotle was a militarist, who gloried in the life of the soldier fighting for a just cause, who held that man's highest

---

(3) Alfred de Vigny, *Servitude et grandeur militaires,* ed. Gauthier-Ferrières (Paris: Bibliothèque Larousse, n.d.), p. 22.

ethical state was laying down his life with courage and devotion on the field of battle and who even went so far as to advocate imperialistic war for the express purpose of reducing to slavery people apparently so destined by nature» (4).

In addition, from time to time a latter-day Elie Faure comes forward, as he himself had done with the publication of his *La Danse sur le feu et l'eau* in 1920, not to oppose war but to argue against its suppression. As a doctor at the front Faure had witnessed human suffering at its worst. Yet, two years later, he was celebrating war as the fountainhead of art. Expressed as a syllogism his thesis would read: everything that stimulates art is good and desirable; war and revolutions stimulate art; therefore, war and revolutions are good and desirable. Peace was in his view a soporific that settled the potentially great artist into a comfortable sleep. Happily, periodic wars and revolutions arouse the sleeper, stir his subconscious mind, mobilize his passions, and kindle his imagination. To prop up his thesis Faure marshalled evidence to demonstrate that art had fallen heir to immense riches with each of what he considered to be the ten capital events of Western history: the conflict of Greece with Asia; Roman expansion, especially in Gaul; the advent of Christianity together with the barbarian invasions; the expansion of Islam; the development of the medieval communes; the Crusades; the Renaissance; the discovery and conquest of America, followed by the political unification of Spain; the Reformation; and the French Revolution. Civil wars and international wars both served the purpose, he argued, and even the loser gained because he too gathered the roses rising out of the ashes. What did it matter if their

---

(4) Everett Colgate Jessup, *War or Sport: an Endeavor to Contribute a Point of View to the Present Widespread Discussion on the Organization and Maintenance of Peace* (Roslyn, N.Y.: n.p., 1940), p. 11.

bloom was fuller, their color richer, for having been fertilized with warriors' bones? The beauty was everything and the price not exorbitant, since «the springing of a lyrical world from the bosom of a great people is sufficient justification for the carnage of a war and the furors of a revolution» (5).

With yet more armaments races in full flower, with nuclear instruments of destruction threatening man's very survival, and with wars following upon wars in an uninterrupted succession, the problem of war elimination enjoys a primacy of global interest. While politicians, statesmen, economists, psychologists, clergymen, and sundry others tirelessly search for a solution, numerous if lesser Tolstoys are warning adventurous youth against the jealous arms of the war Circe and attempting to chart a course to safer islands. On the other hand, for every film of the *Grand Illusion* and *Paths of Glory* type there are a score or more spotlighting war heroes and accenting the thrills of combat. Also, if their names are different, there are still some Kiplings, D'Annunzios, and Jüngers about, glorifiers of war that is a far cry from the blossom-decked institution described in the romances of chivalry, and the Agamemnons of today readily find their Homers.

Over the centuries the literary champions of peace—the likes of Rabelais, La Bruyère, Voltaire, Stendhal, Tolstoy, Melville, Brecht, and Böll—have been badly outnumbered. The butchery of the First World War was, however, to go a long way toward turning the balance. While it is true that after 1918 most of the literary profession in the countries most directly concerned dwelt on themes which, if anything, were intended to distract a haggard humanity from its mourn-

---

(5) Elie Faure, *La Danse sur le feu et l'eau* (Paris: Crès, 1920), p. 15. Cf. «... la guerre est la substance du lyrisme et de sa fortune. Oter la guerre aux lyriques, c'est leur ôter le pain de la

ing clothes, it is likewise true that of the authors who wrote on the war a far greater number than ever before rose up in verbal arms against it. Particularly in France, Germany, Great Britain, and the United States, a great number of anti-war works appeared, and not a few writers emerged from the holocaust as determined pacifists.

Noteworthy indeed are the antiwar currents in French prose in the inter-world wars years. Where such crusading for peace is concerned, no nation, with the possible exception of Germany, had more resolute representation. In his multitudinous essays Jean Guéhenno, first co-editor, then editor (from 1926 to 1929) of the internationalist review *Europe,* spoke religiously of his «patriotisme internationaliste» and contemptuously of the *patrie* concept, all the while making much of the grave responsibility of elders to impress the futility of wars upon the minds of restless youth (6). Surgeon Luc Durtain, also a stout internationalist, contributed a commendable novel, *La Guerre n'existe pas* (1939), in which he exalted life in the manner of Giono and cultivated the tone of *tendresse* and *sympathie* that had distinguished the best pages of the war books of Georges Duhamel. One of the earliest winners of the Médaille militaire in the First World War, Louis-Ferdinand Céline (*né* Destouches), bitterly assailed war and warmakers in his heavily autobiographic novel, *Voyage au bout de la nuit* (1932). Poet Pierre-Jean Jouve, France's second best known literary pacifist of World War I, used his rather lifeless biography of her leading pacifist of

---

bouche.» Julien Benda, *Billets de Sirius* (Paris: Le Divan, 1925), p. 90. Cited by Robert J. Niess, *Julien Benda* (Ann Arbor: The University of Michigan Press, 1956), p. 228.

(6) With France prostrate, Guéhenno made this entry in his diary on June 25, 1940. «I didn't know that I loved my country so much. I am full of grief, wrath, and shame.» *Journal des années noires, 1940-44* (Paris: Gallimard, 1947), p. 15.

the war, *Romain Rolland vivant, 1914-1919* (1920), as a springboard for an assault on war. Maxence Van der Meersch, only seven years of age when the Germans overran his native Flanders, produced a bulky, pacifist-slanted novel, *Invasion 14* (1935), which gave a vivid account of the material and moral destitution brought by war to people living in German-conquered territory. The prolific Victor Margueritte became one of France's most vocal advocates of revision of the Versailles Treaty and mounted a great attack on capitalists and militarists in *Non* (1931), *La Patrie humaine* (1931), and *Debout les vivants* (1932). A liberal ration of antiwar and in some cases merely antimilitarist novels was turned out by Paul Vaillant-Couturier, Léon Werth, Louis Guilloux, Claire Géniaux, Gabriel Chevalier, André Thérive, Raymond Escholier, René Arcos, Joseph Jolinon, Ernest Florian-Parmentier, Henry Poulaille, Paul Reboux, Raymond Lefebvre, Michel Corday, René Naegelen, Marcel Berger, Marcel Grancher, and Charles Delvert. By and large these emitted noisy cries of protest, too often drowning their messages in floods of oratory punctuated with coarse epithets and shrill fulminations.

Alain: War, a Crime of Passion

For philosopher-teacher-journalist Émile-Auguste Chartier (1868-1951), better known under the pseudonym Alain, writing about war without having taken part in it bordered on the obscene. Thus, he enlisted as a private at the age of forty-six despite his pacifist convictions. Turned down for infantry duty, he served for three years in the artillery before being invalided out with a foot injury. Not once did he lament his decision or complain about the suffering and dangers to which it had exposed him. But what he saw of war made of him, as it had made of the *ancien combattant* Hector of Giraudoux's play *La Guerre de Troie n'aura pas lieu,* a militant pacifist for the rest of his days. So intent was he on keeping his defenses up against the war monster that he blindly played into the hand of Hitler by preaching against French rearmament in the late thirties, and by promoting, early in the *drôle de guerre,* a pro-peace manifesto of which one of his cosignatories was Marcel Déat, a notorious collaborator in 1940-44.

It is chiefly in the several hundred essays—he called them «Propos»—of his *Mars ou la guerre jugée* (1921) and in its two-volume sequel, *Convulsion de la force* and *Échec de la force* (1939), that Alain waged his war on war. These severely pondered, densely packed, brief pieces are too abstract to have attracted a broad readership, even though they initially appeared in newspapers. As such, it is highly unlikely that they could have had appeal for the rank and file for whom Alain had felt a close affinity in and outside the trenches.

Liberally scattered throughout Alain's books are dogma dear to pacifist evangelists: on the preventability of war; on the sacred obligation to preserve independent judgment; on the need for standing firm against war propagandists, for rejecting the soporific of fatalistic resignation, for recognizing the power of international reconciliation through negotiation, for banning all but territorial armies, etc. On the other hand, Alain parts company with orthodox pacifists —if the species exists—in playing down the role of conflicting national interests, of big business, of munitions makers, and of militarists in causing wars. «Conflicts of interest,» he flatly states, «are the occasion of war; they are not at all its cause» (7). The cause, he never wearies of repeating, resides in the passions, the word being used in its broadest

---

(7)   Alain, *Mars ou la guerre jugée* (Paris: Gallimard, 1936), p. 41.

4

sense. Or, as he puts it, «... War is really a crime of passion» (8).

Probing unremittingly the soul of man, Alain finds that the passions, ignoble and noble alike, are leagued against him in sweeping him toward the abyss. Vanity, self-importance, cupidity, anger, fear, ambition, generosity, courage, pride, the sense of beauty, adaptability, self-discipline, honor —these are all mainsprings in war's great wheelworks. What most exercises him is the degree to which the nobler side of man contributes to the perpetuation of war. In fact, in his eyes it is this side of him that most betrays him where war prevention is concerned. Wars could not arise, he would assure us, if man in his generosity were less inclined to pay homage to a brave enemy; if he were not richly dowered of the courage that he admires in others and wants others to admire in him, of the pride that impels him to endeavor to surpass himself against even desperate odds, of the aesthetic sense that titillates him as he witnesses marching troops or the swirl of battle, of the adaptability and self-discipline that keep him from cracking under the strain of combat and exhaustion, and, above all, of a sense of honor, seen by him as war's prime instigator. But, since Alain succeeds in demonstrating that man is a hopeless bundle of passions, his urging that we cease being the tool of our passions, that we arrest their wayward impulses by a sharper exercise of the judgment and a stricter control of the will, seems utterly unavailing. We are forced to conclude that the volumes housing the antiwar lessons of this constitutionally optimistic moralist may as well be bordered in black.

---

(8) *Ibid.,* p. 85.

Roland Dorgelès, Short-Term Pacifist

No participant in the pacifist movements of his day, Roland Dorgelès (1886-1973), né Roland Léclavelé, temporarily allied himself with the cause of pacifism with the publication of his novel *Le Réveil des morts* (1923). As a machine-gunner in General Mangin's much battered Fifth Division he had lived war at its worst. In 1919 Dorgelès scored a great success with his war novel *Les Croix de bois,* universally acclaimed as one of the best of France's disappointingly few first-rate works of fiction issuing from the Great War. There is a distinct lest-we-forget note about the book, with the author leaning heavily on the mud and blood element, on military ruthlessness, civilian ingratitude, and so on. This is not to suggest, however, that *Les Croix de bois* is a pacifist work. At no time do its warriors allow personal hardship to influence their viewpoint on the validity of the war they are fighting; pride regularly conquers their indignation; and officers have no trouble finding volunteers for hazardous missions. And there is much else in it to win the favor of even a Déroulède or a Barrès.

In sharp contrast with the earlier book, *Le Réveil des morts* is a philippic replete with what may be termed a cynical pacifism, one that finds outlet in curses, cries, and jeremiads. Again the setting is a battle zone, Crécy, in the Aisne. But the fighting armies are gone now, and armies of laborers have invaded the area to rebuild the ruins and to disinter from fields and reinter in cemeteries the once hastily buried bodies of the many thousands of victims of the Chemin des Dames slaughter. When a law is passed compensating war damages, a pack of profiteers descends upon the devastated area. Agents, speculators, and shysters of every variety proceed to make quick work of emptying the purses of the *sinistrés*. In this jaded atmosphere even the higher principled become contaminated. The smell is pestilential, the catastrophe is complete, and the message is clear: a war from whose ashes so many vultures could rise simply was not worth waging.

Jules Romains, Man of Good Will

Jules Romains (1885-1972), whose real name was Louis Farigoule, was teaching philosophy in a Paris *lycée* when the First World War broke out—a bitter disappointment for this father of unanimism, a literary school having the efficacy of group action and the fraternal love of man for man among its main sources of inspiration. Declared unfit for active service, Romains was discharged after a short stint in uniform as an auxiliary. Although he had not seen the horrors of war through the eyes of a combatant, he recognized them for what they were and vowed always to be a laborer in the atelier of peace.

With aching heart he mourned, in his poem of epic breadth, «Europe» (1916), the dissevering of Europe, and declared war on warmakers. While implying no diminution of his love for France, he made it plain that the continent was his true fatherland. Continental kinship and the brightness of the peace of bygone years reflected against the blackness of war similarly made up the substance of the sprawling verses of his «Le Voyage des amants» (1925) and of his «Ode génois» (1925). In the mid-twenties Romains was already lecturing in Germany on the need for Franco-German collaboration. In the thirties he made frequent good-will lecture trips there as part of his private program for the rapprochement which he regarded as the key to European peace. The political essays of his *Le Couple France-Allemagne* (1934), originally published in newspapers, bore out his passionate concern for the common destiny of the two nations. As the book's title suggests, his ardor for French partnership with Germany in the peace effort remained undamped. Understandably, this left him wide open to criticism, since he seemed blind to the fact that the Beasts of Berlin were hardly men of good will; that partnership with Nazi Germany was one thing and the partnership championed by the poet Lamartine with the Germany of his day quite another (9). Sinking deeper into the morass of appeasement, in 1938 Romains made speeches in justification of the Munich Pact, sincerely believing that war had been averted by it.

His *Sept Mystères du destin de l'Europe* (1940) pictured him dashing about Western Europe during the years 1933 1939 to confer secretly with political notables as a self-appointed master engineer of world peace. This diplomatic amateur, this unofficial representative of and adviser to the Quai d'Orsay everywhere fought a rearguard action and lost. He was taken in rather badly by such old hands at the game as von Ribbentrop and especially Otto Abetz—the latter would become the German ambassador to Vichy France— totally unaware that he was dealing with Hitler-commissioned subverters of the French will to fight. Another prominent figure with whom he had close dealings was Belgian cabinet minister Henri de Man, a notorious appeaser and future head of the Belgian government of capitulation. *Sept Mystères* is, in sum, a sorry book, all the more so that it is bathed in acrimony and shows its well-meaning author

---

(9) Ironically, in his review of the book, socialist Pierre Brossolette supported Romains' initiatives. In 1944, Brossolette, who became an important Resistance leader during the German occupation, hurled himself to his death through a window of a Gestapo bureau on the sixth floor of an Avenue Foch building rather than risk betraying his comrades under torture. See «Le Couple France-Allemagne,» *Europe Nouvelle,* 18 (Feb. 16, 1935), 163-166.

living in a world of illusion and magnifying his errors by a deadly tone of self-exaltation that antagonizes the reader from cover to cover.

Pacifism bulks large in Romains' enormous *roman-fleuve,* the twenty-seven volume *Les Hommes de bonne volonté.* Well it might because it was published between 1932 and 1946 and aimed at giving a panoramic view of French society between October 6, 1908, and October 7, 1933. The best of the men of good will in it, fictional and historical, are those exerting themselves to contain the war menace. Their efforts come to naught, of course, since there is no way that fiction can get around the facts of history. As regards the series' fictional heroes, the best that they can manage in their effort to save Europe is to form a secret society with an élite membership handpicked for honesty, intelligence, courage, and boldness, devoted to war prevention by, amongst and above other things, the assassination of men in high places holding the diplomatic dynamite in any war situation. As this patently mirrors Romains' own thinking on the matter, it may be concluded both that he had never lost his fascination with the notion that an individual had unlimited power to change history through covert activity and that he himself was quite willing to vault over moralistic fences to preserve peace.

There can be no question that it was to awaken the consciousness of Europeans to the threat of war that Romains wrote *Prélude à Verdun* and *Verdun,* volumes 15 and 16 of his series. There is, of course, not a little irony in the fact that these volumes appeared in the year of Munich. *Prélude à Verdun* is concerned with the entire period of the war leading up to the titanic battle; *Verdun* with the first two months of the nine-months battle. Amongst their characters are such familiar figures from the cycle's earlier installments as the greedy manipulator Haverkamp, now raking in millions in war profits; Laulerque, both the chief believer in the efficacy of activism by secret societies and the chief activist; *Normalien agrégés* and inseparable friends, Jallez and Jerphanion, and the schoolteacher Clanricard. The last had been warning his pupils in 1933, fourteen volumes earlier, that Europe was once more standing at the brink of war. Here, as in the preceding volumes, Jerphanion is the principal articulator of the author's opinions. What, then, is the picture of war that Romains paints?

Melancholy is the lot of warriors who are again and again obliged to try to pierce the stubborn enemy defenses. It is like «hurtling toward a great wall of quarry stones to tear it apart with your fingernails» (10). But what do a few thousand deaths amount to if a hundred yards may be gained and the prospects for promotion of an energetic commander are improved? Besides, the men have to be kept in fighting trim. And in a war of attrition, as the sloganeers were phrasing it, the side that holds out for one last quarter of an hour is the side that wins. So much the worse if to feed the French war machine during the first half of 1915 five thousand men a day were being sacrificed —«as many as a city as big as Poitiers was able to supply at the mobilization» (11). So much the worse too if war contractors were dining in plush restaurants on partridge, oysters, and vintage wines and «fortunes were springing from the public ruins like obscene mushrooms» (12).

Truly, the rot was all-pervading. Villagers behind the lines were cheerfully filling their coffers at the expense of the hapless troops. Well-connected rear echelon officers were strutting about like heroes and scheming for decorations,

---

(10) Jules Romains, *Prélude à Verdun* (Paris: Flammarion, 1938), p. 19.

(11) *Ibid.,* p. 50.

(12) *Ibid.,* p. 56.

choice billets, and power. At headquarters offices bureaucratic muddle and red tape were the rule. Back home, war
widows, real and synthetic, were carrying on shamelessly,
and second-guessing jingoistic civilians were blasting commanders for not ordering yet more massive assaults on the
enemy lines. In Paris, military careers were being made
and unmade in the power center that was Madame Godorp's
salon and, to be sure, Barrès, Lavedan, and Richepin were
dutifully applying themselves to the task of propelling fighting
men toward their deaths against an enemy which, they were
telling them, was poorly equipped, starving, and hanging on
the ropes.

Romains gives his readers a full measure of war-born
degradation and quite enough death, even if he allows only
one of the characters of his *Les Hommes de bonne volonté*
cycle, Wazemmes, to die. And Romains early signals what
he is about: infantry lieutenant Jerphanion, describing life
in the trenches to Jallez, observes, «*Nothing is worth that ...*
That is the last word on the wisdom of war. All the rest
is literature» (13). The novelist's art serves him well. He
makes us amply conscious of the Gehenna of the Western
Front without thrusting himself onto his pages, without
aiming to shock us with visions of the macabre, and—as
though he were aping Tolstoy—without even showing us
much of actual battle. He narrates quietly, piles evidence
on evidence, and employs satire, frequently of a stinging
variety, to accomplish what many an antiwar writer has
attempted to accomplish by means of an eternity of ghastly
scenes and the fiery rhetoric of rebellious soldiers. His
lesson is no less effective for his choosing to rub it into us
gently. Viewed more broadly, *Prélude à Verdun* and *Verdun*
together not only represent the high watermark of the *Les*

(13) *Ibid.,* p. 171.

Hommes de bonne volonté series but constitute one of the finest works of fiction on World War I published in any language.

Romain Rolland above and in the Mêlée

Towering above all laborers for peace among the French literary set was the indefatigable Romain Rolland (1866-1944.) From the moment he mounted an assault on war in his drama *Le Temps viendra* (1903) until the earliest squalls of the Hitlerian tempest his voice carried a message of peace to every continent. He penned more antiwar lines than any other writer of fiction of our century, and his field of inquiry was so wide as to embrace within its bounds everything from the encouragement of experiments with ants on the war instinct at one extreme to the endorsement of communist revolution at the other. Rolland's position among the antiwar writers figuring in this study is also unique because his peace crusading during the First World War attracted far more notice than that done by him after the war.

The action of *Le Temps viendra* unfolds during the British conquest of Transvaal and centers upon the conflict of individual conscience with allegiance to the fatherland. The leading character, Lord Clifford, commander in chief of the British forces, tries to reconcile his sense of duty with his sense of fair play, only to die by the hand of an unforgiving enemy—a six-year-old boy! The accused here is Great Britain and the crime is the Boer War. Imperialism is the accessory before the fact, since Rolland projects the guilt to all nations bent on colonial conquest. Their machinations he regards not only as an indefensible abuse of power but also the spark that inevitably kindles the conflagration of war. The play's British heroes are less numerous than its villains, but the villainy of the latter is partly mitigated by the honest soul-searching which they do with respect to the war they are waging, and, Rolland intimates, by the fatality which impels them to continue. Although fighting for a just cause, the Boers are not above sin either, with the reader being pointedly reminded that they too had once subjugated and enslaved an innocent people. Rollandian ideology is here embodied in a pair of minor characters. One is a diehard Italian volunteer in the Boer forces who braves death to shout in the faces of his captors: «Everything unjust is my enemy ... My fatherland is everywhere that liberty is violated» (14). The other is a youthful Scot ruled by Christian principles. Refusing to be a party any longer to badly tarnished patriotism, he quits the fight. Condemned to death for his defiance, he is heard saying as he is being taken away with Boer prisoners: «The time will come when all men will know the truth, when they shall beat their swords into plowshares and their spears into pruning hooks, when the lion shall lie down by the lamb ... The time will come» (15).

It could not have been for the literary virtues of his ten-volume novel, *Jean-Christophe* (1904-12), that Romain Rolland was awarded the Nobel Foundation's prize for literature in 1915. A wild discursiveness, a total lack of compression, and an insipid style—to mention but some of its shortcomings—make the reading of its several thousand pages quite a challenging proposition. Notwithstanding that, it is a powerful plea for brotherly concord between the French and the Germans and, by extension, between the citizens of all European nations. Having a Tolstoyan fervor and an absolute sincerity as its earmarks, this magnificently idealistic work has deservedly been numbered among the noblest of

---

(14) Romain Rolland, *Le Temps viendra*, in *Cahiers de la Quinzaine*, 14e cahier de la IVe série (March 10, 1903), p. 116.
(15) *Ibid.*, p. 148.

our century. Like the Heinrich Heine of earlier years, so fondly remembered by the French, its leading character, Jean-Christophe Krafft, is a German who settles in France and dedicates himself to the task of bringing the French and the Germans closer together. Like him too, he is a sworn adversary of militarism. Christophe is not, however, a writer, but a composer of genius modelled on Beethoven.

There were rather enough tensions on the international scene from 1900 to 1912, the years during which the action of *Jean-Christophe* occurs, to add the dimension of timeliness to the work. Moreover, Rolland perceived all too clearly the menace lurking beneath the festering sores of a nationalism that the War of 1870-71 had further aggravated. For that reason he embarked on the mission of awakening Europeans to the fact that they were inhabiting a tottering structure. Speaking through the mouth of his hero, he thus phrased it: «... If you wonder why a man should give himself so much trouble, why he should struggle ... well, be informed: because France is dying, because our civilization, the admirable edifice constructed at the cost of so many centuries of effort by us humans, would otherwise be engulfed ... The fatherland is in danger, our European fatherland ...» (16).

To inculcate in Christophe a sympathetic understanding of other peoples, Rolland dispatched him on a leisurely odyssey through France, Switzerland, and Italy, the three countries that he himself knew best. Because Rolland recognized in the ever-smoldering animosity of the French and Germans the principal obstacle to European peace, he imposed upon himself the monumental burden of interpreting these two peoples to each other with the intent of demonstrating that

---

(16) Rolland, *Jean-Christophe*, vol. 7: *Dans la maison* (Paris: Ollendorff, 1909), p. 201.

theirs was an inescapable interdependence (17). To that end he joined his German protagonist with Olivier, a young French writer-musician, in a deep and abiding friendship. Radical differences of background and temperament, personal habits and biases, heated quarrels—nothing would destroy it. A harsh critic of his native Germany, Christophe is at the same time critical of his adopted country to the point of inconoclasm until Olivier becomes his bosom friend and patient mentor. If ultimately Christophe acquires a «European» soul and the myths of racial superiority are demolished, this is mainly due to the exemplary devotion of Olivier and to the equally exemplary receptivity of Christophe to salutary influence.

It is an older and, Rolland would assure us, wiser Christophe who, in the final volume of this *Bildungsroman,* vows his neutrality in the war that he no longer considers avoidable. In France, a new generation is flexing its muscles and readying itself for combat. In Italy, the indolent, indifferent youth of yesterday now dream of Roman eagles soaring above the sands of Libya. In Germany and in Eastern Europe, the demons of nationalism are making ominous noises. Exhibiting a talent for prognostication, Rolland prefaced the volume with the warning: «I have written the tragedy of a generation which is going to disappear» (18).

Twice in the pages of *Jean-Christophe* the European powder keg was on the verge of exploding. When in August

---

(17) Many years later, Nazi authorities frowned on Rolland's missionary undertaking. He observed: «At the Oranienburg concentration camp, which Vildrac visited in 1934, *Jean-Christophe* was displayed in a glass case, with the works of Marx, Engels, and of German or Russian communists, in the «museum» of banned books, burned or to be burned.» «Préface,» *Quinze Ans de combat, 1919-1934* (Paris: Rieder, 1935), lxxix.

(18) Rolland, «Préface,» *Jean-Christophe,* vol. 10: *La Nouvelle Journée* (Paris: Ollendorff, 1912), i.

1914 it actually did explode, Rolland was in Switzerland, in which country he had been spending his summer vacations for some time. Exempt from military service for reasons of age and health, he did not return to France. From October 1914 to July 1915 he worked as a clerk and letter writer for the Geneva Red Cross in a bureau whose business was the maintenance of communications between prisoners and their families and the repatriation of refugees. In 1916 he donated forty thousand dollars, his Nobel Prize money, to a fund for the relief of war victims.

In the tumultuous days following the outbreak of war, when millions of socialist and syndicalist pacifists of the warring nations were, like everybody else, submitting to military conscription; when old rebels Anatole France, Gustave Hervé, and Octave Mirbeau were parading their loyalty to the *patrie* and the army, Rolland adamantly refused to surrender moral principle to practical necessity. The war was affording him an unwanted opportunity to demonstrate how profoundly he was imbued with the principles upheld by his fictional sons, Jean-Christophe and Olivier. In Switzerland, he immediately undertook to write articles and open letters in which he made it clear that to his mind a narrow patriotism was an evil to be exorcised even on the part of those engaged in a just war. Most of these appeared in the *Journal de Genève* during the early months of hostilities. However, because for nearly a year the French public had been reading only garbled excerpts of these writings in the press, Rolland assembled them for publication in a book. It appeared in October 1915 and was named *Au-dessus de la Mêlée* after one of its articles, originally published in September 1914.

To the guardians of national solidarity it mattered not at all that Rolland, in addressing French combatants, spoke of the inevitability of their victory in a cause wherein, he contended, human liberty was at stake; that he publicly castigated the Germans for their violation of Belgian neutrality and for their bombardment of the cathedral of Rheims and the destruction of Louvain; that he distributed the blame for the provocation of war among three «rapacious eagles» —Austria, czarist Russia, and Prussia—styling the last «brutal Prussia;» (19) that he noisily condemned the ninety-three German intellectuals who had signed a manifesto pledging unconditional support to their nation in its war effort. What mattered very much to them was his resolve to keep an open mind, to sit in judgment on both sides in an hour when the national existence was fairly hanging in the balance. But the managers of the French war effort were not to be impressed by sermons on the need for respecting spiritual and intellectual values by an individual who, they thought, was taking delight in viewing himself as a moral force. About the only moral force interesting them was that displayed by soldiers in the fighting lines, the one Napoleon had reckoned to be three times as important as physical force in war.

Quite unmindful of the fact that the air of neutral Belgium was still heavy with the smoke of German-lit fires and that patriotic feeling in France had mounted to an unprecedented pitch, Rolland insisted upon drawing a sharp distinction between the German people and their rulers. In an hour when the *Mercure de France* was under attack for keeping its pages free of the derogatory appellation *Boche,* he was publicly expressing sentiments of chivalry and magnanimity toward the enemy. At a time when the French were desperately trying to rally their forces to halt the invader, Rolland was generously saluting the Germans as brothers. With Paris almost within earshot of booming

---

(19) Rolland, «Au-dessus de la Mêlée,» *Au-dessus de la Mêlée* (Paris: Ollendorff, 1915), p. 32.

artillery, he had words of praise for «heroic» German youth fighting «to defend the thought and city of Kant against the flood of Cossack horsemen» (20). And although he repprimanded German intellectuals for fanning the flames of nationalism, he no less severely took to task French cultural leaders for surrendering to the military machine.

Never were conditions less propitious for the spreading of a gospel of fraternity. Pacifism was bankrupt in all the belligerent countries. The minds of intellectuals were just as mobilized as were those of the population at large. On powers bent only on victory and impregnated with the dogma of von Clausewitz on how wars are won all talk of minimizing spiritual wounds and of preparing for the reconciliations of tomorrow was lost. The crowning irony was that in Germany, Otto Grautoff, the translator of *Jean-Christophe,* was willfully distorting Rolland's lines and denouncing him as an abettor of a lying French press. There a holy war was being preached, with the unlikely figure of Thomas Mann emerging as one of many modern counterparts of Peter the Hermit and even lauding war as a regenerator of life-sustaining forces. In England, an enraptured Kipling was singing war hymns; H. G. Wells, John Galsworthy, and Alfred Noyes were busy rallying their countrymen round the union jack, and the old champion of peace, George Bernard Shaw, had rejected out of hand Rolland's invitation to him to unite with other European intellectuals in a show of protest against the destruction of Louvain and the bombardment of the cathedral of Rheims (21). In France, Maeterlinck had sought

---

(20) *Ibid.,* p. 21.
(21) In explaining his wartime position, Shaw stated: «In my own case conscientious objection did not arise: I was past military age. I did not counsel others to object, and should not have objected myself if I had been liable to serve; for intensely as I loathed the war, and free as I was from any illusions as to its

to enlist for combat at fifty-two, Anatole France at seventy. Saint-Saëns had placed himself on record as having put off all composing of music for the duration. Vincent d'Indy was glorifying war as a regenerative force. There was clamor in some quarters for the suppression of the study of German in the schools. Some good patriots were proposing that eau de Cologne be renamed «eau de Pologne.» Philosopher Henri Bergson had joined Maeterlinck, Lucien Daudet, and numerous other men of letters in heaping scorn upon the Teutonic enemy, and as president of the Academy of Moral Sciences he had enlisted its support in «the struggle... of civilization against barbarism» (22). In the *Écho de Paris* of December 27, 1914, it was proposed that there be devised a «complete system of extermination» for use on the Germans, alleged to be «more ferocious than sewer rats,» and deserving a sewer rat as the «emblem of their race» (23). Barrès, long the literati's chief advocate of *revanche* and the energetic promoter of «la terre et les morts» ideology, was in his glory. Helping initiate the Croix de guerre as a medal for military valor, tirelessly calling down evil upon the «vile [German] Beast» and the «bloodstained Tartuffes» in pointed helmets, and filling so many newspaper columns with war propaganda that ultimately it would take the fourteen volumes of his *Chronique de la Grande Guerre* (1920-1924) to hold them,

---

character, and from the patriotic urge ..., I knew that when war is once let loose, and it becomes a question of kill or be killed, there is no stopping to argue about it: one must just stand by one's neighbors and take a hand with the rest.» «War madness», in *Shaw: An Autobiography: 1898-1950*, vol. 2: *The Playwright Years*. Selected from his writings by Stanley Weintraub (New York: Weybright and Talley, 1970), p. 99.

(22) Cited by Rolland in «Au-dessus de la Mêlée,» *Au-dessus de la Mêlée*, p. 27.

(23) Reported by Rolland in *Journal des années de guerre 1914-1919*, ed. Marie Romain Rolland, with a Preface by Louis Martin-Chauffier (Paris: Albin Michel, 1952), Cahier IV, p. 199.

he was in a class by himself as an animator of nationalist sentiment. Praised by his admirers as the principal artisan of France's «union sacrée» of wartime, he was derided by others as the «generalissimo of the home front,» as a «serviceman of the rear,» and the like. To Rolland he was «the nightingale of the carnage» (24).

There was, to be sure, a great deal in Rolland's predicatory pieces of which an imperilled France was duly wary. Knowing that their context would be deliberately falsified in enemy countries, fearing that they would be damaging to French interests in the neutral ones and that some of his words might not fall on deaf ears domestically, war propagandists launched an all-out assault against him in the press. He was branded a deserter, a defeatist, a *Boche,* a *métèque,* a Judas acting in secret complicity with the Germans. Reference to «thirty pieces of silver» became a veritable leitmotif of the attacks on him. It was suggested that he give thought to changing his name from Rolland to Ganelon, and he received mail addressed to such as «Herr Professeur Rolland, auteur de *Jean-Allboche.*» Chauvinist propagandists Paul Souday and Henri Massis found it necessary to inform their readers that the creator of Jean-Christophe was French, not Swiss. Massis took the trouble to publish an entire volume, *Romain Rolland contre la France* (1915), to hold him up to proper reprobation. He was the recipient of postcards depicting the cathedral of Rheims in flames on which were inscribed the words «The work of your friends» (25). Most venomous of his vituperators was Paul-Hyacinthe Loyson. With his book *Etes-vous neutres devant le crime?* (1916), boldly prefaced with the words «by a logical pacifist,» Loyson attempted to prove that since the beginning of the war

---

(24) *Ibid.,* Cahier II, p. 131.
(25) *Ibid.,* Cahier II, p. 100.

5

Rolland had become a member of the enemy's Bund Neues Vaterland. Of him Rolland wrote: «Setting out for war from the rear to cut the dragon in two, entering the lists with a great crash, and sounding the horn, was the most enormous of those Saint Georges, Paul-Hyacinthe Loyson. There is no way of knowing when he would have finished the job because, after a few years, death had disposed of him. Anyhow, he surely had hopes of disposing of me» (26). In short, the unambiguous message communicated to Rolland by his compatriots was essentially the same as that communicated by their compatriots to Wilhelm Foerster in Germany, to Norman Angell in England, and to Jane Addams in the United States, namely, that nations at war sometimes tend to regard their outspoken champions of the spirit of brotherhood between opposing belligerents as more dangerous enemies than those firing bullets at their sons.

Nor are psychological factors to be discounted in the matter. Rolland's repeatedly addressing himself to a European «élite intellectuelle,» to an «élite intelligente,» and his referring to himself as a member of a «little lay church» privileged in having «the most extensive ties with the entire universe» (27), could not but provoke resentment on all sides. Also, the French were much too busy grappling with the hard realities of survival to be impressed by the pronouncements of a citizen of their nation who from his lofty perch on Alpine slopes was vociferously attesting to the strength of his resolve to remain a faithful servant of the cause of peace. It was all too easy for one so sheltered to preach «inter arma caritas» and to raise his voice in protest against the «defections» of intellectual, political, and religious leaders.

_____

(26) Rolland, «Adieu au passé,» _Europe_, no. 26 (1931), p. 192.
(27) Rolland, «Lettre à ceux qui m'accusent,» _Au-dessus de la Mêlée_, p. 83.

The very title *Au-dessus de la Mêlée* was offensive to those in the real *mêlée* below (28). Finally, the self-meritorious note evident on dozens of pages of his writings of 1914 and 1915 betrays the fact that he found quite bearable his martyrdom of those years.

That Rolland had been spending his energy to no avail is nowhere better illustrated than in the German reaction to his «Lettre ouverte à Gerhart Hauptmann» of August 29, 1914, in which he had denounced the invasion of Belgium as well as alleged German atrocities.   In speaking of the bombardment of Malines and of the destruction of Louvain, he had asked the Germans if they considered themselves to be «the grandsons of Goethe or of Attila» (29).   It was bad enough that in his reply, published in the *Corriere della Sera*, Hauptmann gave him no satisfaction, electing rather to sound a *Krieg ist Krieg* note (30).   What particularly upset him, however, was the insidious manner in which elements of the French press reacted to it.   He duly observed that in reaction to the question addressed by him to the Germans on their spiritual lineage the French press accused him of flattering the enemy as being «the sons of Goethe,» while the German Press assailed him for denominating Germans «sons of Attila» (31).   In the end Rolland's outspokenness on various issues related to the war was to draw the fire of all: of conservatives, socialists, and communists, of belligerents and neutrals, of

---

(28) Writing in support of «national unanimity» in his own country, H. G. Wells thus derided those assuming an above-the-battle posture in time of national danger: «'Au-dessus de la Mêlée' —as the man said when they asked him where he was when the bull gored his sister.» H. G. Wells, *Italy, France and Britain at War* (New York: Macmillan, 1917), p. 196.
(29) «Lettre ouverte à Gerhart Hauptmann,» *Au-dessus de la Mêlée*, p. 7.
(30) See Rolland, *Journal des années de guerre*, Cahier II, pp. 48-49.
(31) *Ibid.*, Cahier II, p. 96.

pacifists who saw him as insufficiently pacifistic, and of revolutionaries who resented his qualified espousal of the Russian Revolution.

Realizing that his words were being wasted on a stubbornly unreceptive audience, Rolland remained silent from early summer, 1915, to November 1916. Then he resumed writing articles and open letters for publication in Swiss newspapers and reviews. A collection of these appeared in 1919 under the title *Les Précurseurs*. Like *Au-dessus de la Mêlée,* the book is made up of heterogeneous pieces, with the author applying himself to everything from promoting a worldwide «internationale» of the mind to berating the histrionic American evangelist Billy Sunday for his fanatical endorsement of the war. Rolland gave this work the title *Les Précurseurs* in tribute to the few European intellectuals who in his estimation had succeeded in preserving the independence of their minds and their international faith during the war. In the front rank of these kindred spirits he placed Henri Barbusse, Andreas Latzko, Stefan Zweig, Maxim Gorki, Auguste Forel, G.-F. Nicolaï, and E. D. Morel. Undeterred by the narrowness of this circle, he spared no effort to maintain contact between them and other like-minded souls and to give impetus to collective antiwar crusading by them.

Les Précurseurs derives its significance from the fact that it marked the expansion of Rolland's ideal from a European to a global scale. Whereas in *Jean-Christophe* he stressed the indispensability of cultural links in the establishment of a European fatherland, in December 1916 he spoke of a United States of Europe and envisioned the eventual union of Europe and Asia (32). A convert to communism in the wake of the Russian Revolution, by March 1918 he was

---

(32) See «La Route en lacets qui monte,» *Les Précurseurs* (Paris: Éditions de «L'Humanité,» 1919), pp. 17-18.

looking forward to the day when the whole world would be as one vast country, pleased that war was speeding its advent.

The year 1919 saw the appearance of Rolland's allegorical drama *Liluli,* a burlesque satire on war and the illusions that make war possible. It recounts the facile victory of the wheedling, blue-eyed, blonde goddess Liluli—anagrammatic for «l'Illusion»—in plunging the Gallipoulets (the French) and the Hurluberloches (the Germans) into war. Prodigal of embraces and of promises of deathless glory, she transforms in a twinkling loving friends into mortal foes, bearing all of them off on gun carriages and driving them to destruction. Ultimately even the play's all-mocking hunchback, Polichinelle, perishes. Up to then he had been immunized against Liluli's charms by his laughter, and was wont to quipping, «Héros en bière, j'aime mieux bière en mon goulot.»

The ardent goddess is ably seconded by energetic lieutenants. Amongst the ablest are: another goddess, Llôp'ih (l'Opinion—public opinion), as powerful as she is intolerant. The selfish Maître-Dieu; appearing in the guise of an oriental peddler, this charlatan holds Truth (la Vérité), a promiscuous lass, in his bondage while spurring men to the slaughter and bestowing his blessings on both camps. The Diplomats; for them diplomacy is a game in which victory demands the casual sacrifice of helpless pawns. The Fat Men (les Gros), chiefly munitions makers reeking of the stench of gunpowder. The Intellectuals; their honeyed phrases swell rivers with blood. The sword-rattling Academicians; their spokesman is Polonius, a member of various pro-peace organizations who so manages things that military authorities have reason to pin decorations on him.

Liluli cannot by any stretch of the imagination be considered a worthy addition to the arsenal of antiwar literature. As an expression of bitterness and demoralization it challenges comparison with Céline's works at their gloomiest. Despair is its keynote, however earthy its wit and lusty its laughter. Unquestionably the book was symptomatic of greatly deepened pessimism on the part of Rolland. Whereas in *Au-dessus de la Mêlée* he had given his nod of approval to his countrymen in what he accounted their fight against Prussian imperialism, he now looks back at the war as a gigantic hoax perpetrated on the French and German populations alike. Whereas his *Jean-Christophe* was a paean to life, love, and fraternity, Life is here portrayed as a sneer-provoking headless male smelling like a menagerie; Love, as a snivelling little idiot; Fraternity, as a voracious cannibal. Yet, even in a farce there are bounds which the farcical cannot with impunity overstep. The intense sympathy and Tolstoyan fervor lighting up the pages of *Jean-Christophe* have here given way to ill-camouflaged biliousness, vindictiveness, and sterile negativism. Whereas in *Les Précurseurs* Rolland had likened progress to a long, winding road, slowly rising toward a distant if at times seemingly unattainable objective, with his *Liluli* he strongly suggests that progress is impossible of realization.

Clerambault, subtitled *Histoire d'une conscience libre pendant la guerre,* was begun by Rolland in 1916 and completed in 1920. His most thoroughly pacifist novel, it was also his worst, so that its shrill, over-articulated message long ago accompanied it to oblivion (33). It is the story of a man's dual struggle during the war: with his conscience and with the mighty forces of prevailing opinion. It is not, however, a novelistic autobiography, even if there are nu-

---

(33) In response to an inquiry by René Cheval concerning his sentiments on Rolland, Albert Camus intimated that Rolland's art had been subverting his ideological purposes. He wrote: «I feel as close to him in conscience as I am remote from him in everything having to do with style.» René Cheval, *Romain Rolland, l'Allemagne et la guerre* (Paris: Presses Universitaires de France, 1963), p. 7.

merous resemblances between Rolland's predicament of the war yars and that of Clerambault, the book's hero.

Clerambault is a self-satisfied poet of dubious talent who claims to be an idealist, humanitarian, and pacifist. When war erupts, his son, Maxime, enlists. Although he does not himself enlist, Clerambault swiftly succumbs before the ubiquity of patriotic emotion. On one occasion he carries his belligerency to the point of shouting «Beat him up!» when he comes upon a mob roughing up an individual whom he assumes to be an antipatriot or a spy. Later, news of Maxime's death at the front causes him to retrace his steps. He now launches a vigorous solo campaign against the war. His evangelistic fervor, which for the most part finds expression in antiwar articles and tracts, meets with violent opposition in the form of estrangement from his family, public slander, and physical beatings. Nevertheless, he stands heroically against the ever-mounting tide until finally, like Jaurès, he is struck down by a fanatical patriot.

As in the case of Rolland, Clerambault's pacifism of wartime had provoked a storm of abuse. A jingoist newspaper nicknamed him «L'Un contre tous.» He was vilified as a «Boche» and a defeatist, and attempts were made to trump up charges of treason against him. Time after time his lines were misquoted and his thoughts misrepresented. Publishers slammed their doors in his face. He was not to be intimidated. He simply went on damning all parties supporting the war effort: the masses, for passively accepting the slaughter; the socialists as the most shameful of shameful abdicators; the bourgeoisie as misusers of power; the intellectuals as distillers of propagandist poisons; the munitions manufacturers and diverse other profiteers; and last but not least, the fair sex, «bacchantes of war,» who had all but pushed their husbands toward the inferno.

In his tautly woven novelette *Pierre et Luce* (1920),

Rolland brought into bold relief the antithesis between the sweetness of young love and the insanity of a war to which it was to fall victim. Pierre, a working-class student of seventeen, and Luce, an aspiring painter of bourgeois origin, meet in a Paris subway station during a shelling by German long-range cannon. They fall deeply in love. In their purity of heart and total lack of sophistication the youthful lovers call to mind the Paul and Virginie of Bernardin de Saint-Pierre. Their idyll is short-lived. Six months later, on Good Friday, 1918, they die together in the Church of Saint Gervais when the Big Berthas make a direct hit on that historic edifice (34).

Try as they had been doing to hide from the specter of war, it everywhere overtook them. With Pierre's class due to be called up for service in a half-year, the prospect of impending combat duty had all but paralyzed him in spirit. Spring's triumphant arrival was for the tender lovers but a grim reminder that their dream of happiness would soon be dissolving, since the joyful music of the birds was accompanied by the muffled roar of distant cannon. As the fateful day of Pierre's induction drew near, they had a presentiment that they would be spared the misery of inhabiting a world doomed, in their eyes, to bloodier butchery and vaster ruins. In the end they died as they wished to die—in each other's arms.

Thus, in *Pierre et Luce* war is primarily indicted on the charge of rubbing out the lives of those most innocent of its evils, the young. But the reader is at the same time made conscious of other damage wrought by it. The widowed mother of Luce had become pregnant after accepting employ-

---

(34) The shelling of the Church of Saint Gervais on that date was not a fiction. Seventy-five persons were killed by it during Tenebrae devotions. Recalled by Harold March in his *Romain Rolland* (New York: Twayne Publishers, 1971), p. 97.

in a munitions plant, an irremissible sin in Rolland's book. She had been, he emphasizes, «crazed by the poison fermenting in the promiscuity» reigning in these «manufactories of lewdness and murder» (35). She was not alone, as moral decay was evident in the form of innumerable broken homes and of widespread drunkenness and dissipation.

The book's pacifist thesis is, to be sure, patent, but it rarely intrudes. Of wordy rhetoric, of heightened effects, there is very little. The story moves along on its own strength and is told with a concision and charm conspicuously absent from the author's other antiwar fiction. It is to be regretted that he did not more often cultivate a gift for delicate artistry that he manifestly possessed.

The central factor influencing Rolland's thinking in the inter-world wars era was his simultaneous attraction to communism and to the teachings of Gandhi. His book *Mahatma Gandhi* (1924) was a sympathetic study of the great Indian leader and an in-depth examination of his productive application of the theory of nonviolent resistance (Satyagraha). Insisting on its dynamic aspect, Rolland preferred to speak of nonresistance as nonviolence. His interest in Satyagraha in particular and in Indian culture in general placed him on intimate terms with Indian notables Gandhi, Tagore, Nehru, Lajpat Rai, and the Boses—Jagadis and Subhas. The first two paid him visits at his Villeneuve, Switzerland, home; Tagore in 1926, Gandhi in 1931.

With the problem of war prevention always uppermost in his mind, Rolland, who was constitutionally inimical to the employment of violence, became obsessed with the question of the suitability of nonviolent resistance for Western civilization. He soon came to regard it as a potent weapon in the war on war. When, in the December 3, 1921 issue

_____
(35) Rolland, *Pierre et Luce* (Paris: Ollendorff,, 1920), p. 138.

of the pacifist review *Clarté*, Henri Barbusse initiated what developed into a widely publicized debate with him by insisting upon the necessity of violence in the revolution which both of them considered requisite to the abolition of war, Rolland countered with the argument that Gandhi's nonviolent techniques had produced impressive results in sapping British domination in India. Barbusse had coined the term «Rolland-istes» for all revolution-craving intellectuals whose «labors» in its behalf were confined to «decorative» recriminations. Barbusse sought to persuade them that recourse to violence in revolutionary action was but a provisional step, altogether justified by the end in view. In his response Rolland took strong exception to that contention, emphasizing that the means were even more important to progress than the end, «because the end (so rarely attained, and always incompletely) only modifies the external relations between men. But the means mold their minds, either in conformity with the rhythm of justice or with the rhythm of violence. And if it is the latter, no form of government will ever prevent the oppression of the weak by the strong» (36). Moral values, he continued, should be even more zealously guarded during a revolution, when men's minds are most susceptible to change. This open letter and succeeding ones on the subject left little doubt that Rolland, while unreservedly approving of communism's declared overall objectives, was strenuously opposed to its policy on violence and to its infringements upon the rights of individuals. He would, he pledged, never condone the subservience of moral or ethical values to the *raison d'état*.

---

(36) Rolland, «Première lettre ouverte de Romain Rolland à Henri Barbusse,» *Quinze Ans de combat, 1919-1934* (Paris: Rieder, 1935), p. 37. Reprinted from an early 1922 issue of the *Art Libre* of Brussels.

There is a large preoccupation with peacemaking in Rolland's last novel, the dull seven-volume cycle *L'Ame enchantée* (1922-33). Its action spans three decades, ending in the early thirties, when events in Nazi Germany and Fascist Italy were foreboding another European blood bath. The story begins as an apologia of ultraindividualism as the most effective means of flouting bourgeois morality and closes with an appeal for the espousal of communism. First and foremost, it pretends to be an anthem to sincerity and liberty. The leading characters are Annette Rivière and her love child, Marc.

The pacifism of *L'Ame enchantée* is for the most part compressed into the two volumes of the cycle's third installment, *Mère et fils* (1927). Covering the war years, this section once again affords Rolland the opportunity of holding forth as a critic of the holocaust. He flays in all directions. Hard blows fall on turncoat socialists and syndicalists, on Christians now dutifully rendering to Caesar what is Caesar's, on parents, sisters, and fiancées, for either tacitly sanctioning the participation of their loved ones in the slaughter or for openly urging them on. Concentrating his attention on the home front throughout the entire six hundred pages of *Mère et fils*, Rolland paints a dark picture of wartime morality. Women are shown nonchalantly cheating on absent husbands, with the author sarcastically excusing their transgressions for patriotically reserving their favors for Allies alone. Children freed from parental surveillance frequent disreputable haunts and bathe in an insalubrious atmosphere of eroticism and excess. Illegitimate births rapidly multiply. And even incest finds a place in the appointed scheme. Unwearying in his denunciation of war leadership and war oratory, Rolland scathingly satirizes, amongst others, Lloyd George and Clemenceau. The former is contemptuously sketched as a «Welsh braggart,» a «little, very little Cromwell crossbred with

Cyrano» (37), holding a Bible in one hand and a sword in the other while preaching a new Genesis to his Baptist brethren. Clemenceau is drawn as a crudely speaking scandalmonger puffed up with personal importance. Fanaticism is over and over again seen raising its ugly head.

As for Annette, in August 1914 she had stoically accepted the war as just another cross to be borne in her lifelong struggle. She had for a spell come dangerously close to being swept into the maelstrom, but she beat a quick retreat once she had witnessed the countless crimes war was bringing in its miserable train. And Marc? Only thirteen when the war began, he had spent a good deal of his time since then responding to the sexual forces that adolescence had loosed within him. Yet he was not so much their slave that he could be blind to the ambient evils of war. Eventually he too rejected war categorically, swearing that he would resist any effort to draft him.

Completed in September 1933, *L'Annonciatrice,* the three-volume concluding section of the series, mirrors Rolland's profound disenchantment with the postwar era that had sprung the seeds of another world cataclysm. In this long-winded panegyric of communism and assault on capitalist society as the mother of fascism and wars, wrath conquers all; the novelist would again mold opinion with an invectival bludgeon, as ringing apostrophes and interminable tirades fill many a page.

From the ideological standpoint the paramount interest of *L'Annonciatrice* lies in its evidence of Rolland's inability ever to satisfactorily reconcile for himself his active support of a proletarian revolution with his temperamental and moral predilection for nonviolent tactics. His dilemma is that of

---

(37) Rolland, *L'Ame enchantée,* part II, vol. 1: *Mère et fils* (Paris: Albin Michel, 1927), pp. 185-86.

his Marc, who is now married to the Russian-born Assia. After much indecision, Marc is absorbed into the communist fold. Nevertheless, he cannot resist the siren voice of Gandhi. Freshly indoctrinated in the Indian leader's teachings, Marc quarrels with Assia over the issue of the use of violence or nonviolence in the revolution, all the while betraying a distinct preference for the nonviolent approach. Expressing disappointment over the West's tendency to look upon nonviolence as nonsense, Marc-Rolland refers to Gandhi as «the Indian Christ» (38). And he bemoans the West's unwillingness to make the sacrifices essential to the successful application of nonviolent methods. In the end Rolland solves the vexing dichotomy by merging the two, by electing to terminate the reign of violence through the use of violence. He affirms: «Violence is too strong a wine for men. A single glass of it is enough to cause them to lose control of their reason ... Nonetheless, the Europe of today can no longer act without it. It has been addicted to such alcohol for too many centuries. What can be done to cure it of it? Words are ineffective. Only the example of action is» (39).

Thus did Rolland's fears of imperialist designs on Russia impel him to speak in the early thirties. Nominally his conversion was complete, but the heart sometimes converts grudgingly. More than enough evidence presents itself to show that he was the most reluctant of revolutionaries. His 1917 endorsement of the Russian Revolution had been accompanied by his emphatic insistence that its leaders avoid the excesses of 1793. In the next several years he persisted in qualifying his commendations of it. Then ensued his aforementioned debate with Barbusse on the place of violence

---

(38) Rolland, *L'Ame enchantée*, part IV, vol. 1: *L'Annonciatrice* (Paris: Albin Michel, 1933), p. 48.
(39) *Ibid.*, part IV, vol. 2: *L'Annonciatrice*, p. 188.

in a revolution. Finally, the collected articles and essays of his *Quinze Ans de combat* (1935), which trace out the development of his thought from 1919 through 1934, substantiate the fact that his was a most uneasy marriage with communism.

Hence, one cannot but conclude that the voice of the revolution-preaching Rolland reverberated dully indeed. Everything points to his boundless admiration for Tolstoy, tireless promulgator of Christ's gospel on nonresistance, and to his temperamental kinship with the fictional Jean-Christophe and the real Gandhi, yet it is the method of Lenin that won his official accolade. In the end this ardent champion of spiritual values threw in his lot with violence and, paradoxically, was willing to become a revolutionary in order to remain a pacifist. He would, it follows, have fought war with war, and resisted evil with evil in the belief that he was destroying in order to construct (40).

In 1932 Rolland was elected chairman of the World Congress Against War. Illness, however, prevented him from chairing its historic Amsterdam meetings of that year. The year 1933 saw him named honorary president of the World Anti-Fascist Committee. One of the first Frenchmen of note to assume a public stance of uncompromising opposition to Nazism and fascism, he remained a vocal critic of both. The Munich Agreement by which Great Britain and France ceded the Czech Sudetenland to Nazi Germany was for him a «diplomatic Sedan.» Upon the German invasion of Czechoslovakia in 1939, he uttered the prophetic warning, «You weep, Prague, but you too will weep, Germany» (41). Prompt-

---

(40) In *The Fall of a Titan*, trans. Mervyn Black (New York: Norton, 1954), anticommunist author Igor Gouzenko portrays Romain Rolland, the Romain Rouen of his novel, as a well-intentioned dreamer and hopelessly credulous dupe.

(41) Reported by Pierre Abraham in «Romain Rolland Romancier et dramaturge,» *Hommage à Romain Rolland*, Pierre Abraham *et al.* (Neuchâtel: Éditions de la Baconnière, 1969), p. 33.

ly after France's entry into the Second World War he addressed a public letter to Premier Édouard Daladier expressing his unqualified support of the war effort of his nation and of its allies. This was a war he could believe in.

It was at Vézelay (Yonne), where he had settled in 1937 (except from May 4, 1919 to April 30, 1921, when he lived in France, he had been living in Switzerland continuously since June of 1914), that Rolland witnessed the defeat. He must have been grievously wounded at the sight of panzer divisions burying in a cloud of dust his dream of brotherhood and peace. And soon thereafter it must have shocked him deeply to see Alphonse de Châteaubriant, who had so loyally stood by him during his 1914-15 ordeal, willingly serving the German destroyers of that dream. Under the occupation Rolland lived quietly and completed a huge biography of his antipacifist friend of other days, Charles Péguy. Surely there is nothing to justify the claim of Pierre-Jean Jouve, who remained a pacifist until 1939, that Rolland had been an «artisan of the Resistance» (42). Whereas Rolland's fatherland had already been liberated, the world was still very much at war when he died on December 30, 1944.

The Radical Pacifism of Henri Barbusse

On the day after France's entry into the First World War, forty-one-year-old socialist Henri Barbusse left a Swiss sanitarium where he had been convalescing from tuberculosis to enlist as a private. His action was prompted by his conviction that an absolutist and militarist Germany stood as the most formidable obstacle on the road to peace. His

---

(42) See Pierre-Jean Jouve, «Réminiscences,» *Hommage à Romain Rolland*, Charles Baudouin *et al.* (Geneva: Éditions du Mont-Blanc, 1945), p. 64.

age and physical condition combined to place him in rear echelon services, but on his own insistence he was sent up to the line. In 1915 he saw action as an infantryman and stretcher-bearer in the Artois and Picardy sectors. Later he was assigned to clerical duty at a corps headquarters in the Verdun area. A frequent volunteer for danger-fraught missions, he was twice decorated for bravery under fire and was awarded the Croix de guerre. Thrice he was invalided out with dysentery, the last time, in June 1917, permanently. He suffered no combat wounds, but the deep emotional scars left in him were to orient his thinking toward pacifism, a direction which he would follow undeviatingly until his death in 1935.

In 1919 Barbusse was named president of the newly founded 'Clarté' group, which had as its object the propagation of antiwar ideas that he had embodied in a novel of the same name, published a few months earlier. Highlighting its original roster were the names of Romain Rolland, Georges Duhamel, Anatole France, Léon Blum, and Henri Bataille. In November 1921 he created, together with Raymond Lefebvre and Paul Vaillant-Couturier, *Clarté,* the group's literary organ.

This hard-hitting communist review—it called itself a «revue de culture révolutionnaire»—gave first priority to antimilitarist and antiwar propaganda. It hammered away relentlessly at its bitterest enemies, the generals, to whom it almost invariably referred as «marchands de cadavres.» On the occasion of General Nivelle's death *Clarté* published a virulent editorial under the heading «Le général Nivelle est mort dans son lit» in which the editorialist bemoaned the fact that this architect of the bloody Chemin des Dames offensive of April 1917 was being panegyrized in the press, maintaining that a grippe-induced death was too comfortable a passing for one who, he contended, should have been made to expiate the sin of inept command before a firing squad (43). In January 1926, after a succession of disputes among members of its editorial committee, the review suspended publication. Barbusse had no affiliation with the *Clarté* that reappeared six months later, only to cease publication for good in December 1927. He subsequently devoted the bulk of his journalistic efforts to two communist newspapers: *Monde*, founded by him in 1928, and *L'Humanité*.

Sympathetically inclined toward communism since the Russian Revolution of 1917, Barbusse became a party member in 1923 and remained a militant communist for the rest of his life. In addition to his prolific writing, his pro-peace activities ranged from lecturing before small peasant audiences to organizing international antiwar groups and congresses, including the important Amsterdam Congress of 1932, which drew delegates from all over the globe. Author of *Jésus* (1927), a story written in the form of a gospel wherein Christ is represented as an atheist and revolutionary social reformer, Barbusse has his place in this study as French communism's foremost peace proponent, one whose formula for peace was rooted in his burning belief that only the world triumph of the international proletariat under a communist banner could ensure an enduring peace.

The peace crusade of Henri Barbusse was launched in August 1916, when his novel *Le Feu: Journal d'une escouade* appeared, in somewhat expurgated form, in the daily *Oeuvre*. It made a second appearance, this time as an unexpurgated book, in December, just in time to capture the coveted Prix Goncourt for that year. It could hardly have been published in better season. French morale was close to its lowest level of the war. The French had greeted the war in August 1914

---

(43) See *Clarté*, no. 3 (1924), pp. 149-50.

6

in a joyous mood, tossing flowers at parading troops who were sticking them into their rifle barrels. All were confident that victory over the Kaiser's «Huns,» «Boches,» and «Barbares» would be won by Christmas. «A Berlin!» was the enthusiastic cry. Now, however, the last pages of France's war log for 1916 were being written with no promise of imminent victory. Anglo-French, Russian, and Italian summer offensives had secured a significant but not decisive military advantage. The heroic stand of the French army at Verdun had caught the world's eye, but the staggering number of casualties muffled French shouting. At the year's close badly decimated divisions were digging in for a third winter of fighting. Despite the dogged resolve of the large majority of the French to carry on the rugged fight to a victorious end, few of them could not see through their government's deception in steadily feeding them a cloying diet of jingoistic claptrap. In addition, in its effort to sustain civilian morale, the government had been sedulously sifting out of wartime publications anything considered even mildly «dangerous,» while sanctioning journalistic depictions of war in which ultra-heroic infantrymen gleefully gutted «sales Boches» with their «Rosalies» (bayonets) between rounds of trench parties featuring endlessly flowing wine and further enlivened by resounding choruses of the «Marseillaise» and the «Madelon.» And if death intruded to terminate their careers of cheerful heroism, they had the good taste to die with smiles on their faces and «Vive la France!» on their lips. The extent to which French wartime censors had either been caught off their guard in the case of *Le Feu* or had temporarily relaxed their standards is, then, remarkable.

With casualties still astronomical and the end of the war nowhere in sight, the public was more than a little weary of the bombastic eloquence of the drumbeaters, of military setbacks poorly disguised as «strategic retreats,» and of journalistic anointing of dead heroes (44). Hence, when *Le Feu,* most famous of French books inspired by the war, appeared, describing at times hyperbolically, but for the most part realistically, the insufficiently known sufferings of front-line troops, it was received with enthusiasm by a large segment of a population long nauseated with war writing of «good spirit,» as well as by exhausted combatants, who finally saw themselves and their lot reflected in a much truer light. These had had more than their fill of the chauvinistic drivel of Claudel («Dix fois qu'on attaque là-dedans, «avec résultat purement local»./ Il faut y aller une fois de plus? Tant que vous voudrez, mon général!») (45), of the hate sermons of Maurras and Léon Daudet, and of the sloganeering and cheerleading of Barrès, Bazin, and Bordeaux. May a brief comparison with another well-known if distinctly inferior war novel serve to underscore the opportuneness of Barbusse's book.

Like *Le Feu,* René Benjamin's *Gaspard,* winner of the Goncourt Prize for 1915, owed much of its success to its timeliness. Reaching the bookstores in November of that year, it was the first novel among the dozen or so war books published in France since the war's outbreak. *Gaspard* was patently made to order for a public demoralized by the failure of French forces, after fifteen months of incredibly bloody warfare, to deliver the knockout blow it had so

---

(44) As regards such anointing, Jean Guéhenno observes ironically: «On the whole the republic of letters had become a profitable funeral business. Never had Maurice Barrès known such alacrity. Emerging from the midst of so many undertakers, he chanced to be promoted to the rank of master of ceremonies. It was he who for four years best managed the funerals of the young, thanks to him first-class funerals.» Guéhenno, *Journal d'un homme de quarante ans* (Paris: Grasset, 1934), p. 185.

(45) Paul Claudel, «Tant que vous voudrez, mon général!», *Poèmes de guerre,* in *Oeuvres complètes,* vol. 2 (Paris: Gallimard, 1952), p. 195.

confidently expected in the early months of hostilities, and which it was now again anticipating in the wake of a successful September offensive in the Champagne sector. Expressly designed as a morale-builder, *Gaspard* also abundantly benefited from the imposition by the military censorship service of a tight lid on any writing that could have had a bad emotional association for the French.

The book's protagonist, after whom it is named, is a Parisian commoner of most uncommon resiliency. This peacetime snail-huckster hurls himself into military life with gusto. Exuding confidence, Gaspard leaves for the battlefront in a forty-and-eight marked «pleasure train for Berlin,» troubled only by the tardiness of his entry into the «ballet.» Blessed with a faculty for finding pearls on the dunghill of war, the carefree hero does two stints at the front, spending less than two full days there. He is twice invalided out, the first time for a mangled buttock; the second, for a seriously injured leg. Brief as is Gaspard's baptism of fire, it enables him to discover that, contrary to his earlier belief, German shells really did explode, to conduct himself in a sublimely heroic way, and to hear his dying captain mumble, «Mourir ...our la ...atrie, c'est la ...lus ...elle mort» (46). He is, moreover, sufficiently moved by the horrors of combat to utter a passionate if brief outcry against the insanity of war. But this buoyant resident of the Rue de la Gaîté quickly weathers his emotional crisis; he lays aside his flail and thereafter confines himself to his more characteristic good-natured grumbling over less weighty matters. In truth, there just isn't much to be angry about in René Benjamin's war. Even soldier-officer relations are exemplary, and life

---

(46) René Benjamín, *Gaspard* (Paris: Fayard, 1915), p. 132. The translation of the fully written utterance would be: «To die for the fatherland is the most beautiful of deaths.»

on troop trains and in military hospitals verges on the idyllic. As for those fine souls on the home front, they have, it is plain, mastered the technique of rolling with war's hard punches.

It was in reaction to the changed war situation and to the nauseating niceties and superficialities of war works whose chief exemplar was *Gaspard* that much of the French reading public welcomed Barbusse's *Le Feu*. The novelist's intimate familiarity with trench life had given him a close grip on reality, so that it was with such descriptions as this that he set about disabusing the uninitiated:

> More than charges that resemble troops on parade, more than sharply outlined battles unfurling like streamers, more even than shout-accompanied hand-to-hand encounters, this war is appalling, inhuman fatigue, and water up to one's belly, and mud, and excrement, and unspeakable filth. It is moldy faces, and tattered flesh, and corpses that no longer even look like corpses, floating on the surface of the voracious earth. It is this; it is the infinite, monotonous train of misery broken by shrill dramas; it is this, and not bayonets sparkling like silver or the cockcrowing of the bugle in the sun (47).

In line with this, Barbusse's method of arousing public opinion against war in *Le Feu* is as simple as it is transparent: he attempts to shock the reader by painting an already ugly enough war in the ugliest colors imaginable. One of his disgruntled fighting men proposes, «It would be a crime to show the nicer side of war» (48) —a precept which the novelist obeys and even transcends.

---

(47) Henri Barbusse, *Le Feu: Journal d'une escouade* (Paris: Flammarion, 1917), p. 357.
(48) *Ibid.*, p. 376.

Horror, physical horror of the ghastliest sort, rates highest on Barbusse's list of propaganda weapons. The dead seem woefully neglected: the members of the squad everywhere come upon huge piles of them. These are almost invariably eviscerated, in shreds, and in an advanced stage of decay. Whenever lengthy exposure to the elements fails to render dead men quite as unsightly as desired, broad-bellied rats are made to finish the job. The living linger by the bodies of their fallen comrades and apparently feel no repugnance at examining them in minutest detail. Because, as will be seen presently, similarly revolting visions were also to figure prominently in the general scheme of the author's later war books, one can to some degree appreciate, without endorsing, the view of Jean Norton Cru that «... His [Barbusse's] war novels are a teratological exhibit rather than a portrayal of real horrors» (49).

---

(49) Jean Norton Cru, *Témoins* (Paris: Les Étincelles, 1929), p. 564. Stern rebukes and corrosive criticism are not the exception but pretty much the rule in *Témoins*, whose author spent twenty-eight months in the trenches. It is a huge book devoted to the criticism of 304 works on war divided by Cru into five groups: diaries, reminiscences, reflections, letters, and novels. Its 727 pages might well have been double that number had the print and format been of average size. With *Témoins* Cru intended to provide an exact image of war by segregating truth from fiction in the accounts of war by those who had witnessed it from the trenches. In order to classify the works concerned according to their documentary value, he read a number of them six or seven times, checking the minutest details in them with a vast scholarly apparatus comprising, amongst other things, military chronologies, divisional histories, army units' tables of organization, and a complete series of maps of the front on a natural scale of 1:50,000. If Cru had restricted himself to his declared objective, few discordant voices would have been heard amidst the paeans of praise to which the book gave rise. But it was his succumbing to the temptation of assessing the literary merits of the works he anatomized that nettled critics and criticized alike. Here his passion for documentary truth led him to slant his conclusions heavily, the upshot being that in not a few cases what was in his estimation a superior work was in fact little more than a

While not descanting upon physical horrors, Barbusse assails war from other angles. The winter sky is uniformly somber, the earth wet, the air stinging cold. Spring, mentioned as being close at hand, never does arrive. The warriors seem to be utterly leaderless: only one noncom is present for any length of time, and a lieutenant appears only long enough to lose their way for them. Significantly, he looks very much like a refugee from one of Courteline's military farces. The men, shabbily clad and infested with vermine, spend at least three-fourths of their military lives in trenches. Endless rounds of the popular card game *manille* only add to a monotony for which murderous bombardments provide occasional if unwelcome relief. They go about their duties faithfully but with an air of melancholy submissiveness, and there is a strong hint that only their awareness of military executions has made them tractable. They can laugh, but in harmony with the author's dark vision, they buoy themselves with relatively little humor—black, cynical, farcical, or other—and with practically none while in the front-line, even when fighting is not in progress. And even when they are sent back for a rest, they never quite shake off the pall of gloom that war has cast over them. As Romain Rolland pertinently observes in his generally commendatory assessment of the book, killing fatigue, weariness, and the roar of cannon have so deadened the sensibilities of Barbusse's warriors that they turn out to be pretty hollow creatures, capable of only the

------

wholly objective, dispassionate, and unadorned record of psychological and physical phenomena observed by its author, whereas a fair number of widely acclaimed works were severely downgraded by him because their authors took liberties with the factual while cultivating the artistic.

Pacifists and patriots, the mighty and the humble, felt the force of Cru's blows. With a fiery eloquence he castigated them, and the loftier the reputation, the more vitriolic the tone. «Stupidities,» «absurdities,» «lies,» «calumnies»—these are but a few of the strong substantives with which the pages of *Témoins* abound.

most elemental reactions (50). Rapacious villagers fleece them in exchange for fourth-rate wines and dingy billets, and they somehow never come upon the victrolas and soccer balls that worked miracles for the morale of Maurois' and Mottram's soldiers. Worse still, their long-awaited Paris furloughs are blighted by uncomprehending civilians who set upon them with drivel about how thrilling it must be to charge into action to the blare of bugles, how inspiriting to see heroes die with smiles lighting up their features, and the like—*ad nauseam*. These are the selfsame home front types who completely alienated Aldington, Owen, Sassoon, Remarque, Céline, Bernanos and other writer-veterans of the trenches, with the fiery Bernanos preferring «derrière» to «arrière» in speaking of them and of their drumbeating auxiliaries.

To recapitulate, Barbusse deliberately elects to paint his picture of war in none but the darkest hues, relying mainly on his uncomplicated technique of suppression of the good and exaggeration of the bad. Notwithstanding that, *Le Feu* has a good deal to commend it as a war novel so long as the squad members perform, however grudgingly, their assigned labors. It is when, in the book's last chapter, they suddenly acquire a deep sense of social consciousness that the story deteriorates badly.

Here the author switches to a highly artificial expository mode. Having hitherto been telling his tale as just another unobtrusive *poilu,* he now thrusts himself to the fore as an impassioned defender of the underdog against the infamous powers that have callously dumped him into the inferno. All action ceases as the newly enlightened squad members seat themselves about their discussion leader. The earlier largely untutored, apathetic combatants now debate like intellectuals well trained in dialectics and at times wax mar-

---

(50) Rolland, «Le Feu,» *Les Précurseurs,* p. 92.

velously eloquent in outlining their panacea for the war disease. Bizarre as is this metamorphosis, it detracts less from the book's artistry than do the embittered tirades delivered by the author himself. Abandoning the tone of warm compassion that had served him well, Barbusse here kicks and protests, rants and rages, until financiers and militarists as well as those whom he regards as their intellectual apologists —the clergymen, economists, historians, and genealogists— are all buried under an avalanche of abuse.

At one with the narrator in his pacifist convictions are his comrades. These emphasize that they are fighting not against a nation but against the tyranny of the ruling classes; not for the economic betterment of a few, but for the progress, through unified action, of the working masses of the world. The arch-villain, the cold-blooded monster that must be destroyed, is capitalism. If Barbusse's *poilus* do not crack under the strains of existence in the blood-soaked, mud-encased hell to which they have been consigned, this is because of their belief that «if the present war has advanced progress by a single step, its miseries and slaughter will count for little» (51).

After conducting the reader through the numerous galleries of his museum of horrors, Barbusse evidently considered him psychologically prepared for a violent rhetorical assault on war and on capitalist war-makers. The net result is that his switch from grim realism to shrill idealism flawed his novel with a finale that is anything but grand, one which from the standpoint of emotional impact is the very antithesis of the close of Remarque's celebrated *All Quiet on the Western Front*. Here, with hostilities practically at a standstill, with rumors of an armistice on everybody's lips, and just as he is meditating upon the possibility of ever recapturing

---

(51) Barbusse, *Le Feu*, p. 378.

his long lost zest for life, Remarque's young soldier-narrator has his rendezvous with death. In probably the most effective and surely the best remembered lines ever to close a war novel, the German pacifist wrote:

> He fell in October, 1918, on a day that was so quiet and still on the whole front, that the army report confined itself to a single sentence: All quiet on the Western Front.
> He had fallen forward and lay on the earth as though sleeping. Turning him over, one saw that he could not have suffered long; his face had an expression of calm, as though glad that the end had come (52).

To carry the comparison a step further, the ending of Roland Dorgelès' *Les Croix de bois* (1919) may be recalled. As in the case of Remarque's close, the fighting is coming to a halt and on all sides the talk is of peace. Sulphart, the last survivor of a squad around whom the action of the book has centered, hears a tipsy citizen mumble, «Peace or no peace, it's too late; it's a defeat. It can't be helped ... the die is cast. For us it's a defeat.» To this Sulphart objects that it is, on the contrary, a victory. «I find that it's a victory because I came out of it alive,» he explains (53).

A second pacifist novel by Barbusse, *Clarté* (1919), describes the transmutation of Simon Paulin, the book's hero, from an irresponsible factory clerk into an ardent pacifist and revolutionary through intimate contact with mechanized war. *Clarté* may be regarded as an ideological extension of *Le Feu* because in it the author further articulates the ideas expressed

---

(52) Erich Maria Remarque, *All Quiet on the Western Front*, trans. A. W. Wheen (Boston: Little, Brown & Co., 1929), p. 291.
(53) Roland Dorgelès, *Les Croix de bois* (Paris: Albin Michel, 1919), p. 340.

in the latter work and fully assumes the stance of a prophet, political theorist, and communist mentor. The propaganda element now emerges as a coherent whole.

Although in *Clarté* the volume of horror-mongering has been substantially reduced, the macabre still predominates. The reader is again offered a full ration of visions of disemboweled men and animals, and of trenches thickly lined with festering cadavers that swarm with maggots of every shape and form; again bursting shells lock the living and the dead in unloving embrace.

This overdrawn picture of war's physical horrors is not, however, the book's only serious shortcoming. For one thing, Simon Paulin makes a most unconvincing reformer. Whatever the impact of war on Simon's soul, the overnight conversion of this insolent, phlegmatic, shiftless, self-centered, unlettered sex-maniac into a thoughtful, eloquent, and fervent champion of the weak and oppressed carries no conviction. Secondly, Simon fairly drowns himself in windy tirades that unbalance the work, and it is only after sixteen pages of pure declamation that Simon proclaims the «inevitable advent of the universal republic» (54). In time the reader is as much exasperated by Barbusse's inexhaustible predication as his shell-shocked hero is by the oily patriotic oratory of the local drumbeaters. Finally, as an antiwar novel *Clarté* also breaks down because of the novelist's inability to harness his fury. The note of pity, plainly discernible in *Le Feu,* is here entirely submerged by his shouts and screams. Wrath and pity, compounded in just proportion, can, of course, make for both artistic excellence and effective propaganda. The war poetry of Wilfred Owen stands as evidence thereof. Barbusse, for his part, was only beginning to apply the formula when he abandoned it.

---

(54) Barbusse, *Clarté* (Paris: Flammarion, 1919), p. 278.

Barbusse's novel, *Les Enchaînements* (1925), traces the exploitation of man by man across the ages. While it can scarcely be classified as a pacifist novel, the antiwar component does bulk large in its structure. Generously endowed with what the author terms «ancestral memory,» the book's hero, Clément Trachel, perceives everywhere the need for man's liberating himself from the chains that have impeded his progress in every age. Never is he more convinced of this than when a chance assignment has him, an officer at a corps headquarters, dashing about a broad sector of the front. Thus, in «Ce qui fut sera,» the book's closing chapter, Barbusse, true to the pattern established in *Le Feu* and *Clarté,* prepares the ground for a savage attack on war by cataloguing every variety of physical horror. Again his soldiers exhibit an uncanny knack for dying in a standing position, again a «smell of broiled meat» emanates from the cadaver-clogged trenches, again the novelist betrays a morbid propensity for examining the entrails of the dead. As for the living, who in typical Barbussian fashion somehow cannot prevent themselves from brushing up against their sacrificed comrades, they are plagued with troubles aplenty. Not the least of these is the barbarous inhumanity of their commanders. In vain will the reader look among them for a latter-day Messire Bernard du Guesclin with a paternal concern for the well-being of the common soldier, or for a kind, compassionate Turenne. Rather, abusing their hierarchal prerogatives as roundly as the heartless officers of Abel Hermant's *Le Cavalier Miserey* (1887), Latzko's *Men in War* (1918), and Dos Passos' *Three Soldiers* (1921), these resort to profuse bloodletting whenever the military whip, lies, and drink are not enough to keep their personnel in line. Thus, a humming soldier on night patrol is silenced by a superior's trench knife, and a middle-aged father of three pays with his life for having fallen asleep on sentry duty despite his having had to go without sleep for better than two days. Thus, every tenth man of an entire company is executed in order to quell the rebelliousness of a scattered few (55). Yet, a general gallantly permits a captured German officer to return to his side with the words «I'll be a sport ... I'm letting you go» (56). Finally, nowhere is the satire more devastating than when the novelist contrasts the magnitude of human sacrifice with the triviality of the officialese employed to report it.

It is more of such satire, of the ironic counterpoint of a Stephen Crane, of the economy of a Stendhal, of the measured tones of a Remarque—they too determined destroyers of myths about the romance of war—that the pacifist writings of Barbusse needed. Of bloated, contorted cadavers, of wrath and rhetoric, there is too much. When the propagandist overpowers the artist, the message is blunted, and the reader whom the artist would have resist war resists the propaganda instead.

What, however, is most plain is that Barbusse was at a long remove from pure pacifism. Whereas Tolstoy's experience of war at first hand had convinced him that all war was an unmitigated evil, and that inasmuch as evil is evil, it should never be placed in the service of even a good end, Barbusse subscribed to civil war and to revolution as long as the ultimate aims of communism were served. He whom war's bloodshed had appalled was able to accept the concept of revolution undeterred by his awareness of its indiscriminate horrors. Revolution was revolution, as he saw it. So much the worse if blood, even innocent blood, should be spilled.

---

(55) Soldier executions figure prominently in Barbusse's *Faits divers* (Paris: Flammarion, 1928), a collection of sketches, all supposedly based on fact, describing the sufferings of citizens at the hands of reactionary governments everywhere, but especially in Eastern Europe and in the Balkans, during and shortly after World War II.

(56) Barbusse, *Les Enchaînements* (Paris: Flammarion, 1925), II, 264.

The end in view was all that mattered. Only with the triumph of international communism would the golden age of peace dawn.

Roger Martin du Gard and the Collapse of Socialist Pacifism

For the sentiments of Roger Martin du Gard (1881-1958) on war we must depend almost exclusively on the content of the two novels by him in which they may be discerned, the three-volume *L'Été 1914* (1936), and *Épilogue* (1940), of his *Les Thibault* series. Otherwise we are severely handicapped because few writers of mark have avoided public living with greater resolve or success than he. The political arena, the lecture platform, interviews, and writing for newspapers and magazines were anathema to him. Only after World War II did he begin taking a public stand on issues of the day to any significant degree. Moreover, except in the case of a handful of close friends, of whom Gide was the closest, he consistently maintained a scrupulous silence about matters pertaining to his personal life and beliefs. It is nevertheless apparent that ideologically this *grand bourgeois* was on the left and that he was greatly fascinated by and sympathetic to socialist efforts to better the lot of mankind.

Throughout the Great War, Martin du Gard served as a truck driver for the First Cavalry Corps, which saw action over a broad area of the front. He was thus able to have a good look at the face of war, and was utterly repelled by it. He early betrayed his pacifist leanings in a letter dated August 25, 1915, which he sent to Romain Rolland to applaud him for his antiwar crusading, as mirrored principally in his *Au-dessus de la Mêlée* (57). Martin du Gard was to remain

---

(57) See Romain Rolland, *Journal des années de guerre 1914-1919*, p. 504.

a convinced pacifist. At the beginning of 1936, in a letter to his friend Marcel Lallemand, he came out strongly for nonintervention in the Spanish Civil War, urging: «Be as unyielding as iron *on the side of neutrality*. Principle: *Anything in preference to war! Anything, anything!* Even fascism in Spain! ... even fascism in France! *Anything*: Hitler in preference to war!» (58).

In 1937 Martin du Gard won world renown when the Swedish Academy awarded him the Nobel prize for literature for his *L'Été 1914* (1936), the seventh part of his *roman-fleuve*. In accepting the prize, he told officials of the Academy that he surmised that they had wished to reward «an independent writer who had escaped the fascination of partisan ideologies, an investigator as objective as is humanly possible, as well as a novelist striving to express the tragic qualities of individual lives» (59). He also took occasion to express his hope that *L'Été 1914* would serve to impress the young with the folly of giving in to a fatalistic acceptance of war and to remind their elders of that folly. Be that as it may, he was no absolute pacifist for whom war was always wrong. With the outbreak of World War II, he considered the message of his prize-inning novel inopportune and only hoped that Hitler's armies would go down to quick defeat. Wanting no part of a *Pax Germanica,* under the occupation he supported the Resistance's Comité National des Écrivains and played a minor role in the underground war.

L'Été 1914 offers a detailed account of historical developments in Europe between June 28, 1914, date of the assassination of Archduke Franz-Ferdinand at Sarajevo, and August 10, 1914, with particular emphasis on the collapse of the Second

---

(58) Cited by Denis Boak, *Roger Martin du Gard* (Oxford: Clarendon Press, 1963), p. 136.
(59) Cited by Howard C. Rice, *Roger Martin du Gard and the World of the Thibaults* (New York: Viking Press, 1941), p. 22.

International's antiwar programs. Of that collapse Martin du Gard conducts a thorough autopsy. With Europe on the threshold of another conflagration and quite conscious of its impending doom, it was natural that this novelistic reconstruction of events taking place on the continent on the eve of the Great War should have attracted a wide readership.

L'Été 1914 differs materially from the seven preceding segments of *Les Thibault*. In them the novelist had portrayed at great length and in meticulous detail the lives of two Parisian bourgeois families, the Catholic Thibaults and the Protestant Fontanins. He had rooted them firmly in their social, economic, and religious environments, subtly demonstrated the influence of heredity on their personalities, and progressively opened them to the reader's gaze under the stress of multifarious circumstances. As is inferable from the cycle's title, the members of the Thibault family play the preponderant role. These are the rich, successful, socially prominent ex-parliamentary deputy Oscar Thibault and his two sons, Antoine and Jacques. A widower, the austere-living Oscar had, up to his death shortly before the war, ruled his household with an iron hand and alienated the affection but retained the respect of his sons.

Antoine, the elder, is a hard-driving, ambitious young physician who manages to free himself from the chains of his profession long enough to carry on a torrid love affair. Personable, poised, disciplined, he differs markedly from his peevish, restless, and indisciplinable brother. Jacques, rebelling against his father's tyrannical dominion, runs away from home at the age of fourteen. After confinement in an Oscar Thibault-endowed reform school and after submitting to further spiritual torture in the stifling atmosphere of home, Jacques departs for good to work in the interest of socialist revolution.

Since the nominal head of the Fontanin family, Jérôme,

an eventual suicide, is a weak-willed, shiftless philanderer, it is to the charming, understanding Madame de Fontanin that devolves the responsibility of keeping the family knit together. Daughter Jenny has always been somewhat of a romantic: morbidly sensitive, melancholy, and self-pitying. Her brother, Daniel, a youth of loose morals, values freedom above all things. He had introduced Jacques to his personal bible, Gide's *Les Nourritures terrestres,* and was cursed by Oscar as his son's evil genius.

With *L'Été 1914* the previous emphasis on the psychological analysis of the cycle's characters yields to the necessity of portraying crises affecting all Europeans. Antoine, who together with and more than his father had been occupying the center of the stage in the preceding volumes, now relinquishes it to his younger brother. The much matured Jacques —his strength of will and intellect had even gained him entry into the élite École Normale Supérieure—emerges here as an ardent socialist with a fanatical faith in the ability of his party's twelve million European members to prevent the imminent conflict. Emancipated from the bourgeois and family ties he loathes, he throws all his latent Thibault energy into the fight against war. Gifted propagandist and orator, trusted contact man, he is regarded as one of the second echelon worthies of the Second International. As such Jacques is obliged to scurry from one major European country to another on important missions. This enables him to discover in short order the many breaches in the party armor. While he slaves to help contain the war menace, many of his confederates squander time and energy in palavers and debate over nonessentials—the definition of offensive and defensive war, for example. They, like Antoine and his assistants and associates in Paris, spend a great deal of time discussing the events leading up to the war and assigning blame. The author's accusatory finger is plainly visible here, even though he at no time departs from his impersonal narrative style. And the reader has no difficulty recognizing how Martin du Gard feels about a number of the subjects related to war prevention which come up for discussion: the part played by the press in whipping up nationalistic fever, the abdication of governmental authority to militarist elements, the machinations, double dealing, and treacheries of governments, the fatalism of the working classes, the disunity of socialists and syndicalists, and the lack of bold initiatives by pacifist forces in general.

At the very hour when the International's most potent weapon, the general strike, could best be employed, the immense organization crumbles. Mass defections occur in all the principal nations threatened by war, and nationalist pride suddenly provokes sharp antagonisms even in the cell of the movement at Geneva. The idealistic Jacques deplores more than ever the lack of a coordinated, Europe-wide program for averting war. The cause of harmony further suffers as members wrangle over the advisability of using violent as opposed to nonviolent methods to bring about revolutionary change, with the Austrian Mithoerg establishing himself as the novel's arch-apostle of violence. In his judgment, Jacques is no more than an aborted revolutionary, a «rationalist dilettante» who is too individualistic to subordinate his person to the needs of tough revolutionary action. Nevertheless, in spite of his instinctive abhorrence of violence, Jacques sees resort to it as justified in a single instance: when the choice is between a Europe-wide war and a preventive insurrection. He does not regard a few thousand deaths at the barricades as an excessive price to pay for the prevention of the massacre of millions. Ultimately, in a gesture epitomizing the party's desertion of pacifism, the Swiss Meynestrel, Jacques' group-leader, consigns to flames a sheaf of secret documents which reveal the collusion of the German and Austrian general staffs to induce Russian mobilization. The «Pilote» does so in his fear that the disclosure of their contents might forestall the war that he believes will inevitably accelerate the demise of capitalism, thus leaving the road open for the victory of international socialism. Whereas this episode also serves to dramatize the divisions in the socialist camp, it is entirely without foundation in historical fact—a bizarre phenomenon, as not a few critics have pointed out, in a book in which historical accuracy is scrupulously honored apropos anything of consequence.

The entry of rabid antimilitarist Gustave Hervé into the *patriotard* fold and the swiftly mounting war fever of late July deeply distress Jacques but, paradoxically, fortify his belief that a general strike will yet save the day. Drawing moral support from the example of the unflagging pro-peace effort of his idol, Jaurès, he redoubles his own effort and transfers his monetary share of the Thibault inheritance to the coffers of the Second International. Stiffening in his resistance, he cries, «For me ... there is no heroism in picking up a rifle and dashing off to the frontier; it is in pointing a rifle butt skyward and in letting yourself be escorted to the execution ground rather than becoming a partner in crime!» (60). Although stunned by the death of Jaurès and by the betrayal of socialism's surviving leaders, he does not give up hope (61). By then, however, he must have felt as solitary

---

(60) Roger Martin du Gard, *L'Été 1914*, in *Oeuvres complètes*, vol. 2 (Paris: Gallimard, 1955), p. 538.

(61) Under the brilliant leadership of Jean Jaurès, French socialists played the leading role in drawing up antiwar resolutions at European socialism's mammoth international congresses at Stuttgart (1907), Copenhagen (1911), Basel (1912), and Berne (1913). At these gatherings plans were laid for averting war through a general strike by the proletariat in the nations concerned. Jaurès was still attempting to rally the continent's socialists round a common flag of peace on the evening of July 31, 1914, when Raoul Villain, a half-crazed chauvinist fanatic, shot him dead as he was

as a drunk who appears briefly on these pages and is heard shouting «Down with war!» (62) as he zigzags down a Paris boulevard against a background of flaming newspaper headlines and of crowds clamoring for mobilization. Finally, with millions of his fellow European socialists already in their nations' fighting forces or about to enter them, this bourgeois revolutionary individually attempts to rise superior to the circumstances. In Switzerland, where he has gone as a military deserter, he arranges to be piloted by Meynestrel over the Alsatian front to scatter about leaflets of his own authorship entreating French and German troops to quit the futile conflict and enumerating reasons for doing so. The flight is planned for the dawn of August 8. For Meynestrel, recently abandoned by his mistress, this is a much better than average way of committing suicide, since it can also serve a broader purpose.

This act of faith on the part of Jacques—it is, in addition, his way of atoning for a largely wasted life—goes for naught as the plane crashes before any portion of its cargo can be released. Meynestrel is killed. Mangled, burned beyond recognition, unable to speak, a dying Jacques is taken for an «alboche,» labelled a spy, and brutally finished off by a French military policeman after being joggled about on a stretcher for a full day by retreating soldiers. The hapless Jacques had been dumped by the wayside so that his stretcher

---

dining at the Café du Croissant. Royalist Charles Maurras, spokesman of the ultranationalist Action Française movement, had all but invited the assassination in his columns of the preceding weeks. He was now quick to press his advantage. Condemning the assassination in one breath, condoning it in another, Maurras applauded the evaporation of the «humanitarian, revolutionary, and romantic dream» of which to him Jaurès was the embodiment. «Après vingt ans. — Paix ou guerre?», *L'Action Française*, Aug. 2, 1914, p. 1.

(62) Martin du Gard, *L'Été 1914*, p. 556.

could be used to transport a wounded major. The M.P., reacting to the suggestion of a noncom that Jacques be done away with and crazed by fear of the swiftly approaching enemy, had mustered courage for the dirty business by shouting, as he fired a bullet into the martyr's head —«Fumier!» (63) By that time Jacques was but an unconscious «bundle of inert, black and blue flesh» (64). Ironically, not only had Jacques' peace effort prevented any killing but he had actually made a killer of his executioner, a war-hating peasant who previously had never so much as killed an animal. With Jacques dead and the initial phase of the slaughter well underway, the rout is complete: personal tragedy has now been coupled with the collective tragedy of millions of Europeans.

In the thirty-page segment concerned with Jacques' ordeal after the crash, Martin du Gard skillfully blends realism and impressionism to produce a picture of war deserving of inclusion in any anthology of war writing. It is not a pretty picture. The troops are made to believe that a «strategic withdrawal» is in progress, but the evidence is that a major defeat has been inflicted on French forces in the general area. All is muddled and disjointed. Awaited liaison agents never arrive, contradictory orders are barked, and the famished, dog-tired troops are at a loss as to what their arrogant, inept officers are up to. Stendhal's young Fabrice del Dongo on the battlefield of Waterloo could scarcely have been more confused. The soldiers have cruelly nicknamed Jacques «Fragil» because a splint improvised from a wooden crate and attached to one of his fractured legs bears that inscription. A youngster throws a fistful of pebbles at the limp Jacques, another burns him with a cigarette, and flies attack him as the surly troopers lug him along for endless miles, fiercely

---

(63) *Ibid.*, p. 758.
(64) *Ibid.*, p. 753.

resentful that this added burden has been imposed upon them. Having early weighed the merits of killing him, they are relieved when eventually they are given what amounts to an order to jettison the surplus freight.

The evils of war are given full treatment in *Épilogue,* a worthy sequel to a Nobel Prize winner and a more directly pacifist work. History played a trick on Martin du Gard at this juncture because, although this final volume of the series was completed before the beginning of World War II, it did not appear in print until January 1940, hardly a propitious moment for the dissemination of antiwar ideas.

The more forcefully to accent the havoc wreaked by war, Martin du Gard built the finale of his symphony on low, somber notes while still adhering to his policy of strict non-intervention. We learn that young Manuel Roy, Antoine's prewar laboratory aide and secretary, is gone, having made the supreme sacrifice as early as the second month of hostilities. He it was who from early childhood had yearned for the opportunity to avenge the Prussian-humbled pride of his father's generation; who, before his exposure to war, had exalted it as a sport without equal. «A good periodic blood-letting,» he held, «was necessary for the health of nations» (65). Daniel de Fontanin, a leg amputee, is back from Aceldama, but it is a bitter, despondent Daniel who is living the life of a recluse and stubbornly concealing from his family the secret of his war-obliterated sexuality. He who once gloried in easy feminine conquests has lost all appetite for life, and vows that, upon the death of his mother, he will take leave by his own hand of a world he no longer understands. Stripped as he is of all illusions as to what war is, his misery is compounded by his fear that the whole thing could happen again.

---

(65) *Ibid.,* p. 340.

The sorriest case of them all is Antoine, who on the first day of mobilization had answered the call to the colors without protest, more irritated by war's disruption of his life style than by anything else. Besides, as a partisan of law and order, he accounted it the duty of a citizen to defend the nation that bestows benefits on him. Now, four years later, the thirty-seven-year-old Antoine suffers from abscessed lungs, a condition contracted by him during a tour of medical inspection on the Champagne front. Doomed to die, he lies in a small hospital for gassed patients that overlooks the Riviera, observing his gradual decline with a sure professional perspicacity.

Antoine too has undergone a gradual maturation, and it is the spirit of Jacques that now dwells in him. Once too absorbed in his work to have given much thought to the approaching war, he is now a confirmed pacifist obsessively concerned with the necessity of preserving peace for those who will be lucky enough to survive the hecatomb. Antoine categorically rejects war. Reacting to criticism of German methods of waging it, he argues, in a passage that could have been scissored right out of Alain's *Mars*: «Look out ... Codifying war, wanting to limit it, to organize it (to *humanize* it, as they say!), to decree: «This is barbaric! This is immoral!», that implies that there is another way of waging war ... a perfectly civilized way ... a perfectly moral way. ... What is monstrous ... is war itself» (66). Earlier, Antoine had been surprised at the alacrity with which he had answered in the negative when Jenny, the mother of Jacques' illegitimate son, asked him if he was scandalized by her censure of her mother for serving as a volunteer nurse, for pursuing a vocation «which consists of caring for and healing young men for the sole

(66) Martin du Gard, *Épilogue*, in *Oeuvres complètes*, vol. 2 (Paris: Gallimard, 1955), p. 872.

purpose of enabling them to go off again and get themselves killed!» (67).

It is in a terse, unfurbished diary which Antoine began keeping upon realizing that he was condemned that *Épilogue's* antiwar message is clearest. Martin du Gard is doubtless telling us here that if we can behold such agonized, needless dying without working to prevent its recurrence, then a kind of death already inhabits us. Truly heartrending is Antoine's log of his fatal illness and of the thoughts running through his mind during those weeks. And since Martin du Gard attaches signal importance to what his protagonist has to communicate to us, he safeguards his lucidity until the final hour.

As Antoine feasts his eyes on the splendors of the semi-tropical vegetation outside his window, his heart pinches at the thought that life is swiftly passing him by. As each new month arrives, he sadly weighs the odds of surviving until its close, and as death draws ever nearer, he muses on the good fortune of those who will live to celebrate Christmas. Pitiful is the image of this man who in his slavish dedication to his profession had not taken the time to make a single true friend and who now looks back with envy upon the friendships of his more gregarious lost brother. Though branding war, Antoine feels a nostalgia for the fellowship afforded by this «shared malediction»—its only virtue. Manifestly construing it as one of war's absurdities, he tells how his gassed hospital-mates, many of whom he knew to be as doomed as himself, rejoiced at a rumor that the war's end would be hastened by the employment of a certain new gas which could only be released over enemy territory on account of its all-destructive qualities. Some of these patients had been willfully retarding their recuperation so as not to be

---

(67) *Ibid.,* p. 848.

sent back into combat. Antoine now wholeheartedly subscribes to the concept of a world court, of a league of nations, of general disarmament. No public figure engages his attention nearly as much as Woodrow Wilson, for whom his admiration borders on idolatry. About the American idealist he jots down in his diary: «Each of Wilson's messages—a big blast of breathable air that passes over Europe. Reminds you of the oxygen shot to the bottom of a mine after a cave-in so that the luckless entombed men might be able to fight off asphyxiation long enough to hold out until the rescue» (68). On the eleventh of November Antoine is in such excruciating pain that he makes no reference to the Armistice. A week later a self-administered injection puts an end to his suffering. Antoine had come to regard his death as absurd. It is plain that Martin du Gard had never regarded it any differently. All the same, he was a realist who did not have to be informed that the destruction of the institution which had snuffed out the lives of the Thibault brothers would not be easy of accomplishment. Their pessimism about the possibility of transforming human nature, he more than intimates, is his own too.

Other grist is brought to the book's antiwar mill. While Antoine is still able to get about, the diplomat Rumelles, a patient of his, takes him to dinner at Maxim's, where the plush ambiance and comfortable *embusqué* clientele contrast vividly with Antoine's image of the poor wretches in the filthy, water-logged trenches of the East. Mazet, one of the doctors

(68) *Ibid.*, pp. 923-24. Cf. Jean-Richard Bloch's comment on Wilson in 1931: «Wilson was the Ossian of hearts weary of war. He brought them an exotic fragrance, an opium indispensable to troubled times. He recolored the pacifism which the dull and realistic phraseology of the Europeans had brought into disrepute. He cast a humanitarian cloak over the coldest political horse-trading, he poetized diplomacy, made of the sale of guns an ode; of monetary loans, an elegy.» *Destin du siècle* (Paris: Rieder, 1931), p. 87.

on duty at the hospital, is enough disturbed by the «atmosphere of official lies» to which the war has given rise to wonder if the populations of the warring nations will ever again be able to make their voices heard and if the European press will ever manage to extricate itself from the morass into which it has sunken. In this connection, Rumelles, in whose person villainy is concretized in *Épilogue,* explains to Antoine how the powers that be had deemed it expedient to sacrifice the lives of some twenty-five thousand soldiers in the Laffaux sector in order to score a slim victory and supposedly repair thereby the morale damage caused by the Chemin des Dames blood bath. After he has finished expounding on how much ingenuity goes into the production of «salutary lies» and enthusing over the remarkable results achieved by such lies in a war situation, Antoine observes, «Between those who wage *it* [and] those who don't wage *it* ... Between them and us never again will reconciliation be possible!» (69). For his part, Daniel, who knows what it means to participate in bayonet attacks, hardly looks at newspapers anymore, since he is all too cognizant of the disparity between the reality and the clipped, distorted, communiqué-fed accounts of happenings at the fighting fronts. Doctor Philip, Antoine's *patron* and collaborator, paints a grim picture of what the French army's medical services were in 1915, in which year he had been charged with the duty of reorganizing them. Amongst other things, the wounded were sometimes being evacuated in cattle cars; soldiers with head wounds were being shipped off to such distant points that gangrene and tetanus were killing them off en route; there was an acute shortage of hospital supplies of every kind, and heading large surgical units were inexperienced careerists who were abusing the perquisites of their rank by performing operations well

(69)   Martin du Gard, *Épilogue,* p. 812.

beyond their competence, amputating left and right, and ignoring the counsel of more knowledgeable reservist colleagues. Bad as all this was, the real culprit for Philip was war itself. Because in his view—and no doubt in that of Martin du Gard—wars rarely settle anything, they can rarely be justified.

Jean Giono, Champion of Peasant Pacifism

Jean Giono answered the call to the colors in January 1915 without—he claimed—believing in the fatherland. Attached to an infantry company whose original complement was virtually wiped out by the time the war ended, he saw action over a broad area of the front, including such bloody sectors as Verdun-Vaux, Chemin des Dames, Noyon-Saint-Quentin, and Mount Kemmel. He never rose above the rank of private, was never seriously wounded, and killed no Germans because, as he boasted, he took part in attacks either without a rifle or with a spiked one. Emotionally war was the crowning experience of his life. His mind haunted by the wholesale slaughter he had witnessed, he became an extreme, an absolute pacifist. He was the sole French writer-pacifist of note who was not to surrender his antiwar pennants before the Second World War.

Upset by Romain Rolland's uniting with Paul Langevin and Francis Jourdain in early September 1938 to address a telegram to Premiers Daladier and Chamberlain urging the taking of «energetic measures» to foil Hitler's designs on Czechoslovakia, Giono caustically reminded Jean-Christophe's creator that «energetic measures» in 1938 usage could only be synonymous with «war.» In a counter telegram of September 11 Giono, in company with Victor Margueritte, Alain, and Georges Pioch, called upon the same statesmen to bring pressure to bear on their governments to «save peace by any equitable arrangement conceivable» and to follow this up with an all-out effort to secure Czechoslovak neutrality (70). So blind and undeviating was Giono in his devotion to his pacifist ideal that he went so far as to urge French disarmament as a first step toward universal disarmament in the wake of the Munich Pact, and he made so bold as to publicly announce to President Lebrun that he had personally organized a team of men to botch and tear up mobilization posters in his native Manosque area. Understandably, his untimely pacifist crusading was ill appreciated by the authorities, who jailed him for a spell.

Giono's pacifist creed is enunciated in his novel, *Le Grand Troupeau* (1931); in the article «Je ne peux pas oublier,» which first appeared in the November 15, 1934 issue of *Europe* and was subsequently joined to four unpublished chapters of *Le Grand Troupeau* to make up the volume *Refus d'obéissance* (1937); in *Lettre aux paysans sur la pauvreté et la paix* (1938); in *Précisions* (1939), a miscellany of open letters, telegrams, meditations, and extracts from his earlier writings; and to a lesser extent in the impassioned essay *Les Vraies Richesses* (1936) and the lyrico-epic pamphlet *Le Poids du ciel* (1938).

In *Le Grand Troupeau*, Giono shows his peasant heroes grappling with war and losing all around. The picture is as unpleasant as the denunciation of war is complete. Torn away from their plows, catapulted from their peaceful fields to smoking battlegrounds, his peasants react with consternation and disgust. Theirs, Giono would assure us, had been the true beatitude; theirs the boon beyond compare of living close to nature and in harmony with it. But now they who had daily luxuriated in the sight of life in all its germination, growth, and efflorescence, see death casting its great shadow

---

(70) Jean Giono, *Précisions* (Paris: Grasset, 1939), pp. 8-10.

over everything and frustrating nature at every turn. Some of them go insane; others stoically bend under the military yoke until death puts an end to their suffering; still others wrench themselves free from the yoke by inflicting wounds on themselves. Olivier, one of the story's leading characters, arranges to have a mate shoot off part of his hand, no doubt hearing, as in an echo chamber, the whisper of his father's parting advice: «Remember what I tell you ... Do no more than you have to. The main thing is that you come back» (71). And the Stygian trenches in which these men of the soil wallow are overrun with crows and rats, ghouls that come to feast on rotting cadavers, with Giono from time to time incorporating into his narrative shock-inspiring visions that surpass in naturalistic horror anything on the pages of Barbusse's *Le Feu*. He does not, for example, hesitate to confront the reader with the spectacle, described in vivid detail, of a pig devouring the corpse of a baby a short distance behind the lines. On several pages of hospital scenes, the novelist contrasts the grotesque visages and mutilated bodies of the soldier patients with the unimpaired beauty of the roses and walks of a hospital garden below, with the roses bearing the names of historic battles and of politicians' wives, and the walks those of generals. The sightless are observed pushing about the wheelchairs of the legless, and a blinded, frightfully disfigured *poilu* runs his fingers over the facial contours of a nursing sister in an effort to visualize what his own face once resembled.

If things are going very badly for these Jacques Bonhommes in arms, they are going no better for the folks on the home front. Government requisitioners prowl the countryside, robbing it of its men and of the food produced by the sweat of peasants' brows. Little Valensole, hundreds of

_____

(71) Giono, *Le Grand Troupeau* (Paris: Gallimard, 1931), p. 84.

kilometers removed from the battle areas, feels the impact of war quite as much, if in a different way, as it would if the opposing armies were dug in on its fields. The messenger bearing death notices becomes an all too familiar figure about the community. Crushed villagers gather to pay their last respects to progeny sacrificed to the war Moloch, in a strange and ancient ceremonial called a «veillée à corps absent.» With the manifold duties of farming now in feebler, women's hands, the wheat sprouts thinly and irregularly, and anemia stunts its growth. Male adolescents early experience carnal pleasures as older females in the bloom of sensuality seek out substitutes for more mature love partners. One of the women gratifies her sexual instincts in the company of an uncouth-appearing deserter who is hiding out in the local woods —toward whom, significantly, the villagers bear no ill will. In the meantime, her husband is losing an arm at the front.

But it is not man alone who pays for man's lunacy, a point exemplified by the showpiece section of *Le Grand Troupeau*. The story opens on an awesome note, with Giono achieving a remarkable epic effect in portraying the downward surge of a mammoth mass of sheep on the eve of battle. These move not in their customary slow, rambling manner, but swiftly and straightaway, as though driven on by a demoniac force. Like a river overflowing its banks, the tremendous herd swarms over the walks and presses up against the houses and garden walls. «Talk about wasting life! Talk about wasting life!» (72)—a frightened villager laments as he watches the panting, sweating, bloody-bottomed animals rumble on for endless hours through a huge cloud of dust, rending the air with agonizing bleats as swarms of bees and flies attack their raw wounds. Some will never reach the lowlands toward which they are being driven,

(72) *Ibid.,* p. 18.

falling out to die lonely deaths. And when, to cap all, the horrified onlookers note that the war has left behind but two patriarchal shepherds to pilot the Gargantuan herd from cool mountain pastures to sun-baked lowland pasturelands, they have a presentiment that, farther off, hell itself is about to break loose. The symbolism of the scene is, of course, obvious: the sheep represent the millions of men being led to the slaughter, mesmerized by or blindly devoted to a handful of leaders. It especially pained Giono that uncounted numbers of peasants were among them, since for him, as for Zola, the peasant was the backbone of the nation and the salt of the earth. But Giono, for his part, could never have seen fit to portray a latter-day Jean Macquart voluntarily presenting himself for possible immolation on the altar of war.

What, above all, Giono could not suffer was the renunciation of life. Because this apostle of joyful and sensual living had celebrated life itself as man's only real glory, for him war, which killed off men in their flower, was murderous madness, whatever the circumstances. Inasmuch as he would thereafter have no part of it, he could even declare unashamedly, «There is no glory in being French. There is but one glory: that of being alive» (73). But that is not enough, for man must also live life properly. So, with his *Les Vraies Richesses* (1936) Giono tries to point the way to happiness. Man, he holds, cannot fail to find it if he only be willing to return to a simple, natural life. Incalculable riches are his for the asking, but he must first throw off the chains of a mechanized, money-governed civilization. Does he not realize that money is a deadly pestilence, that his thirst for it has made of him a drudge and chattel of the machine,

---

(73) Giono, *Jean le Bleu*, in *Oeuvres romanesques complètes*, vol. 2, ed. Robert Ricotte (Paris: Gallimard, 1972), p. 180.

has stripped him of his priceless individuality? Does he not know that real living and worldly success are mutually exclusive terms? Such are the reminders with which Giono covers the pages of his hymn to happiness. Hence, his lyrical evocation of nature as the dispenser of inexhaustible pleasures: let every man exult in the touch of his toes on mother earth, in the harvest of his own golden wheat; let him take time to examine the natural perfection of its kernels, a perfection unmatched by the most brilliant of human inventors; let him bake bread of flour milled with his own hands and tan hides obtained from his own cattle.

Consistent with this philosophy Giono was to continue to make a frontal assault on modern civilization, with its political and social tyrannies, its urbanization, commercialism, and soul-destroying machines—a civilization which was transforming the peasant into an agricultural entrepreneur and driving the craftsman out of his little shop onto the assembly line of the factory, with, as he saw it, disastrous consequences for both. Yet, it was chiefly on peasant foundations that Giono would have erected his temple of peace. Preaching the essential identity of peasants everywhere, he repeatedly hailed the peasantry as a «nation above all nations,» invincible by its very *raison d'être* and its great numerical superiority. He could not condone what he judged to be the lack of self-consciousness of a peasant class which, buttressed with such inborn strength, should, he stressed, have enjoyed a preponderance of authority in regulating the destinies of nations rather than again and again acquiescing, sheep-like, in its own slaughter. Would French peasants, he implied, again be content to lament, as their forefathers had done during the Napoleonic wars, that they had only been born to become cannonfodder?

Until 1938 Giono's war on war had been restricted to his campaign of awakening the peasant from a slumber which in his view had made him the bondsman of the money-mad, technology-mad minority that had reserved for him a special place at Mars' blood banquets, that had made him the eternal loser who was marched off to do battle by government agents cognizant that his wife would unfailingly replace him in the fields and his children shepherd his flocks, while the factory hand remained at his bench to assemble the tools of war and even to enjoy increased prosperity. But Giono did not have to lean on statistics: the French farming population was well aware that in the Great War it had suffered the highest per capita losses of any group, one peasant having been killed for every half-dozen mobilized (74). Then, with his *Lettre aux paysans* of the same year, Giono spiritedly expounded what he considered to be a simple method for preventing war: all that was necessary was the universal adoption by peasants of poverty—poverty understood not as genuine want but rather as an economic condition a step above that ordinarily associated with day-to-day living. This seemingly impossible trick could be turned if only farm populations in every land agreed, as soon as a dangerous international crisis impended, to destroy all food supplies over and above those required by their family consumption. And because, as the saying goes, an army fights on its stomach, the bellicose powers would be up against the impossibility of unleashing the dogs of war. Moreover, a permanent solution had to be striven for, with the peasant vowing never again to produce more than a bare sufficiency. As a result, industry, which favors wars to multiply profits, would collapse as the workers migrated back to the soil whence they came, and

---

(74) D. W. Brogan writes: «... Over 3,700,000 agricultural workers had been mobilized and of these over 600,000 had been killed ... And, of course, the great war losses among the peasant class, when coupled with the limitation of the size of families, meant in many cases that the only son for whom the holding had been destined had been killed. *The Development of Modern France, 1870-1939* (New York: Harper & Row, 1966), p. 60.

— 113 —

where, Giono would have us know, they belong. Giono's peacetime peasant revolution would, therefore, neutralize the power of the capitalist state without ushering in the communist rule which he likewise abhorred.

In speaking of Giono's revolt against war and capitalism, Pierre Brodin makes the valid point that his is «basically the revolt of a poet—not of an economist or theoretician,» (75) implying that the author, in his boundless love of life and of nature can be excused if he enormously overestimates the efficacy of his cure. And where his peasant-centered scheme for frustrating war-makers is concerned, it is precisely because he addressed himself to a poetized, idealized peasant that it had no chance of working (76). It can be readily imagined how a *real* French peasant of the thirties would have reacted to all his inflated talk about money being nothing but useless paper whose acquisition could only impoverish and de-peasantize him. In his eagerness to sway his *campagnard* brothers, Giono conveniently overlooked the fact that: to ask them to cease trading with the outer world was to ask them to cease doing what they had been doing since ancient times; that they were by nature dark pessimists for whom the ultra-severe limitation of crops could only be viewed as an invitation to pauperization; that for all but a small minority of them the prime ambition was to enlarge their fields in order to expand production and profits; that to the golden age of pastoral living to which he would have had them return they preferred the banknotes that made it possible for them to meet the mechanizing competition; that to the rudimentary

---

(75) Pierre Brodin, «Jean Giono,» *Présences contemporaines* (Paris: Éditions Debresse, 1956), I, 135.
(76) W. D. Redfern may not be overstating the case in affirming that Giono's peasants «are obviously less like peasants than anyone has ever encountered in life or even in literature.» *The Private World of Jean Giono* (Durham, North Carolina: Duke University Press, 1967), p. 97.

tools he glorified they preferred the tractors he execrated; that their sons had been steadily abandoning the soil since the late nineteenth century (77); that if they loved their *mas,* their cattle, and their crops, they also loved the automobiles, radios, and newspapers that were opening up to them the world beyond their villages; that, finally, their common sense would surely cause them to reject out of hand any scheme that would leave their fields open to invasion by a powerful, industrialized, agriculturally deficient neighbor bent on finding *Lebensraum.* Was it not more for that reason than any other that they had so stubbornly held their ground at Verdun? Was not that one of the reasons that tens of housands of their sons were to join the Maquis under the German occupation?

Never until France again mobilized for war did this visionary betray any pessimism as to the fallibility of his remedy. Only with his *Précisions* (1939), published almost on the eve of a second great war—in which, as much as anything else, the lack of the machines he loathed condemned his countrymen to defeat—did Giono finally admit the industrial worker into his scheme. In it he apologized to him for having neglected to assign him his due role in preventing war, claiming that he had expressly done so in the hope that labor would thereby be shaken of its inertia. He now proposed an alliance of farm and factory workers to form a new proletariat that he defined as «the collectivity of men who refuse all wars» (78).

With German military might swelling at an alarming rate and Hitler's hysterical voice riding the airwaves, the hour

---

(77) John Ardagh notes: «In one recent national survey of fifteen-to-twenty-nine-year-olds still on the land, half the boys and three-quarters of the girls intended to leave.» *The New French Revolution* (New York: Harper & Row, 1968), p. 79.

(78) Giono, *Précisions,* p. 42.

was late for preaching mutiny, and, as Giono well knew, the mutineers of mortally endangered nations end up in jail. As a rule neither governments nor many of the governed have much patience with those who in such circumstances put staying alive at any cost above all else, even above living in abject servitude. Another declared doctrinaire pacifist, Albert Einstein, had, as early as 1933, with Hitler's rise to power, arrived at the conclusion that dogged adherence to an ideal in radically altered circumstances can be tantamount to entertaining a death wish—for the soul if not for the body. There can be little doubt that it was Giono's stubborn cast of mind joined to his total unconcern with public opinion rather than any degree of personal admiration for Nazism or Vichyism that led him, during the German occupation, to make a few rather harmless if ill-advised contributions to two collaborationist publications, the *Nouvelle Revue Française* and *La Gerbe*. At any rate, under the dominion of his naïve pacifism he had made quite enough misguided moves in the late thirties and after the *débâcle* to attract the attention of post-Liberation justiciaries. In addition, his *Triomphe de la vie* (1942), while extolling the joys of the plow and of the artisan's workbench neither more nor less than he had been doing for years, read too much like Vichy's own back-to-the-soil and back-to-the-craftsman's atelier propaganda to please them. As a result, Giono was blacklisted by the Resistance's Comité National des Écrivains and again found himself behind prison bars, this time for six months.

Having met with nothing but frustration as a substantially *engagé* author, Giono totally abandoned that orientation when he resumed writing in 1947. The new Giono was still a pacifist in heart and mind, but now he could weave militarist adventurers into the fabric of his stories quite as comfortably as nature-loving peasants, while showing favoritism to neither.

André Chamson and Religious Pacifism

«The generation without elders, the adolescents separated from men» (79)—thus did André Chamson qualify, in his *La Révolution de dix-neuf* (1930), his own generation, eighteen-year-olds in 1918. Too young to be called up for military service, these lads were, as he hastens to add, old enough to recognize war as the crime of crimes. These were the youths who, while poring over lessons in logic, were baffled by the gross unreason of the world about them, who learned of the obscenity of war through the glum uncommunicativeness of furloughing brothers and the knock of the death-notice bearer.

Born of peasant parents in Nîmes, Chamson grew up in a severely Protestant atmosphere on the slopes of the nearby Cévennes mountains. Here he came to know well the hardy, austere-living Protestant descendants of Camisard religious rebels who raised sheep and cultivated miniature farms on eroded foothills, isolated from and largely indifferent to the changing world about them. Although Chamson at an early age stopped practicing the religion of his childhood and left the Cévennes to study and settle in Paris, the impress on his writings of his Protestant consciousness and of his native environment has been very heavy.

As a politically *engagé* author, Chamson's place was to be on the left. An early admirer of Romain Rolland, he became a militant pacifist and a contributor to the review *Europe* with which Rolland was prominently associated. In the thirties he was an active member of the Association des Écrivains et des Artistes Révolutionnaires. He strongly supported the Spanish Republic and Léon Blum's Front Populaire govern-

---

(79) André Chamson, *La Révolution de dix-neuf* (Paris: Hartmann, 1930), p. 25.

ment, which appointed him assistant curator of the National Museum at Versailles. From 1935 to 1938 he co-edited, with Jean Guéhenno and André Viollis, the weekly *Vendredi,* a forum for anti-fascist intellectuals.

At twenty-five Chamson made an impressive entry on the literary scene with the publication of his novelette *Roux le bandit* (1925). This is a tale, supposedly rooted in reality, of a mountaineer's mutiny against war, a tale that caught the imagination of Cévenol peasants and made of Roux a legendary figure and of his case a moral lesson of considerable fascination for these Bible-imbued folk. If the narrative contains any mythical accretions, embellishments that might well slip into stories that make and remake the rounds of these mountain fastnesses, the reader is unaware of them as Finiels, an old villager of reputedly unblemished integrity, gives his version of Roux's rebellion.

When in the summer of 1914 the tocsin for mobilization rang and the area's young men, flushed with excitement, went off to become tiny cogs ~~in an~~ enormous military machine, Roux, then thirty, responded with an emphatic «No!» Ignoring social pressures, refusing to succumb to the common emotion, this woodsman withdrew to the mountains he knew so well, doing so in the full realization that his government would doggedly pursue him and, upon capture, pitilessly prosecute him. Roux de Sauveplane would thereafter be know exclusively as Roux le bandit, not for being a thief or murderer but rather as one living apart from the community of men, a sort of poacher at large in the woods and hills.

Roux's display of extraordinary individualism caused his Cévenol neighbors to rise up in wrath despite their own well-justified reputation as uncompromising individualists. With the German peril staring them in the face, with their neglected crops going to wrack and ruin, and with the village's morale at half-mast over killed, mutilated, and missing sons and husbands, Roux's action was damned as an indefensible flight from responsibility. «Traitor,» «coward,» «monster»—such were the epithets showered upon the absent woodsman. Hunted like a beast by the implacable gendarmerie, hemmed in by the elements, and reduced to a subhuman level of living, Roux got no sympathy from the beleaguered peasantry. Even the fugitive's mother and sister, high honored in the vicinity for their tough moral fiber, suddenly found themselves social castaways.

But time works many changes. In Roux's case it took three years to overcome the hostility of his neighbors. By then the god of war had exacted a terrible tribute in the region and there could no longer be any question of cowardice on the part of a man who had passed three bitterly cold winters in the Cévennes snows. By then, above all, it had been conclusively established that Roux's nonconformity was based on his conviction that war was inconsonant with his interpretation of Biblical passages relative to it and to the use of violence, and, by inference, with the spirit of Christ. For, as the months and years dragged on, Roux would come out onto the edge of the forest to meet trusted acquaintances, and when inevitably they would subject him to searching interrogations on the reasons for his escape, he would discuss them fully and frankly. A peasant to the bone and marrow, he could give no complex explanations, present no erudite disquisitions; nor could he have been expected to be familiar with the doctrine of a «just war» that Christianity had been refining ever since Saint Augustine first attempted to enunciate it. Yet, that may not have mattered to him anyway. What obviously very much did matter to him was his ability to find Biblical lines in support of his antiwar position and to recite them verbatim in reply to his interlocutors' questions. What these lines are we are never told, but it is apparent that his Bible-revering peasant neighbors were satisfied that the outlaw had made a sincere effort to interpret the word of God correctly. Accordingly, none of them took the trouble to point out to him—though it is unlikely that some of them were not aware of it—that more than one Biblical passage is either ambiguous on war or even suggests its inevitability (80).

With first a combat soldier, then two venerated townsmen coming to his defense, Roux disarmed all rancor toward him. With their abiding respect for things spiritual the chief impellent, these mountaineers completely exonerated him whom they had dispossessed in 1914, reproving themselves for having so hastily branded him a slacker. And had not the merciful, forgiving, peace-loving Roux amply demostrated that, by braving cold, starvation, and the gendarmes' bullets, he, like Christ, was willing to die a martyr's death if need be? One of them, the narrator's son, now swore that he would never again leave the family *mas* for war. Surely we may surmise that those famous sons of peasants whose names were so conspicuously linked with the war—Clemenceau, Joffre, and Pétain—were no heroes in his eyes. The young man swore, at the same time, that nobody would ever succeed in driving him away to a mountain hideout. As though transplanted from Giono's Manosque, he declared: «A peasant, you understand, is meant to remain close to the soil. I have no greater desire to go tearing about the mountains with the gendarmes on my tail than to go back into combat. I must stay with my grapevines and my animals, and if ever I have to do any shooting, it'll be in front of my door and

_____

(80) In his book *The New Testament Basis of Pacifism* (n.p.: The Fellowship of Reconciliation, 1942), G. H. C. MacGregor reviews the antiwar arguments commonly advanced on the basis of Scriptural passages and makes the point that «Even the Devil can quote Scripture, and to cite isolated passages wrested from their context is to use a boomerang which is apt to recoil on the head of the user.» p. 9.

at the first person who comes to tell me what I must do» (81).

Conscious of the population's readiness to make common cause with him, Roux had by now been sufficiently emboldened to pay sporadic visits to his home and to lend a hand to nearby shepherds, loggers, and terrace farmers. Ultimately his own carelessness and the loose talk of an eleven-year-old girl combined to draw him into the constabulary's trap. Brought to trial after the Armistice, the outlaw defied his judges. In Finiels' words, his message to them was that «they could kill him but he would kill no one» (82). The price of his pacifism? Twenty years in prison.

Chamson wisely chooses to plead his antiwar case by striving to engage the reader's sympathy for his hero, all the while building up the notion of the futility of an institution that kills off men while giving rise to despondency in their survivors. He eschews didactic intervention; instead he lets his indictment tacitly emerge from his narrative. A powerful indictment it is, all the more so that his peasant mountaineers, who speak in the quaint idiom of the Cévennes while also speaking like people closer to nature than to books, have all the earmarks of authentic country folk. They are living types. It is a moving story. Without seeming to strain for effect, Chamson has achieved it. *Roux le bandit* is, in short, a little *chef-d'oeuvre,* one worthy of a much older mind than that of the fledgling that Chamson was when he wrote it. As propaganda in a literary frame it cannot easily be faulted.

Perhaps Chamson tried all the harder to portray his «bandit» in a sympathetic light in his awareness that religious conscientious objectors, like political conscientious objectors, have always had a difficult road to travel. Religions them-

---

(81) Chamson, *Roux le bandit* (Paris: Grasset, 1925), p. 143.
(82) *Ibid.,* p. 208.

selves, old and new, as well as their representatives and adherents, so often stand in their way. Beginning with Christian humanist Erasmus in the Renaissance, if not earlier, and right up to the present, the lament of many has been that war is made to wear the cloak of religion. German troops rush westward to the cry «nach Paris,» with «Gott mit uns!» inscribed on the buckles of their garrison belts, and French armies rush eastward shouting «à Berlin,» assured that God is on their side. Christ becomes a general in the army of Mars. Caesar is rendered his due, and God is invoked to help in the rendering. Newspaper editors of belligerent nations urge on the combatants in the field as well as lathe-operators at home, reminding them that it is for God and country that they are extending themselves. To be sure, bellicose Archbishop Turpins are no longer seen joyously slashing away on bloody battlegrounds, relying on their swords as much as their scepters, but a Cardinal Spellman can be heard voicing his approval of Stephen Decatur's «my country right or wrong.» There are still some twentieth-century Joseph de Maistres around to insist that nowhere is the hand of God more visible than on the field of strife and to list reasons why war must be considered a manifestation of divine law, just as there are twentieth-century Hegels to argue that war is indispensable to the moral development of man-kind. There is no shortage of priests to promote reverence for the Victoria Cross, the Iron Cross, and the Croix de guerre. And it is now known that a new high priest can arrive on the scene, write a new bible, replace the Cross of Christ with the crooked cross of the swastika, the Gospels with Wagnerian legends, the hymnal with military marches, and processions with torchlight parades; stock department stores with an abundance of toy guns, tanks, and planes in the Christmas season, and condemn heretics and unbelievers to earthly hells and to death.

Four books later, and after having earned a place beside Alphonse de Châteaubriant and Henri Pourrat as one of the foremost regionalist writers of France, Chamson published *L'Auberge de l'abîme* (1933), a romantic mystery story with pronounced pacifist overtones. It too has the Cévennes as its setting, but the action (it would necessitate lengthy recounting and is not especially pertinent to our purposes) occurs in the wake of the Napoleonic wars. Here Chamson shows Roux's Cévenol ancestors giving vent to their bitterness over the legacy that fifteen years of the Emperor's campaigns has left them. Kindling their ire is the arrival in their village of a transient lieutenant escapee from the recent military slaughters. In no time at all the village's entire population learns that one of the «brigands,» one of the «cutthroats,» has put up at a local inn. Civilian tempers boil, since the region had been drained of its manpower by Bonaparte's repeated drafts. So severe have the incursions been that the area's tiny workshops have had to close down, and ghost towns have mushroomed on the slopes. Besides, these Cévenols are incensed over the sacrifice of lives without number to an effort that had come to national grief, one for which they had small use to begin with. Therefore, to them the stranger's presence can only signal further conscription, plunder, and the setting off of riots. The leading inciter against him is the innkeeper himself, who had for a decade resisted every attempt by the authorities to conscript his sons. His antiwar credo is simple. «The others,» he declares, «were leaving [for war] only to return as deserters a year or two later. My boys deserted nothing at all ... There was no reason in the world to make all the men go. Who, then, would have attended to the girls, the houses, the land?» (83).

---

(83) Chamson, *L'Auberge de l'abîme* (Paris: Ferenczi, 1935), p. 28.

From beginning to end, the narrative is studded with passages that reflect the war-weariness of the populace.

In his novel, *L'Année des vaincus* (1934), Chamson indicted Nazi Germany for girding for war. Carrière, its principal character, had felt no antipathy for the Germans in the trenches across the way from him during World War I, since they too belonged to the great fraternity of helpless sufferers. Pacific by instinct and a pacifist by choice, Carrière had made every effort to eradicate ill feeling toward a group of technicians imported from Hitler's Germany to work in a mill in his home town. In fact, he had invited a pair of them to live in his home, with the resultant perfect harmony between them symbolizing the amity that could be realized by their governments and compatriots if they too cultivated a sense of tolerance, understanding, and compromise.

All goes awry, however, when Carrière accompanies his guests to Stuttgart on a purchasing mission. There he is able to observe how deeply they have drunk of the poisons of Nazism. There he watches columns of swashbuckling troopers overrun the squares against a background of swastikas and blaring bands. And he hears Janus-faced Hitlerian apostles assure him of their government's noble intentions while in the streets storm troopers gather the politically unregenerate into their dragnets. Upon apprising his townsmen of his dreary findings and witnessing the breakdown of Franco-German relations in the town, Carrière concludes, «... At present I'm afraid of everything, of the war that can return, of all sorts of troubles. I'm afraid of this year and of those ahead. We are all losers now» (84).

Unwilling to sit back and await the impending catastrophe with fatalistic resignation, in July 1937 Chamson travelled through eastern and central Spain to take the pulse of the

---

(84) Chamson, *L'Année des vaincus* (Paris: Grasset, 1934), p. 255.

war there. His *Retour d'Espagne, Rien qu'un témoignage* (1937) is an emotional account of his findings. In it he emphasized that previously his detestation of war had been founded on abstractions, chiefly on his love for the citizens of his own and other nations, inasmuch as he had had no direct experience of war. This detestation had now been intensified by his witnessing war in all its hideous reality. Victory won by Franco's nationalist forces would, he believed, mark the beginning of a Europe-wide death struggle. He felt particularly obliged to awaken public opinion to that menace because of the terrifying visage of modern war—war in which lever-manipulating crews of high-soaring planes held whole populations at their mercy, quite unfeeling about the mass extinction of humans they could not see, war fought by technicians operating precision instruments of destruction. And if, as he claimed, the war in Spain, in July 1937, was much more than a civil war, a bloody clash between intransigent supporters of opposing ideologies, this was because it involved a new and unprecedentedly dangerous nation, a «nation without its own territory, without culture, civilization, or responsibility ... but a terrible nation united by nothing except the servicing and use of the machines of massacre that have become its fatherland» (85).

Whereas, like Giono, Chamson established himself as a champion of peasant pacifism and on occasion resorted to a line of reasoning similar to that of the son of Manosque, he primarily focussed on the right of the individual to decline military service on religious grounds, an issue that Giono does not touch upon. And if, with memories of the slaughter of 1914-18 fresh in his mind, Chamson portrayed his Roux as a popular hero, a tower of moral strength, and a symbol

---

(85) Chamson, *Retour d'Espagne, Rien qu'un témoignage* (Paris: Grasset, 1937), p. 108.

of spiritual resistance, he did so without placing himself on record as supporting the contention of Benjamin Franklin that there has never been a good war or a bad peace. Rather, it is evident that he would have passionately endorsed the view expressed by Vauvenargues' maxim that «War is not as onerous as servitude.» Consequently, for him the war against Hitler was a good war—as it was for the same Bertrand Russell who had gone to jail for his antiwar stance of World War I, and as it was for Dresden firebombing survivor Kurt Vonnegut, Jr., who, however, has since served notice that he can no longer justify going to war (86). As a result, Chamson not only served his country in the Second World War but he served it well beyond the call of ordinary duty: as a liaison officer during the «drôle de guerre,» then as a key Resistance leader in the South of France, and, finally, with De Lattre de Tassigny's French First Army in the Alsace sector. In 1940, reckoning the French «the most pacifistic and the most pacific people on earth» (87), he went on record as enthusiastically approving, as the only way out of a false peace, his government's September 3, 1939 decision to enter the war. He now launched a scathing attack on Giono for not giving the war his blessing, declaring: «Of what importance is G... to me today? He is faithful to his pride. He is not faithful to the peasants. What he has done could have been great, but at bottom he is but an Epicurean, a vain, gifted—wonderfully gifted—man, who, it appears, is complaining about his fate. His fate is of no interest to me» (88). Clearly, the spreading viruses of Nazism and fascism had moved André Chamson a long way from his

---

(86) See *The Vonnegut Statement,* eds. Jerome Klinkowitz and John Somer (New York: Delacorte Press, 1973), p. 118.
(87) Chamson, *Quatre mois, Carnet d'un officier de liaison* (Paris: Flammarion, 1940), p. 70.
(88) *Ibid.,* p. 16.

militant pacifism. For his personal contribution to bringing about peace by distinguishing himself in warfare, he was awarded the Croix de guerre and the Médaille de la Résistance.

The Sentimental Pacifism of Georges Duhamel

Exempted from military duty in peacetime, Paris-born Georges Duhamel volunteered for service in an ambulance unit at the beginning of the war of 1914-18. Though he had been a licensed physician since 1909, he had not practiced medecine, having embarked on a literary career instead. As a field surgeon with the rank of major he performed some 2,300 operations during his fifty months at or near the front. At the close of his working day, often at midnight, sometimes at dawn, his surgical garments would be crimson with the blood of those whom he called «martyrs.» After that grim experience Duhamel was not disposed to argue, as some have done, that one of the reasons that war can be justified is that it accelerates progress in the medical and surgical sciences. The disproportion was simply too great.

A member of the 'Clarté' group for a few years after the Armistice, Duhamel collaborated with Barbusse and Rolland in waging war on war. But, temperamentally unsuited for collective action of any kind, he resigned from the group in early 1920. To all appearances a heated quarrel with Barbusse provided him with a convenient pretext for doing so. This was a time when Duhamel was identifying himself as a passionate believer in European federalism and intercontinental union as the surest guarantors of peace, a conviction that he abandoned only when Hitler's divisions were on the march. After dissociating himself from 'Clarté,' Duhamel remained outside the public arena, letting his books and, in the late thirties, his columns in Le Figaro do the speaking for him. In the essays of his *Défense des lettres* (1937) and especially in those of his *Mémorial de la guerre blanche* (1938), Duhamel aired his bitterness over developments in Nazi Germany and sounded his personal alarm on the deadly menace it posed for France in particular and civilized society in general. This gentle lover of mankind could not in the slightest condone the brutality, ruthlessness, and racism of the Hitlerian regime. Continuing to nourish his broad humanistic vision—he had earlier described himself as «a French citizen of the world» and a «European of Paris» (89)—he remained totally unaffiliated politically. Mistrustful of all political systems, he looked to them for few remedies; for the war disease, none whatever.

With France again at war, Jean Giraudoux, as director of the Ministry of Information, placed Duhamel in charge of its radio section. After giving medical aid to hundreds of ailing and injured civilian refugees in a hospital near Rennes during and just after the *débâcle,* Duhamel retired to his Valmandois estate in the Ile-de-France. Under the occupation his home was searched by the Germans on two occasions. He made a limited number of contributions to the German-controlled press, all of a strictly nonpartisan nature. With characteristic solicitude for the weal of others, he carried on a voluminous correspondence with French prisoners of war and presided over the Comité de Sauvegarde des Oeuvres Créées en Captivité.

Duhamel's reputation as a pacifist was established with the publication of two books he managed to write in the brief periods of respite from medical duties stingily allowed him by Mars: *Vie des martyrs* (1917) and *Civilisation* (1918). The former is made up of short sketches or vignettes. Its

---

(89) Georges Duhamel, «Introduction,» *Géographie cordiale de l'Europe* (Paris: Mercure de France, 1931), pp. 25, 32.

subject is the unutterable suffering of war's chief victims as witnessed by the author himself in a hospital setting. Its characters are wounded and dying soldiers, ordinary soldiers from the rank of private to lieutenant, peasants and laborers for the most part, humble of station but great of heart.

Duhamel narrates in the first person, usually addressing his «sons» and his «brothers» in the familiar *tu* form. As he moves from bed to bed lavishing comforting smiles and words upon them, he comes through as a warm, kindly father or missionary rather than as what many another might well have been in such circumstances, i.e., a surgeon pure and simple, one drained of all emotion through the long cultivation of clinical coolness under the pressures of the operating room. While Duhamel certainly does not close his eyes or ours to physical horrors and while he mournfully discloses that «under their dressings there are wounds of which you cannot conceive» (90), he is equally intent on plumbing the depths of the souls of the suffering. Of realistic details he is not frugal, but nowhere does one find anything to compare with the brutal realism of the lengthy field hospital scenes of Zola's *La Débâcle,* whose ghastliness fairly overwhelms the reader. Thus, whether it is as his deft hand attacks gangrenous limbs and rent tissue or as he makes his daily rounds in the wards, he fastens on his patients' every reaction, for not only do these victims of man's bloody ways deserve more than pious attention, but present and future generations must not be spared this grim memento. Rinaldi, the military surgeon of Hemingway's *A Farewell to Arms,* felt less bad about the war when he was performing operations continuously because this gave him less time to think about its abominations. Contrarily, Duhamel the memorialist will not allow himself

---

(90) Duhamel, *Vie des martyrs 1914-1916,* 81st ed. (Paris: Mercure de France, 1918), p. 6.

9

the luxury of so feeling, even with scalpel, probe, or forceps in hand.

For Duhamel the acquittal of his sacred obligation is all the easier that he possesses an exceptional capacity for sharing in the tribulations of humans. And nowhere in his voluminous literary output is this quality more in evidence than in *Vie des martyrs*. An alloy of profound pity and *tendresse,* Duhamel's sympathy carries no suggestion of the maudlin or of the gushing. It is the same openhearted *tendresse* that civilian Walt Whitman showed the sick and wounded of the American Civil War while attending them as a volunteer male nurse. It is the same profound if untrembling pity that Tolstoy's Prince Andrey, badly injured in the Borodino slaughter, experienced while observing the sobbing Anatol Kuragin, a man he had detested, lying forlorn on a table in a field hospital, his amputated, still booted leg in a receptacle nearby. It is incontestably not the «purely literary pity» of a writer who «exploits pity like other writers exploit adultery» (91), of which animal-lover Paul Léautaud, irked that Duhamel did not concern himself with the sufferings of animals in his war books, accused him.

For Duhamel the truth communicates its message well enough, so he does no tampering with it. Some of his «martyrs» stand out by their moral nobility, but among them are also found the weak of will, the cross-grained, and the ingrate. Be that as it may, he cheerfully lends an ear to their gripes and shows them no less compassion, since in his eyes they too are heroes, not by virtue of deeds accomplished on the field of battle but on account of their suffering. He is impatient only of those humans who can contemplate their sacrifice and remain untouched by it, or of those who profane

---

(91) Paul Léautaud, *Journal littéraire, VII June, 1928-July, 1929,* p. 318.

it through incomprehension—such, for example, as the perfume-drenched society woman whose haughty manner and whose offer to a soldier-patient of any gift of his choosing combine to infuriate him.

Present on every page, Duhamel does not, however, offend by his presence, for he is unobtrusive of manner and restrained of voice. Describing in simple, succinct language the death pangs of a soldier begging to be saved so that he might yet savor a measure of earthly happiness, he sighs, «It is tough to have been unlucky for forty years and to have to give up forever the humble joy of smelling the bitter scent of junipers» (92). He fires no broadsides against the makers of war, although there can be no doubt as to where they stand with him. His spare commentary leaves plenty of room for afterthoughts and for the drawing of inferences. Nor is all gloom and darkness. He lends further verisimilitude to his sketches by complementing his portrayal of large-scale human agony with a liberal injection of the comic wit that can spring from the deepest recesses of men's souls when their spirits are lowest. It is, of course, a wit more than tinged with the tragic. To cite a single instance, when a legless soldier is teased that his disability pension will enable him to live «like a small *rentier*,» he quips, «Oh! a very small *rentier*, a very small one» (93). Aiming to strike a blow at the collective conscience of men, Duhamel invites them to take a good look at his suffering and dying soldiers, to catch a pain-distorted smile here, a last utterance there, trusting that if they see only a fraction of what he has seen, war will have forever divested itself of all glory and poetry for them.

Civilisation, Goncourt Prize awardee for 1918, was pub-

---

(92) Duhamel, *Vie des martyrs,* p. 108.
(93) *Ibid.,* p. 172.

lished by Duhamel under the pseudonym Denis Thévenin. Much akin to *Vie des martyrs,* this ironically titled work may be regarded as an extension of it. Nevertheless, some significant differences are apparent. The setting is more diversified, with the author no longer confining the reader to hospital wards and operating rooms. He now also takes him on excursions to the morgue, cemetery, and even the battlefield. By and large the selections are longer, about half of them may be categorized as full-fledged short stories, and a few of them have no tendentious object whatsoever. Finally, *Civilisation* is more of a grudge book than its predecessor, and the satire has a sharper sting.

In neither book is there even a glimmer of hatred for the German enemy, while, on the other hand, self-inflated visiting dignitaries are consistently held up to shame. In *Civilisation* a queenly «lady in green» causes a chronic depressive to laugh uncontrollably when she tells him how fortunate he is to have won glory, to have known «the exquisite anguish of bounding forward, bayonet shining in the sun; the voluptuous sensation of driving an avenging blade into the bloody side of the enemy, added to the divine suffering endured for all; the holy wound which makes a god of a hero!» (94). And a dying soldier is thus consoled by a prosperous-appearing male visitor: «You seem to be badly hurt, my good fellow! But if you only knew what wounds we are inflicting on them with our 75's! Terrible wounds, my dear man, terrible wounds!» (95). There is harsh treat-

---

(94) Duhamel, *Civilisation,* 64th ed. (Paris: Mercure de France, 1925), p. 113.
(95) *Ibid.,* p. 55. Another physician-writer with little use for war, Austrian Arthur Schnitzler (1862-1931), makes an interesting semantic observation on the expression *mutilés de guerre.* Contrasting the treatment shown dead victims of war with that shown its crippled survivors, he reasons: «They say he died the death of a hero. Why do they never say he suffered the magnificent

ment too for those callous souls who go on shamelessly enjoying themselves in the usual worldly ways, closing their eyes and their hearts to the suffering of the unsheltered, for those who neither have smelled nor would want to smell the ether, chloroform, and putrefying flesh of operating rooms and wards, and who have not seen men expiring of gaping head and stomach wounds and of gangrene while one of them whispers «dodo» and «bobo» as a baby would. The spread of the gangrene of indifference, it too must be checked.

Throughout his *Vie des martyrs* and up to the final chapter of *Civilisation* Duhamel had managed to suppress the wrath which had steadily been mounting in his breast. For the finale, an explosive unburdening, he assumes the guise of an operating-room technician. Nauseated with the horrors that a mechanistic civilization has wrought, a civilization in which humans are pitted against the machines that annihilate their souls at all times and, in time of war, their bodies as well, he concludes: «People are mistaken about happiness and goodness... I have had a chance to look at the monstrous autoclave [mobile operating unit] on its throne. I tell you the truth: civilization is no more to be found in that object than in the surgeon's shiny forceps. Civilization cannot be found in all that terrible junk, and if it is not in the heart of man, well, it just isn't anywhere» (96).

The war was still in progress when Duhamel was completing the writing of his *La Possession du monde* (1919). A type of moral handbook, it prescribes pretty shopworn, idealistic panaceas for the world's afflictions with lyric verve.

---

mutilation of a hero? They say he has given his life for his country. Why do they never say he had both legs amputated for his country?» *Some Day Peace Will Return: Notes on War and Peace,* trans. and ed. Robert O. Weiss (New York: Frederick Ungar Publishing Co., 1972), p. 78.

(96) Duhamel, *Civilisation,* p. 272.

To rescue humans from the miasmas in which they are suffocating on account of their obsession with mechanistic progress and material prosperity, humanist Duhamel proposes the establishment of a «reign of the heart.» Under this reign the authority of our errant intellects, inventors of dehumanizing machines and of engines of death, will be sapped. We shall cease pursuing counterfeit values but win possession of inexhaustible mines of love and knowledge, a very intimate knowledge of other humans and of nature with its unsurpassed beauties. Thus shall we grow in spirit and in love for one another and for our planet; thus will reform from within do away with the ills that the spiritually undernourished would cure with *coups d'état,* revolutions, and wars. A visionary program indeed.

Duhamel's *Entretiens dans le tumulte,* also published in 1919, is in large part made up of fragments of conversations overheard or participated in by him at an officers mess and of his own random thoughts. Together with much else, he again concerns himself with war and peace. This is no longer the soft-spoken surgeon inviting our pity for luckless soldiers. Remonstrances galore have been compressed into the pages of *Entretiens.* Drawing Duhamel's thickest fire are the *bourreurs de crâne,* the professional poets and salaried sycophants whose lies have glamorized war for the uninitiated and prostituted the suffering of the tragedy's real players. Yet, however fraternal his sentiments toward the victims, he cannot wholly exculpate them, for he notes with misgiving that as early as on the morning of November 11, 1918, they had begun to construct the fatal legend of war. The mere fact that they had employed the past imperfect tense in chatting about the experiences of yesteryear and even of yesterday was for him proof sufficient that the carnage was already being consigned to oblivion by them; that, therefore, the victims themselves had already turned *bourreurs* for the next holocaust. Cautioning against the dangers of steeling the heart to suffering and of banishing it from the memory, he stresses: «So that the sacrifice may have its full impact, its full significance, it must leave a bitter taste, a very bitter taste, until the very end; the cup must really be drained to the dregs—even of the dregs» (97). In a postwar essay, *Guerre et littérature* (1920), he once more took up the theme of human forgetfulness and pessimistically predicted that twenty years later those who fought the war would be told how they fought it by non-veterans.

With his *Les Sept Dernières Plaies* (1928) Duhamel reverted to the genre of *Vie des martyrs* and *Civilisation,* appearing in the person of the *aide-major* Cauchois   However, this later work suffers in comparison with its distinguished forerunners, mainly because of its overdependence on a somewhat heavy-footed satire and because of a diminution of the *sympathie* that had served him admirably before. This is most visible when for long stretches he neglects to speak of the sick and wounded soldiers whom he understands so well in order to square accounts with their unfaithful wives, white-livered colonels, muddling hospital administrators, and sundry others. The empathetic author is again at his best in describing the selflessness of a dying *poilu* in allowing a ward party to go on as scheduled («Un Concert»), and in his moving account of the passing of Cauchois' last patient, ambulanced away from the hospital while at death's door to foster the illusion that he too was being evacuated to another locale («Le Dernier»).

Since for Duhamel the role of the heart was always dominant, he placed his trust in its imperatives more than in those of the intellect. Thus, he did not aim to present

---

(97) Duhamel, *Entretiens dans le tumulte* (Paris: Mercure de France, 1919), p. 113.

any tightly reasoned case against war. Rather, he preferred to assume the stance of an evangelist of brotherly love and preached on the virtues of a «reign of the heart,» of personal conversion, moral disarmament, and moral revolution while focussing on the sanctity of human life and the need to lift spiritual frontiers to create a true brotherhood of man. But Duhamel was far too intelligent to have thought that this alone would provide a solution to the war puzzle. He was, then, probably content that he had done his bit to discourage the unwary from looking for beauty or majesty where the only majesty, as Vigny would have put it, was «the majesty of human suffering,» and where the only beauty Duhamel himself found was the beauty in the hearts of men against whom the cards were hopelessly stacked. They were, to be sure, stacked against him too, for if he could influence some people, what could he have done to impress a Napoleon Bonaparte, who, meditating on casualties on the eve of a battle, could snap, «Bah, a single Paris night will repair all that!»? (98). Or a Joffre, who, while commander in chief of the French army, refused access to his headquarters to any combat soldier, wounded or unwounded, lest the vivid reminder of the plight of the unfortunate fellow affect his powers of concentration? (99). Or a Hitler, who never once set foot inside a military hospital? Or even an Emerson, for whom sentimentality was to be scorned as abject weakness and who «was unmoved by tearful descriptions of war's physical horrors?» (100).

---

(98) Cited by Gaston Bouthoul, *La Population dans le monde* (Paris: Payot, 1935), p. 212.

(99) See Jean Galtier-Boissière, *Histoire de la Grande Guerre, 1914-1918* (Paris: Les Productions de Paris, n.d.), p. 207.

(100) William A. Huggard, *Emerson and the Problem of War and Peace*, University of Iowa Humanistic Studies, vol. 5, no. 5 (Iowa City: University of Iowa Press, 1938), p. 45.

CHAPTER III

IN OCCUPIED AND LIBERATED FRANCE WITH JEAN-LOUIS CURTIS

In 1945 Jean-Louis Bory, age twenty-six, won the Prix Goncourt for his novel *Mon Village à l'heure allemande.* It was a portrayal of the conduct in 1941 of the inhabitants of Jumainville, an imaginary village of the Beauce. Shallow, disjointed, and overwritten, it awkwardly combined the tragic with the caricatural and the semi-farcical while leaning heavily upon gratuitous realism. In 1947 another Jean-Louis, this one Béarnais Jean-Louis Curtis, Bory's senior by two years and, like him, a teacher, was awarded the same prize for his *Les Forêts de la nuit,* also a novelistic portrayal of Frenchmen's deportment under the German occupation (1). In this book, whose merit clearly commended it to the favor of the Goncourt jury, the occupied fictional town is Saint-Clar, situated on the boundary between the Béarn and the Basque country. In due course we shall examine the conduct of the Clarois under the stresses of the occupation and of the subsequent Liberation. In the meantime, to give ample perspective

---

(1) A second prestigious prize was conferred on Curtis in 1972, when the French Academy awarded him its Grand Prix de Littérature for the aggregate of his writings.

to our examination, let us see how those tragic years were lived by the French and how French writers reacted to the events and conditions associated with them.

For the great majority of the French people the German occupation evokes a flood of nightmarish memories whether they experienced it first-hand for fifty months in what was initially known as the Occupied Zone or for less than two years in what up to November 8, 1942, had been familiarly called the «Zone Nono,» i.e., the Unoccupied Zone, or Free Zone. The degree to which a French citizen suffered physical privation was in goodly measure dependent on whether he lived in a big city or a small city or in the largely self-sustaining countryside, on the extent to which his economic means enabled him to deal in the black market, and on his *débrouillardise,* a sort of heightened and somewhat devious resourcefulness that he would summon up in an effort to cope with the relentlessly deteriorating conditions of daily life. It was a time when, if Parisians were not reduced to eating the animals of the Jardin des Plantes, as in early 1871, probably more rutabaga was eaten per capita than during any other period of French history; when tomatoes and cabbage were grown in the Jardin du Luxembourg, when pumpkins could be seen ripening in the shadows of the Louvre, when the sight of rabbits and chickens in cages resting on window sills of apartment houses startled no one. And it was a time when the *crémier* on the block was truly a king (2). But

---

(2) In dwelling on the *crémier-roi* theme, Henri Amouroux, prolific historian of the German occupation of France, appropriately remarks: «Butter, eggs, and cheese—these were the three jewels of his crown.» *Quatre Ans d'Histoire de France* (Paris: Hachette, 1966), p. 87. In his novel *Au Bon Beurre* (Paris: Gallimard, 1952), a Prix Interallié winner, Jean Dutourd subtly blends comedy, caricature, and satire in his bitter condemnation of such royalty. So successful were Dutourd's *crémier* protagonist, Charles-Hubert Poissonard, and his energetic wife, Julie, in their licit and illicit

having an empty stomach is not the worst fate that can befall human beings.

The ignominy of a swift, crushing defeat at the hands of Hitler's highly mechanized, well-trained legions in June 1940, weighed heavily on a proud people, as did the presence of hundreds of thousands of wearers of the *feldgrau* in their land. The few inhabitants of an all but deserted Paris present at the scene recoiled in horror on June 14, 1940, at the sight of a swastika flag being hoisted to the top of the Arc de Triomphe and of German troops marching down the Champs-Élysées, as they were to march daily thereafter. Five days later many an Alsatian heart bled while another swastika flag was being raised above the cathedral of Strasbourg. And whereas Nazi flags all but covered the façades of the arcaded buildings of the beautiful Rue de Rivoli, a ban was soon placed on the carrying of the tricolor at French funerals. Joseph Meister, first recipient of Louis Pasteur's epoque-making antirabies treatment and gatekeeper of the Pasteur Institute, as staunch a patriot as Pasteur himself had been, committed suicide to avoid being forced to open for the German occupier the crypt where the celebrated scientist is buried. So cruel a blow was the entry of German troops into Paris for Thierry de Martel, great-grandson of Mirabeau and one of France's leading brain surgeons, that he too chose the route of suicide—as much a victim of war as was his only son, killed in World War I combat.

In his allegorical novel *La Peste* (1947), Camus symbolically represented the occupation, with its poisonous excrescences, as a plague, because that is how he experienced it. For Mauriac, who prided himself on never for a minute

---

commercial dealings in occupied Paris that they were able to amass a fortune of 47 million francs by 1950 and to marry off their daughter to a deputy of the National Assembly.

having left the Occupied Zone, these were years of unremitting anguish. He confessed that he had never been able to look at the Nazi flags on the Place de la Concorde «except through a mist of tears,» flags whose swastika resembled «a blood-swollen, sated spider» (3). Fervent Christian that he was, Mauriac seems, however, to have been unable to honor the Biblical injunction against yielding to a hatred of one's enemy, and, in print at least, he made little distinction between Germans as such and Germans who were also Nazis—a posture that was quite unusual among French writers who had participated in the underground war (4). He who had filled his novels with characters who must endlessly do battle with the forces of evil believed that he was seeing evil in its most sinister cast. Writing under his *nom de guerre,* Forez, he closed his *Cahier noir* (1943) with an appeal to his compatriots to postpone planning for the post-war years in favor of dedicating the national effort, as he put it, to «first tearing ourselves free from the giant's grip, to getting his hands off our throat and his knee off our chest» (5). «Filthy» is the epithet Mauriac applied to the Nazi flag. A month after the Liberation, he complained about the «sticky mud» that had been left behind by the «filthy tide» as it went out (6). Two years later, reminiscing on the German occupiers' days in France, he again gave vent to his feeling about them. «Ah! how the Germans loved France. How

(3) François Mauriac, «Les Années sombres,» *Mémoires politiques* (Paris: Grasset, 1967), p. 134.

(4) Konrad F. Bieber underscores the fact that there was a quite remarkable absence of hatred of the enemy on the part of these writers and points out that most of them were careful to differentiate between Germans and German Nazis in his distinguished study *L'Allemagne vue par les écrivains de la Résistance française* (Genève: Droz, and Lille: Giard, 1954).

(5) Mauriac, *Le Cahier noir* (Paris: Éditions de Minuit, 1943), p. 49.

(6) Mauriac, «Le Visiteur,» *Mémoires politiques,* p. 162.

comfortable they felt in it. They rolled over and over in it, they wallowed in it» (7), he wrote. Jean Galtier-Boissière, long-term editor of *Crapouillot* and author of a well-received wartime diary, *Mon Journal pendant l'Occupation* (1944), also drank to the dregs the bitter cup of defeat and occupation. He too viewed with repugnance the omnipresent German uniforms, and it was not color blindness that caused him to prefer «caca d'oie» to «vert-de-gris» as a color label for them. Pillar of French republicanism, Jean Guéhenno, who also authored a widely praised diary, *Journal des années noires* (1946), saw, like all Parisians, German troopers marching down boulevards to the tune of the «Horst Wessel Lied» and rubbed elbows with them at street crossings and in subway cars. Like many of them too, Guéhenno neither much loved nor much hated the invaders. Addressing an imaginary German soldier, he says, «I pretend not to see you. I act as though you don't exist. I have promised myself never to speak to you. I understand your language, but if you speak to me, I raise my arms skyward and play the role of a man who doesn't understand» (8). It is not surprising that Mauriac likewise adopted a policy of simulated blindness. In June 1940, upon observing that his compatriots were witnessing the arrival of the victorious Germans with the same feeling of excitement with which in the past they had watched the passing of Tour de France cyclists through their towns, he excused as «natural» their gaping curiosity. Nevertheless, lest their gaping become a habit, he tacitly advised: «Have eyes in order not to see ... The propriety of conduct that we must show these uninvited visitors must be counter-

---

(7) Mauriac, *Le Bâillon dénoué* (Paris: Grasset, 1946), p. 22.
(8) Jean Guéhenno, *Journal des années noires, 1940-44* (Paris: Gallimard, 1946), Feb. 22, 1943, p. 242.

balanced by the absence of our glances and by our complete inattention» (9).

Premier of France from 1938 to 1940, Édouard Daladier, conscience-troubled signer of the Munich Pact, had warned General Maxime Weygand, supreme commander of the French Army during the *débâcle,* that he would be well-advised to take Hitler for a Genghis Khan rather than for a younger version of gentlemanly Kaiser Wilhelm I, who had appropriated Alsace-Lorraine to his realm in 1870. History was, of course, to confirm the validity of Daladier's appraisal. But «Polandization» was not part of Hitler's strategy for France. «Korrektion» having been enjoined upon them, the German forces serving in France in the early months of the occupation could nowise have been associated in the popular mind with the hordes of Attila, the «blond beasts» of Nietzsche, or the Erich von Stroheim of Jean Renoir's film *La Grande Illusion.* Posters appeared everywhere, inviting the «abandoned» population to place its trust in the German soldier, who, for his part, appeared to be doing his utmost to merit it (10). Not for long, however. As the Resistance

---

(9) Mauriac, «Ce qui reste de fierté,» *Mémoires politiques,* pp. 126-27.

(10) Cf. «To start with, France experienced none of the atrocities which the Germans committed in Eastern Europe, and, closing their eyes to the horrors of the Polish campaign, the French could claim to have encountered a humane invader. Indeed, in the first months of occupation more German soldiers appear to have been shot for breaches of discipline than Frenchmen executed for acts of terrorism or sabotage.» Alastair Hamilton, *The Appeal of Fascism* (New York: Macmillan, 1971), p. 238.

Putting down the wild rumors reminiscent of those of 1914 that she had heard circulated among civilians fleeing the onrushing German divisions, Simone de Beauvoir thus described her initial observation of enemy soldiers freshly arrived in a village of the Maine-et-Loire: «The Germans were not cutting off children's hands, they were paying for their drinks and for the eggs that they purchased on the farms, they spoke politely ...» *La Force de l'âge* (Paris: Gallimard, 1960), p. 458.

took hold, then grew, the German authorities resorted to repressive measures whose severity quickly tarnished the shining image of the decent fellow in enemy dress (11). SS influence and tactics saw to that. The French came to understand only too well that the same sentimental Germans who put up Christmas trees on their public squares, who patted their children and gave up their seats in *métro* cars to women, posed a mortal threat to any one of them who dared shelter an escaped prisoner or forward a message for a Resistance unit or even listen to a BBC broadcast. *Pax Swasticana,* as Koestler termed it, was fast becoming a nightmare. Small wonder that World War I hero Ernst Jünger, a staunch nationalist but not a Nazi, on occupation duty in Paris as a member of General von Stülpnagel's staff, noted, in October 1953, that when, in uniform, he passed by French citizens lined up in front of stores or offices, they gave him looks «stamped with a deep passive aversion and a desire to kill» (12). The knock in the night, trademark of totalitarianism, had become a common occurrence, and it mattered little to the victim that the arresting troopers frequently addressed him and his family politely, since he did not have to be told that a prison or a Gestapo interrogation center was to be his immediate destination (13). Common too now

---

(11) André Gide, a witness of the German occupation of Tunis, described a similar change of strategy. On May 27, 1943, he wrote: «'Make yourself liked' was the watchword launched by a German newspaper in Tunis during the early days of the German occupation. The newspaper (which was not for sale and circulated only within the army) added: 'Even by the French.' This watchword did not succeed, any more than it did in France itself, and was soon replaced by: 'Make yourself feared.' Behind the feigned politeness one remained too well aware of the need to dominate, which their smiles could not disguise.» Gide, *Journal 1942-49* (Paris: Gallimard, 1950), p. 184.

(12) Ernst Jünger, «Journées parisiennes,» *Les Lettres Nouvelles,* Oct., 1953, p. 935.

(13) At one of the notorious Paris Gestapo interrogation centers,

was the sight of red and black notices, in French and in German, on police station walls and on *mairies,* announcing the execution of «terrorists»—so common, in fact, that the charge was to be made at the Nuremberg trials of 1945-46 that 29,600 Frenchmen and women had been executed by the occupying forces. French Jews in particular discovered how expendable human beings were in the eyes of the Hitlers and the Himmlers. Appalled by the sight of names of notorious anti-Semites on street signs which had borne the names of distinguished Jews, excluded from the professions, deprived of virtually all of their civil rights, obliged to wear a large yellow star on their breasts to brand them publicly as some sort of subhumans, theirs was a living death, with nearly 150,000 of them subsequently suffering physical death in concentration camps before liberating Allied armies arrived (14). Finally, with nearly a million and a half of their fellow countrymen wasting away in German prisoner of war camps, with Gauleiter Sauckel making relentless demands for transferring ever larger numbers of French workers to duty in the Reich's munition factories, and with a thousand other things to demoralize them daily, it is not surprising that Sartre, while intent upon dispelling the myths that had grown

---

located at 180 rue de la Pompe, Frenchmen suffering the agonies of torture sometimes heard the music of Mozart being played by a German officer on a grand piano in the salon. Reported in Francis Steegmuller, *Cocteau: A Biography* (Boston: Little, Brown, and Co., 1970), p. 448.

(14) As early as January 1941, when the plight of the Jews in France was not nearly as bad as it was later to become, Paul Valéry's oration at the Académie Française on the occasion of Henri Bergson's death was regarded as a courageous act of resistance. In it Valéry lauded the Jewish Bergson for having condemned pan-Germanism. A few days before, this giant amongst twentieth-century philosophers was buried at Garches as quietly and as unobtrusively as the occupying authorities demanded, with about thirty persons on hand—in painful contrast to the national funeral, following a lying in state on the esplanade of the Palais de Chaillot, given his eulogist in the liberated Paris of January 1945.

up around the occupation, should have emphasized that it had indeed been a «terrible ordeal,» one from which, he thought, France might never recover (15). Sartre too it was who best highlighted the magnitude of his compatriots' tribulations in observing that «there wasn't a person in Paris who did not have a relative or a friend who had been arrested or deported or shot (16). Neither is it surprising that it took less than two years for all but the blindest of them to see that their promised partnership in a German-sponsored new order in Europe could never be.

Marshal Pétain, octogenarian hero of Verdun, had been brought to power as head of the German-authorized Vichy government and given an all but universal mandate by his *concitoyens* to «limit the damage,» to «save the furniture,» as they quaintly put it (17). He was to be faced with the unenviable challenge of maintaining balance on a tightrope, of trying to please both the authorities bent on exploiting France for their purposes and his French brothers and sisters, who were ever on guard against any form of exploitation that could only worsen their already tragic lot. Pétainism ran riot, with even many an anti-Vichyite being a *maréchaliste*. Thousands of streets and boulevards were renamed to bear his name. France was inundated with photos of the «chef d'état,» with even the nation's postmen offering a variety

---

(15) Jean-Paul Sartre, «Paris sous l'Occupation,» *Situations, III* (Paris: Gallimard, 1949), p. 16.

(16) *Ibid.*, p. 22.

(17) In his *Vichy France: Old Guard and New Order* (1972), Robert Paxton forcefully argues that Pétain and his Vichy cohorts did a poor job of limiting the damage. Marshalling a wealth of evidence, he dismisses as substantially illusory the familiar thesis that Vichy collaboration saved France from a much worse fate, materially and otherwise. His comprehensive examination of German archives brought to light the fact that Vichy leaders not infrequently took initiatives highly detrimental to the weal of France, their public pronouncements to the contrary.

— 145 —

of them for sale on their daily rounds. A spate of books appeared in which the Marshal was compared to Joan of Arc, Henri IV, Louis XIV, and Napoleon Bonaparte, with some of the incense-burners seemingly regarding him as all four of these national heroes rolled into one (18). Amateurs and professionals vied in composing poetic hymns in his honor. No doubt the most avid incense-burner of them all was a Georges Gérard, author of a personal «Lord's Prayer» entitled «Notre Père.» It reads as follows:

Notre Père qui êtes
A notre tête,
Que votre nom soit glorifié
Que votre règne arrive,
Que votre volonté
Soit faite
Sur la terre pour qu'on vive.

---

(18) A well-known resister in her own right, Joan of Arc was played up as a heroine by both sides, with Resistance groups hailing her as one of their own and collaborationists lauding her for delivering France from the English. See Michèle Cotta, *La Collaboration 1940-1944* (Paris: Librairie Colin, 1964), p. 169.

Reacting to the flood tide of tributes equating his patriotic virtues with those of the Maid of Orleans, Pétain quipped, «The end result of their comparing me to Joan of Arc will be their burning me at some stake.» Quoted in Jean Plumyène, *Pétain* (Paris: Éditions du Seuil, 1964), p. 124.

Péguy too was being pulled in both directions, with the Pétain-istes in particular apotheosizing him as the martyred champion of all that was good about the old France. His son Marcel travelled much further down the road of collaboration than did the ordinary Vichyite. In the August 5, 1941 issue of *La Gerbe*, he hailed the Germans as Christian warriors seeking to establish a new order in a tired old Europe, deserving both the gratitude and the apologies of the French, who «had for twenty years been betraying God» and allowing themselves to be «dominated by English Masonry.» (Cited by Cotta, p. 188.) With his 1941 book *Le Destin de Charles Péguy* he further desecrated his father's memory by subscribing to Nazi anti-Semitism and by twisting the meaning of his writings to give him the appearance of a before-the-fact National Socialist.

Demeurez sans retour,
Notre pain de chaque jour,
Redonnez
L'existence
A la France,
Ne nous laissez pas retomber
Dans le vain songe
Et le mensonge
Et délivrez-nous du mal
O Maréchal! (19).

Paul Claudel too caught the fever. With his poem «Paroles au Maréchal» (1940) he saluted Pétain in the same slick fashion in which, four years later, he would salute France's most famous resister in his óde «Au général de Gaulle.» Paul Valéry had words of public praise for the aged idol. The Académie Française was enthusiastically pro-Pétain, Mauriac excepted, and, in the judgment of historian Alexander Werth, Duhamel partially excepted (20).

But there were those who did not care to magnify the Marshal. Mauriac, the sole Academician to actually enter the ranks of the Resistance, was, of course, of their number, although initially he too penned a few soon to be regretted lines in laudation of the new chief of state. *Résistant* Jean Dutourd, who delivered a blistering attack on Pétain and a host of other «défaitistes» in his *Taxis de la Marne* (1956), remarks: «Our king of hearts was named Pétain. We believed

---

(19) Cited by Le Marquis d'Argenson in his *Pétain et le Pétinisme: Essai de psychologie* (Paris: Éditions Créator, 1953), p. 170.
(20) See Alexander Werth, *France 1940-1955* (New York: Henry Holt & Co., 1956), p. 44.
In 1975, seven years after his election to the Academy, poet Pierre Emmanuel, a veteran of the Resistance, resigned from it in protest over the election to it of Félicien Marceau. A naturalized French citizen, Belgian-born Marceau had been in the employ of the German-controlled Belgian state radio under the occupation.

that this foxy old fellow would put Hitler into his pocket because he was handsome, because he was touching, and because he was old. Pétain, the Old Man Goriot of France, the Christ of patriotism, had made us a gift of his person» (21). Hard-hitting Étiemble made it plain that he was not prepared to regard Montoire as Pétain's second Verdun and saw much irony in the fact that the aging «Feld Marshall» [sic] aimed to deliver France from gerontocracy. Guéhenno could not forgive him for «making of dishonor a temptation for a whole nation» (22). To Guéhenno the Vichy government was «Vichy-Tartuffe,» and, like Pétain's former protégé De Gaulle, he saw the Marshal as the «father of the defeat.» The Revolution's «Liberté, Égalité, Fraternité» had yielded to the Vichy motto «Travail, Famille, Patrie,» which wags were soon to alter to read, «Travail: Introuvable. Famille: Dispersée. Patrie: Humiliée.» According to historian Henri Amouroux, the communist interpretation of the Vichy slogan was, rather: «Travail: Forcé. Patrie: Vendue. 200 Familles» (23).

The oppressed French were sickened by the eagerness with which some of their compatriots had placed themselves in the service of the Germans, although out-and-out collaborators made up but a relatively small segment of the population (24). Marcel Déat, an unabashed pro-Nazi of

---

(21) Jean Dutourd, *Les Taxis de la Marne* (Paris: Gallimard, 1956), p. 121.

(22) Guéhenno, «Préface,» *Journal des années noires*, p. 10.

(23) Henri Amouroux, *La Vie des Français sous l'Occupation* (Paris: Fayard, 1961), p. 537.

(24) Sartre's comments on genuine collaborators mirror his philosophic acceptance of their inevitability. He writes: «There has been a good deal of talk about 'collaborators,' and certainly there were authentic traitors in our midst. We are not ashamed of them: every nation has its scum, that fringe of human failures and of embittered individuals who profit for a brief spell from disasters and revolutions. The existence of a Quisling or a Laval

cabinet rank, had estimated their number at no more than fifty thousand. Of these, he believed, no better than half could be depended on in a genuine emergency. Déat, Jacques Doriot, and Joseph Darnand were the notorious «Three D's» who had ascended to posts of great power under the aegis of the Nazis. Doriot, ex-communist mayor of Saint-Denis and founder, in 1936, of what became the ultracollaborationist Parti Populaire Français, waged relentless war on his former party associates while serving the Gestapo and SS with fanatical devotion. Never a man of half measures, Doriot further demeaned himself by donning a German uniform to fight on the Russian front, as had done aristocrat Christian de la Mazière of the highly praised documentary film of Marcel Ophuls on the German occupation, *Le Chagrin et la Pitié* (1969). The most pathetic collaborator of them all, Darnand, who had distinguished himself in combat during both the Great War and in 1940, had sunken from Pétainist idolatry to personally organizing, then heading, the hated *Milice,* the para-military right arm of the Gestapo in its terrorist anti-Resistance activities (25). Other leading henchmen of the German occupiers were: Marcel Bucard, leader of the fascist Francistes; Jew-baiting poison penman Lucien Rebatet; Darquier de Pellepoix, zealous helper of the Nazis in the deportation of Jews to concentration camps; Hérold-Paquis, head of the German-controlled radio in Paris; Jean Luchaire, czar of the collaborationist press (unlovingly referred to by many as «Louche (shifty) Herr»),

---

in a national body is a *normal* phenomenon, like the incidence of suicide or of crime.» Sartre, «Paris sous l'Occupation,» p. 36.

(25) Acerbic in his commentary on what he reckoned French lack of combativeness during the pre-armistice German offensive, Georges Bernanos observed: «... If all the soldiers of 1940 had fought like Darnand, there probably never would have been any militia issue.» Bernanos, *Français, si vous saviez... (1945-1948)* (Paris: Gallimard, 1961), p. 286.

and Philippe Henriot, who as Minister of Information was the chief French disseminator of enemy propaganda.

Pierre Laval, the Vichy Government's second most prominent figure and its head in 1942, had no love for Germans. He had nevertheless bet on the German horse, urged close collaboration with the occupiers, and hopelessly compromised himself by publicly proclaiming his confidence in and wish for a German victory. Ever the opportunist, Admiral Darlan, who ranked third in the Vichy hierarchy, had shown himself to be quite willing to serve the Germans so long as this enabled him to serve himself. Far from shrinking from military collaboration, he enthusiastically endorsed the idea. Thousands of bourgeois reactionaries, particularly those of the upper tiers of their class, vividly recalling the sit-down strikes and dagger-in-teeth posters of the Front Populaire years and blaming the forty-hour work week and the paid vacations instituted by the Front for the 1940 collapse, became tools of the enemy. «Better Hitler than Blum» was their motto. These it was who, in Mauriac's words, «considered Hitler and his legions as exterminating and avenging angels» (26). And whereas collaboration was not a monopoly of the bourgeoisie, there were not many bourgeois who would have preferred «a red France to a blushing France» (27), as did the wealthy *Résistant* baron of Joseph Kessel's *L'Armée des ombres* (1944). On the other hand, probably no other mayor of a French town had gone to such an extreme as the mayor of Barbizon, who had had a plaque fastened to his door inscribed «Burgermeister,» and few boudoir collaborators wore swastikas of gold over their breasts after the fashion

---

(26) Mauriac, «Préface,» *Mémoires politiques*, p. 20.
(27) Joseph Kessel, *L'Armée des ombres* (New York: Pantheon, 1944), p. 131.

of the slutty Denise Véchard of Bory's aforementioned novel, *Mon Village à l'heure allemande* (28).

Although collaboration by the French did not so much as begin to assume the epidemic proportions of the collaboration to which succumbed the characters of Ionesco's brilliantly successful play *Rhinocéros* (1960), collaborators could be found in the banks and in the black market, in the press and the pulpit, in concierges' *gîtes*, and elsewhere. There were venal collaborators and disinterested collaborators; there were Nazis in French clothing as there were high-minded but misguided patriots. At one extreme stood the enemy's hired killers and torturers; at the other, Frenchmen who had actively supported the Vichy government in a diversity of small ways in their sincere belief that no treason was involved in serving a legitimately constituted government. And sometimes it was impossible to tell whether a man could properly be stamped as a collaborator, so blurry was the line separating guilt from innocence. Sartre conceded as much in his article «Qu'est-ce qu'un collaborateur?» and could come up with no full answer to his own question (29). But Galtier-Boissière had defined collaboration very simply, i.e., as a case of asking a man for his watch with the promise that you would then tell him the time. Playwright-actor Sacha Guitry, indicted for «intelligence with the enemy» because it was thought that he had been too politely receiving the German officers frequenting his theatre, argued in his defense that there was such a thing as «unintelligence with the enemy» (30).

---

(28) In her sycophancy Bory's Mademoiselle Véchard had a real-life counterpart in Bunau-Varilla, publisher of the newspaper *Matin*, who, Alexander Werth reports, «used to throw dinner parties in honour of the Germans, with flowers arranged in a large swastika in the center of the table.» Werth, *op. cit.*, p. 240.

(29) Sartre, «Qu'est-ce qu'un collaborateur?, *Situations, III*, pp. 43-61.

(30) Reported by Sisley Huddleston in his *France: The Tragic Years, 1939-1947* (New York: Devin-Adair, 1955), p. 337.

Étiemble, having treated at some length of the complexities entailed in bringing justice to bear on writer collaborationists, made a recommendation that implies a definition of collaboration. He urged that only those writers and journalists be prosecuted who had preached «hatred of Blacks, Jews, and Arabs, or who, either by stool pigeoning or by inciting to collective murder, were responsible for the assassination of a single patriot or for the deportation of a single Jew to a concentration camp» (31).

Some writers of mark shamed their names through collaboration. Though he had not actually enrolled in the service of the Germans, Céline would have to be placed high on the list. Awarded the *Médaille militaire* for bravery in combat in World War I, Céline greatly sullied his honor during World War II. For him the occupation provided a forum for venting his wrath on his three sworn enemies: capitalism, communism, and the Jews. In his hatred of the Jews he heaped criticism on them in his lampoon *Les Beaux Draps* (1941), as he had earlier done in his sulfurous pamphlet *Bagatelles pour un massacre* (1937). Star-crossed, weak-willed, confused Drieu la Rochelle welcomed the German triumph, convinced that it could regenerate continental Western Europe and unify it to serve as a dual bulwark against Russian and American power. He who had always worshipped force was dazzled by the show of German force that had so swiftly overwhelmed his countrymen. Royalist Charles Maurras, champion of integral nationalism, of «la France seule,» made no pretense of his dislike of the Germans. At the same time, he had had nothing but scorn for the Third Republic, «la Gueuse,» as he and his royalist cohorts were wont to call it. In the words of Georges Bonneville, Maurras «had the infallible advantage

---

(31) Étiemble, «Justice pour les collabos,» *Hygiène des lettres, II* (Paris: Gallimard, 1955), p. 175.

of attributing victories to the fatherland, and defeats to the Republic» (32). Always on the side of national discipline and authoritarianism, and long committed to the overthrow of the Republic, Maurras had become a fanatical supporter of Vichy. Whereas he was to remain innocent of intelligence with the German enemy, he played into its hands by dispensing the poisons of hate in his influential daily, the *Action Française,* by pushing for the strict enforcement of anti-Semitic legislation, and by demanding the death penalty for *Résistants.* Talented young novelist and critic Robert Brasillach completed his conversion to fascism in 1937 when he got drunk on the pomp and pageantry of the massive National Socialist Congress of Nuremberg. Eight years later Brasillach, a self-proclaimed National Socialist whose career officer father had fallen in battle in 1914, fell before a French firing squad for his rabidly collaborationist and sometimes violence-bidding contributions to such newspapers as *Je Suis Partout* (of which he had become editor in 1937), *Action Française, Révolution Nationale, L'Écho de la France,* and the literary journal *La Gerbe.* The measure of Brasillach's animus vis-à-vis the Third Republic and of its supporters is manifest in such lines by him as these:

> Shall we finally have an end to the unpleasant smells of perfumed putrescence that are still being given off by the moribund old harlot, the syphilitic bitch smelling of patchouli and of leucorrhea, the Republic forever standing on her sidewalk? She still remains there on her doorstep, this ill-washed, creaking, crackling wreck, surrounded by her over-paying customers and her pimps, the young ones just as eager in their attentions as the old ones.

---

(32) Georges Bonneville, *Prophètes et témoins de l'Europe: Essai de l'idée d'Europe dans la littérature française de 1914 à nos jours* (Leiden: A. W. Synthoff, 1961), p. 43.

She has been so useful to them, has brought them so many bank notes in her garters. How could they have the courage to give her up in spite of her recurrent gonorrhea and her chancres? (33).

Stern antidemocrat Alphonse de Châteaubriant had become intoxicated with Nazism during a four-months stay in Germany in 1937. In his book *La Gerbe des forces* of the same year he urged Franco-German rapprochement and presented Hitler as the incarnation of the German race, a political genius, enlightened statesman, and as an «immensely good» human being of unimpeachable sincerity, totally unlike the menacing Hitler who had written *Mein Kampf* behind prison bars during the French occupation of the Rhineland (34). Understandably the Germans were happy to have him become their flunky editor of the review *La Gerbe* under the occupation. Also a target for severe censure by the Resistance-formed Comité National des Écrivains, Jean Giono had incurred its ire because some of his writings had appeared in Châteaubriant's review and because of his unconcealed enthusiasm for some facets of Vichy dogma and his stubborn refusal in 1939 to abandon his pacifist stance. Montherlant, worshipper of physical prowess and energy and sworn believer in the laws of force, had escaped with but a slap on the wrist—a one-year ban on publishing—for his overt admiration of German force in the early days of the occupation. Other well-known personalities in the world of letters who had in varying degrees diminished their reputations by their deportment

---

(33) *Je Suis Partout*, July 2, 1942. Cited by Cotta, *op. cit.*, p. 80.
(34) A sample of the sort of claptrap the book contains reads: «His [Hitler's] eyes have the deep blue color of the waters of his Lake Königsee when the lake, surrounding Sankt Bartholoma, reflects the mighty, cloud-streaked geologic faults of his native Tyrol.» Alphonse de Châteaubriant, *La Gerbe des forces* (Paris: Grasset, 1937), p. 68.

under the occupation were: Raymond Abellio, Marcel Aymé, René Benjamín, Pierre Benoit, Henri Béraud, Henry Bordeaux, Paul Chack, Jacques Chardonne, Alfred Fabre-Luce, Ramon Fernandez, André Fraigneau, Gustave Hervé (35), Marcel Jouhandeau, Jacques de Lacretelle, Jean de la Varende, Pierre Mac Orlan, Paul Morand, Roger Peyrefitte, and the two Abels: Bonnard and Hermant, whose common *prénom* had been changed by underground patriots to «Caïn.» Corrupt Academician Bonnard, Vichy Minister of Education, an especially zealous lackey, was also referred to as «Abetz» Bonnard after Otto Abetz, Hitler's ambassador to occupied France.

The vast majority of the French neither collaborated with nor resisted the occupying power. While they had no desire to serve their conquerors, their instinct toward self-preservation was stronger than their will to go on fighting them. They merely acquiesced to the changed conditions and went about their daily business, which, they felt, was quite enough to absorb energies sapped by multiple privations and frustrations. If they did anything risky—and millions of them did—it was tuning in on the daily BBC broadcasts to France, always introduced by the familiar dot, dot, dot, dash of Beethoven's Fifth Symphony. Others rose above the circumstances by escaping to England or to Africa to join General de Gaulle's Free French forces or by going underground to

---

(35) Hervé was not unhappy about seeing simultaneously wafted in the breeze the swastika flag and the tricolor that he had once boldly advocated consigning to a dunghill. The former socialist had begun chanting the praises of a new variety of socialism, National Socialism, and of its leader even before Hitler became chancellor of the Third Reich. As a matter of fact, he went so far as to pretend that Christ had been the first Nazi. The once fierce antimilitarist was overjoyed to have Marshal Pétain at the head of the civil government. This was for him the fulfillment of a long-nursed dream. In his distaste for parliamentary democracy Hervé had, since the mid-thirties, been so ardently propagandizing Pétain as an ideal strong-man chief of state that André

fight the Germans at the peril of their lives (36). Among the purest of the *purs* were: Jean Moulin, a resister of the first hour and founder of the Conseil National de la Résistance (Malraux labelled him «the Carnot of the Resistance») (37), who died a martyr's death and was the only participant in the underground war whose remains were to be buried in the Pantheon; Colonel Rémy (Gilbert Renault), master builder of spy networks, today a legendary hero of the Resistance; historian Marc Bloch, a leader in the large Francs-Tireurs et Partisans wing of the clandestine forces, who died before a German firing squad after refusing to talk under torture; and Jacques Chaban-Delmas. The last, destined to be a premier of France in the Fifth Republic, was amongst the earliest to resist. De Gaulle's military delegate in occupied France, he became a general in the underground army at twenty-nine. These and tens of thousands of more obscure French citizens could not live with the memory of a German band striking up «Deutschland über alles» at Rethondes in the Compiègne forest on July 22, 1940, nor rest until the Nazis' swastikas and black eagles no longer defaced the French

---

Schwob, who devoted a book to the subject, dubbed him the «[P. T.] Barnum of the 'Pétain mystique.'» *L'Affaire Pétain* (New York: Éditions de la Maison Française, 1944), p. 199.

(36) Because internal resistance to the German occupiers posed a constant challenge to human inventiveness, it assumed a large variety of shapes and forms. Nobleman Philippe de Vomécourt, a most active underground warrior, struck upon the idea of having French prostitutes feed heroin to German night-fighter pilots based in the Tours area to impair their vision. The results were little short of spectacular, but before long German army doctors succeeded in identifying the cause of the problem and in tracing the source of supply. A pair of prostitutes died thereby, martyrs to the cause of freedom. See De Vomécourt, *Who Lived to See the Day: France in Arms 1940-45* (London: Hutchinson and Co., 1961), pp. 81-82.

(37) Malraux, in an address on the occasion of the transfer of the remains of Jean Moulin to the Pantheon, Dec. 19, 1964. *Oraisons funèbres* (Paris: Gallimard, 1971), p. 126.

landscape. Eventually, Fighting French victories at Bir Hakeim, in Italy, Provence, Alsace, and elsewhere, coupled with the solid contribution of the Resistance to the Allied victory—General Eisenhower equated it with the work of fifteen divisions—restored a measure of sorely needed French pride (38).

The number of members of the French literary community who entered the Resistance was much greater than that of those who can be classified as collaborators. For some of them—Sartre and Simone de Beauvoir are cases in point—joining the ranks of the underground army was their first firm step on the road to long careers as «engagé» writers whose acute sense of responsibility for bettering society was to be mirrored in their art and in their public acts. Raising the spirits of the population, sustaining its hopes at an hour when it was easy to surrender to despair, and galvanizing its energies for the fight for liberty while striking at the conscience of those who might be tempted by treason—this was the primary task French *Résistant* writers assigned themselves. Whereas some of their writing was done in the open, with the poets in particular performing prodigies of cryptic communication, the bulk of their publishing effort forced them into the dangerous business of setting up underground printing presses and of distributing tracts and their message-bearing works of prose and of poetry. A small number of them took part in the actual fighting: in addition to Malraux there were Louis Aragon, René Char, Pierre Fisson, Jacques Perret, and Jean Prévost, the last having been killed in the Vercors *maquis* in 1944. The year 1942 was marked

---

(38) Accounting as paramount the spiritual significance of the Resistance, underground fighter Malraux writes: «We were France in tatters; our significance did not lie in the achievements of our networks but in the fact that we had been *witnesses*.» *Anti-mémoires, I* (Paris: Gallimard, 1967), p. 118.

by the dramatic appearance of Vercors' *Le Silence de la mer,* the first work published by the clandestine publishing house Éditions de Minuit. Together with the periodical *Lettres Françaises* it was to play the leading role in promoting the Resistance of the literary set. In addition to the afore-mentioned writers, any roster of members of the literary Resistance would have to include the names of Georges Adam, Claude Aveline, Hervé Bazin, Samuel Beckett, Julien Benda, Pierre Binard, Jean Blanzat, Alain Borde, Pierre Bost, Albert Camus, Jean Cassou, Jean Cayrol, André Chamson, Pierre Courtade, Jacques Debû-Bridel, Jacques Decour (Decourdemanche), Noël Devaulx, Jean-Marie Domenach, Pierre de Lescure, Robert Desnos, Jean Dutourd, Paul Éluard, Pierre Emmanuel, Max-Pol Fouchet, André Frénaud, Stanislas Fumet, Roger Giron, Serge Groussard, Jean Guéhenno, Guillevic, René Hardy, Georges Hugnet, Étienne Lalou, René Laporte, Jean Lartéguy, Jacques Laurent, Lucienne Laurentie, Michel Leiris, Jean Lescure, Pierre Leyris, Henri Malerbe, Jean Marcenac, Marietta Martin, Louis Martin-Chauffier, Roger Martin du Gard, Roger Massip, Loys Masson, Micheline Maurel, François Mauriac, Jean Maydieu, Rouben Melik, Maurice Merleau-Ponty, Edmond Michelet, Raymond Millet, Robert Morel, Claude Morgan, Emmanuel Mounier, Georges Mounin, Léon Moussinac, Louis Parrot, Jean Paulhan, Georges Politzer, Dominique Ponchardier, Francis Ponge, Raymond Queneau, André Rousseaux, Jean Rousselot, Claude Roy, Georges Sadoul, Lucien Scheler, André Schwarz-Bart, Pierre Seghers, Claude Sernet, Roger Stéphane, Jean Tardieu, René Tavernier, Marcel Thiry, Edith Thomas, Paul Tillard, Elsa Triolet, Tristan Tzara, Roger Vailland, Jean Vaudal, François Vernet, Charles Vildrac, and Bernard Zimmer.

However, the Resistance had never been entirely free of assorted criminals and unprincipled opportunists, and more came rushing in at the eleventh hour. When, at the Liberation, banditry, looting, and even murder were committed by these elements on a large scale; when, in addition, self-appointed Resistance arbiters of justice took the initiative in ordering the wholesale execution of compatriots known to have or alleged to have thrown in their lot with Vichy or with the Germans directly, the clandestine army's image became badly tarnished in the public mind.

Passions rose to a paroxysm at the Liberation, for memories were fresh of betrayals, of Gestapo and *Milice* terrorism, of deportations of relatives and friends to concentration camps and to slave labor camps. It was therefore easy for victims of oppression to be impatient in their demands for justice, and since in many communities neither the local administration nor the police were in control in the wake of the German departure, illegal arrests, drumhead trials, packed juries, and summary executions became a commonplace.

The purge or *épuration,* as it was known, had, however, begun before the Liberation and continued for many months thereafter. An *épurateur* could be anyone from a nationally prominent high court justice to an untutored laborer sitting on an irregular tribunal or a spectator suddenly turned killer under the sway of mob frenzy, and an *épuré* could be anyone from a Pétain or a Laval on down to a female who had carnally collaborated. For having so collaborated, and sometimes only on the suspicion thereof, thousands of French women had their hair shorn off in public, like the heroine of Marguerite Duras' *Hiroshima, mon amour* (1960), with some of them being subjected to the added humiliation of being paraded, half-naked, through the streets (39). No matter

---

(39) Paul Éluard, who had witnessed such a shearing on the rue de Grenelle and who was anything but tender on political collaborators in the matter of *épuration,* expressed his disgust with such proceedings in his poem «Comprenne qui voudra.» Éluard, *Oeuvres complètes, I* (Paris: Gallimard, 1968), p. 1261.

how abased they felt, theirs was a kindlier fate than that which befell the better than 400,000 French citizens imprisoned after the Liberation, to say nothing of the thirty to forty thousand historian Robert Aron estimates to have been victims of summary executions before and after the Liberation, a figure he arrived at after exhaustive research and which appears to have gained wide acceptance. «One in a thousand massacred, one in a hundred deprived of liberty» (40), he emphasized. Even the Revolution's Reign of Terror and the Commune of 1871 had not accounted for massacre on so vast a scale.

The Resistance had long planned for a purge, considering it indispensable to the building of a new France through vast political, economic, and social reform; of a republic that would be «pure» and «dure,» one radically different from the «République des camarades» which had left the country wide open to enemy attack. But the danger was that if partisan fury gained the upper hand, if the meting out of justice became a mockery, and if Draconian tactics became the rule, the already badly divided nation might be irreparably harmed. The circumstances notwithstanding, for Étiemble the law was sacred. «Justice for the *collabos*,» he wrote, «let us absolve those who have nothing on their conscience save having chosen the side of Créon because they declined the fate of Antigone; let us condemn those who have violated and are still violating the law» (41). Sin-obsessed Bernanos bridled at what to his mind were the excesses, inconsistencies, and pharisaism of the *épuration*. Mauriac pressed for the tempering of justice with a large measure of mercy and showed himself at his Christian best in leading the fight, supported

(40) Robert Aron, *Histoire de l'épuration: De l'indulgence aux massacres, I* (Paris: Fayard, 1967), p. 433.
(41) Étiemble, *op. cit.,* p. 177.

by Jean Anouilh, Colette, Dorgelès, Duhamel, Paulhan, Daniel Rops, Jean Schlumberger, Valéry, and numerous other writers, to spare the life of Brasillach, who had so often and so roundly insulted him in his collaborationist role. Unsuccessful in this venture, Mauriac was, at any rate, credited with saving the life of the deeply compromised Henri Béraud. At the same time, Mauriac saw himself as a pragmatist. If he persisted in appealing for «charité,» if he soberly warned the Fourth Republic against «putting on the boots of the Gestapo,» he did so in his conviction that a strong France could not be built until «the two Frances» to which the ravages of the occupation had given birth were joined. In the meantime Camus, editor of the clandestine-born newspaper *Combat,* was implacably demanding justice. It was his unshakable belief that the cornerstone of a new French society could not be laid until proportionate and, he hoped, prompt payment, was exacted of the guilty for their crimes. To do otherwise was, in his view, to foster the development of a nation of «traitors» and «*médiocres*» and to insult the memory of his fallen comrades of the underground war. These were months during which, owing to his stance as a hard-liner, Camus —who did, however, sign a petition asking clemency for Brasillach—was being compared to Saint-Just, while Mauriac, on the other hand, was being referred to as «Saint François des Assises.»

The repression ground on inexorably, with some factions ceaselessly stoking its fires. The communist Resistance newspaper *Franc-Tireur* went so far as to daily publish the legend «Pourvu que ça dure» under the rubric «ÉPURATION.» All manner of crimes continued to be committed in the name or under the cloak of *épuration,* and justice continued to be travestied, so that the binding of the nation's wounds was to become an interminable process. In 1951, Paulhan, a resister of the first hour, roundly denounced the excesses of the Comités d'Épuration and of their courts of justice in his *Lettre aux directeurs de la Résistance.* In his novel of the same year *Les Fins dernières,* whose hero is a journalist collaborator, distinguished literary critic Pierre de Boisdeffre also expressed moral indignation over the temper of post-Liberation justice while making no attempt to whitewash collaborationists. And the issue of the purge was still very much alive when in 1956 Anouilh's bitter dramatic satire of it, *Pauvre Bitos,* was first performed. Though the pace had slowed, groups and individuals were still bloodily settling accounts in streets and woods, with private vendettas sometimes being conducted that had no connection with their victims' behavior under the occupation. As for the courts, many of them were in fact conducting trials according to the highest traditions of French justice, but, often, stacked juries and Resistance-installed judges used them as a base for liquidating political opponents. And nobody was so blind as not to notice that some «vedettes de la trahison» were being let off with token sentences while «lampistes» were being made to pay for them, or that «economic» collaborators and captains of the black market were frequently escaping prosecution whereas literary collaborators were being shown no quarter. Camus too was to sour on the *épuration.* Without his saying so directly, in his August 30, 1945 article in *Combat* he conceded the rightness of Mauriac's consistent stand on the matter. Giving voice to his disappointment with the thoughtlessness and vindictiveness with which the purge had been carried out, with the unevenness of its justice, and with its political taint, he now termed its failure «complete» (42).

Let us now return to the Saint-Clar of Jean-Louis Curtis, viewing the town and its inhabitants against this backdrop.

---

(42) Camus, *Actuelles: Chroniques 1944-1948* (Paris: Gallimard, 1950), p. 79.

The action of *Les Forêts de la nuit* primarily revolves about the lives during the German occupation of three members of the Balansun family: Count Pierre-Auguste-Léon-Martin de Balansun, his son, Francis, and his daughter, Hélène. The count's wife, Émilie, is simply there, a model wife and mother, hardly noticed and seldom entering the action. While the Balansuns have an inherited nobility, it is a senior citizen of the town, Victor Lardenne, and the Costellots, widowed mother, Marguerite, and son, Jacques, Lardenne's son-in-law, who have the wealth. Completing the bourgeois element of the story are a second widow, Madame Cécile Delahaye, her son, Gérard, Saint-Cyr graduate Jean de Lavoncourt, and enterprising politician Justin Darricade. Repesenting the third estate are transplanted Parisienne Fernande Arréguy, her son, Philippe, and Madame Delahaye's housemaid, Berthe.

A true patriot was Hélène de Balansun's fiancé, Jean de Lavoncourt. There would be no fence-straddling by him, and flag-waving would have been alien to his nature. This «Cyrien» and former scoutmaster had always had an admirable sense of duty and his strength of will seemed well-nigh inhuman. Consequently, the Pyrenees, the oceans, a woman's love—nothing could prevent him from responding to De Gaulle's call to arms. The only Clarois to join the overseas Free French, Jean was to die in the glorious blue uniform of the R.A.F. But, although he was on a military mission at the time, it was not the war Moloch that devoured him. Having been apprised by Hélène that she was breaking off her engagement to him, Jean plunged his Spitfire into the earth from a high altitude.

The pure *Résistant* of the story and by far its most sympathetic character is schoolboy Francis de Balansun. In the classroom, at the tender age of fifteen he had pluckily taken to task his *maréchaliste* teacher. At seventeen he was already cutting classes to help escapees cross over to the

Free Zone. He did not have to wait for the Allied invasion of North Africa, Stalingrad, or D-Day to make up his mind as to where his duty lay. True, initially, in his adolescent exuberance, he seemed a little casual, a little careless in how he went about getting a patriot or a refugee over the line of demarcation. But he learned rapidly, and as time passed he was entrusted with more and more hazardous liaison missions in Bordeaux, Bayonne, Pau, and elsewhere. And if he felt no hatred for the Germans and saw no reason why he should call them «Boches,» «Alboches,» or «Chleuhs,» he did not have to be told that the part of honor was the part of active opposition, of energetic participation. More-over, he was no *miles gloriosus,* even preferring to play down the importance of his clandestine responsibilities. Shortly before the Liberation Francis died a martyr's death upon being lured into an anti-Resistance trap. He had shown his mettle by refusing to talk despite the unmerciful beating administered him by French brutes in the service of the Gestapo. No stirring strains of the «Chant des partisans» accompanied Francis to his grave. After his death, his body was mutilated beyond recognition and dumped into a pine forest, leading the Clarois to believe that he had died in deportation, especially since a band of schoolboy Resistants had fallen into the clutches of the enemy almost simulta-neously. The nameless death of this loyal servant of national honor was all the more lamented because he had also been unswerving in his loyalty to his parents and friends. Perhaps —though the author doesn't suggest it—someday the Clarois would name a street after him, inasmuch as dead local heroes of the underground war could be just as heroic as those of national repute, the Gabriel Péris, Jean Moulins, and General Delestraints who have given their names to so many streets.

No selfless patriot was public works engineer Justin

Darricade, head of a tiny regional Resistance unit. Civic mindedness and public spirit he had in abundance—on the surface. Truth to tell, the Resistance was for him all *politique* and no *mystique*. Deep down, he would surely have preferred staying alive to living in dishonor if he had thought that it could come down to that. As insolent, egocentric, and cynical an underground combatant as Marat, the hero of Roger Vailland's highly rated novel *Drôle de jeu* (1945), Darricade is not, however, redeemed by the fearless bravery with which Marat is endowed. Therefore, Darricade was not given to bold personal initiatives, leaving the work in the field to «two or three» trusty young Clarois, including the lucklesss Francis. Nor did he have to be told that, if he had permitted himself to roam all over the Basque countryside, it might have been a lot harder for him to build bridges to post-Liberation power. He knew, as everybody knows, that in politics the earth can shift quickly, so one must stay close enough to home and constantly keep an ear to the ground. And, noting that the wind «was blowing in from the Russian steppes» as well as «from the vast American plains,» this former supporter of the Croix de Feu realized that he would have to move a good deal to the left in order to ascend the political ladder with maximum speed. Caring little about the dangerous business of dissidence, he had nothing in common with underground patriots of the Gabriel Péri stamp and would have scoffed at their dream of fashioning happy morrows (43). In the turmoil of the Liberation Darricade swiftly moved into the vacuum created by the departure of the Germans and in no time at all he was carving out a handsome political career for himself, helped immeasurably by the publication of his memoirs on

_____

(43) Péri's often cited line, «Nous préparons des lendemains qui chantent.», became a sort of *cri de ralliement* of Resistants.

the area's clandestine struggle against the occupying forces. In them he made certain to pay due tribute to his fallen comrade in the underground war, Francis. Yet Darricade was so unfeeling as to have been unmoved by the boy's tragic fate and he brutally refused to help the brokenhearted Count de Balansun in his effort to locate his missing son. If the «Republic of Silence» of which Sartre spoke were to have any chance of acquiring a voice in post-Liberation France, it was not the likes of Darricade who could be counted on. Manifestly he was not of that breed of men to whom French resisters had been looking to renew their country's proud humanist and humanitarian tradition.

A tragic-comic figure was the count, a lawyer by profession and the novel's main character. This proud descendant of a proud clan which over the years had supplied the *patrie* with many a heroic defender didn't much care to be reminded that, at sixty, as a major in the reserve, he had managed to lose his battalion in the pandemonium of the 1940 exodus. Yet, neither military humiliation nor the decay of his family's economic fortunes had undermined his spirit. Perhaps his buoyancy would have deserted him if he had been able to perceive the reality that to just about everybody around him he was nothing but a pompous old fool incurably addicted to rhetoric that was as wearisome as it was flamboyant. In the aftermath of the *débâcle* he, like millions of his compatriots, had had a firm faith in the ability of Marshal Pétain to hold his own and thereby to preserve much of the nation's own in his dealings with the Nazi conquerors. Conservative by family tradition, the count had become a passionate Pétainist. He eagerly accepted the whole package: the hero of Verdun, the bulwark against Bolshevism, the National Revolution, the «Patrie-Famille-Travail» concept, and the rest. He had even blanched in reflecting that «the hideous mating of the [British] lion and the Soviet bear defied the imagination» (44). But as soon as he learned of his son's affiliation with the Gaullist underground, he espoused Gaullism; perfidious Albion» was now cleansed of all perfidy, and the man who had been to him the odious «Tartar boss of the Kremlin» now elicited his admiration. Blood will tell, of course. Not allowing the burden of his years to stand in his way, the count volunteered his services to the regional *maquis*. However, no action was taken on his request; this, the reader supposes, because of his uncontrollable garrulity. Never, then, would he enjoy the matchless fraternity of underground warriors or live as dangerously as only they can live, although nothing could prevent him from living Francis's war vicariously. Sadly, the count did not realize that these were years when words could kill, so that his failure to restrain his tongue was to contribute in substantial measure to his beloved son's death.

Now, who were the Germans on duty in Saint-Clar whom Francis and Darricade had been attempting to outwit and with whom some of the Clarois were to collaborate? Whereas we know that there were enough Germans in the town to have occupied both of its hotels and that, in addition, some officers were billeted in private homes—one with the Balansuns—only a few of them emerge from the shadows. The monocled colonel heading the local *Kommandantur* comes into the story only long enough to convey the impression that he is surely too careless about his public image and probably too bent on taking his pleasure where he finds it to worry overmuch about how well or ill he might be serving the Führer. He unselfconsciously squires his mistress, Coryse Salomé, propietor of a perfumery and a very scarlet woman, to the local cinema. Still, he can afford to affect an insou-

---

(44) Jean-Louis Curtis, *Les Forêts de la nuit* (Paris: Julliard, 1947), p. 56.

ciant attitude, seconded as he is by the devious and cunning von Brackner, a most efficient secret service officer. Of imposing presence and, it would seem, as handsome as Kurt Franz, commandant of the concentration camp Treblinka, as dashing and as urbane as «Hangman» Reinhard Heydrich was reputed to be, as jovial and charming a conversationalist as Goering, and probably as dangerous as all three of them, the blue-blooded Brackner charms Marguerite Costellot, one of the story's leading characters, over cups of tea, to draw out secrets concerning the city's residents, about whom he already knows far too much. In polite company Brackner exudes old world politesse and is the soul of cordiality, but because his heart belongs to Hitler he loses no time in weaving the web that catches Francis. Then, though knowing the youth to be dead, he cynically promises to exert himself to locate him and to bring about his release.

Fort his part, Lieutenant Friedrich Rustiger, billeted at the home of Madame Cécile Delahaye, has as much use for Nazism as had the verdigris-clad Marlon Brando of the film *The Young Lions* and as have had not a few other «good» German men of arms turned out in Hollywood studios after the Second World War. Like Werner von Ebrennac, protagonist of Vercors' *Le Silence de la mer* (1942) and one of the best known fictional German soldiers born of World War II, Rustiger is a sensitive, cultured, gentle and gentlemanly devotee of music who, after falling out of favor with his comrades, is en route to the inferno of the Eastern front, in his case not as a volunteer, albeit willingly (45).

---

(45) In an obvious gesture of self-immolation, Vercors' Werner, shattered by his discovery that his government was wooing the French, the better to control and ultimately to enslave them, rather than, as he had naïvely believed, to seek their privileged partnership in a new and salutary European order, gave up his cushy desk job in a *Kommandantur* to volunteer for combat in

He had been found to be «too much the musician and too little the soldier.» Besides, the *Kommandantur* had belatedly learned that the lieutenant was guilty of a most odious crime, that of having a Jewish grandmother. Also shipped off to the Russian front was Werner, the noncom in charge of the military post at the line of demarcation. Madame Arréguy had had tongues wagging in Saint-Clar because of her liaison with him.

Throughout their stay in the town the victors show themselves to be as «correct» as were the Germans whose deportment so favorably impressed Gide, Sartre, and Simone de Beauvoir during the initial stages of the occupation. In truth, the Clarois can find little fault with the behavior of either the handsome Aryans of the earlier years of the occupation or with that of the «pale, rickety adolescents» and «gloomy, old, and stunted Thuringian peasants» who succeeded them when their able bodies were needed at the fighting fronts. But then, Saint-Clar was not a Marseille in miniature; the docile population was posing no threat to the occupiers' lives. And if, before the line of demarcation was done away with, a Clarois now and then got caught trying to cross over into the Free Zone, a slight reprimand could bring him into line, and if a few mixed-up schoolboys were giving the Germans some trouble, that was the concern of Brackner. The swastika floating in the breeze above the

---

Russia. Vercors cautions, however, against taking his book's hero for something that he is not. He writes: «Vis-à-vis Nazism any German remaining free could only affect a posture of reprobation or, if not one of allegiance, one of obedience. The immensity of German obedience was the drama of Germany and of Europe. Ernst Jünger loved France, yet he obeyed. If my hero had been a man of character, he could not have been either free or an officer. Incapable of disobeying, he had no choice but to go and get himself killed for masters whose machinations nevertheless terrified him.» Vercors, *La Bataille du silence* (Paris: Presses de la Cité, 1967), p. 182.

Kommandantur of Saint-Clar provoked no violent reaction in Clarois breasts. The citizens of this «minuscule Arcadia asleep for centuries along the Gave» were not prepared to panic because of the imposition of a curfew or because the hobnailed boots of German night patrols were now beating out a dull rhythm in their streets. These good people had all the earmarks of partisans of the quiet life, the sort of folk who would rather be spectators of history than makers of it. At the same time, they were not suffering great privation. Theirs was a fertile, favored countryside; they all had gardens, they had solidified trade relations with their peasant neighbors, and butchers were obliging them by engaging in illegal clandestine slaughtering. Moreover, in a day when *débrouillardise* could be a Frenchman's stoutest ally, they could be as effective *débrouillards* as any, anywhere. So blessed, why should they not have elected to remain above the battle, especially since the Germans were keeping out of their hair? Indeed, if Madame Costellot could be believed, the merchants were exploiting the enemy soldiers, the peasants were receiving them with open arms, the working girls were fighting over them, and the men were joking with them in the local café. All in all, then, life under the German boot would not have been too unpleasant if heightened partisan passions, caste rivalries, and the jealousies spawned by the sudden-won fortunes of greedy profiteers had not remained a constant source of exacerbation.

The sharp-tongued sophisticate, Marguerite Costellot, who loathed the common herd and who doubtless believed that France had been fighting a losing battle ever since the storming of the Bastille in 1789, saw herself as a patriot. In point of fact she was a collaborator and a traitor. More than any other resident of Saint-Clar she was an abettor of Brackner in his secret service work. The mild anglophobia to which Marguerite had yielded in 1939, when some British aristocrats had snubbed her at Biarritz, had ripened into a malignancy, fed as it was by her wartime reading in Maurras, Bainville, Béraud, and Drumont, to say nothing of the poisons distilled in the fascist *Je Suis Partout*. So, it followed that she should look with venomous scorn upon the likes of Francis: Gaullist adolescents, disturbers of law and order, and potential subverters of society's well-defined structures. And why should she not have wanted to take full revenge on the haughty British by holding out the hand of friendship to Brackner, member of the oldest European nobility and friend of the Kronprinz himself? Whatever else may be said of Marguerite, it cannot be said that she was inconsistent, for she hoped for a German victory to the bitter end.

Urbane, asthmatic old Victor Lardenne, the town's richest citizen, was wholly in accord with Marguerite in matters political and social. The Marshal was for him «a gift of God, a providential blessing,» the personification of all good things, and if he adapted readily to the presence of Brackner —billeted in his home—he no doubt did so in his dread of seeing, in the twilight of his years, the «red rabble» swarming like locusts over the land, effacing social boundaries, and expropriating his hard-earned wealth. Be that as it may, he was a collaborator in spirit only, and he sensed real danger in Marguerite's free-spoken ways with Brackner. On the face of the evidence there was no cause for Lardenne to live in the mortal fear that he would be hung on a meat hook at the Liberation.

Lardenne's son-in-law, Jacques, feared nothing and nobody. It is to this handsome patrician dandy, as cynical as he was cultured, that Curtis has assigned the role of *raisonneur*. If he had done his military bit before the *débâcle,* he had done so out of «simple decency» rather than out of a personal sense of duty. And if, several years later, Jacques courageously steered David Horsman, a parachuted British intelligence agent, clear of watchful Germans—an offense punishable by death in the enemy book—and even slyly arranged to have him dined at the same table with Brackner and sheltered for a night under the same roof, he wanted it understood that he would have rendered a similar service to a German in distress. Now in his late twenties, Jacques wears an air of skeptical superiority, and his posture is one of nonchalant detachment. Rare is the individual who is not a target for his sardonic shafts. These he directs at *Résistants* and Vichyssois alike. He takes particular delight in putting his father-in-law and his mother in their place for their Pétainist hero-worship, as here:

> ... Consider the maudlin comedy that is being played in France today: the visits of the victor of Verdun to the large martyred cities, the counterfeit cheers with which the grand old man is greeted, the kids presenting him with bouquets, ... the idiotic refrains bleated in the schools, the tricolor portraits, the Frankish battle-axes in—be it noted well—empty shop windows, the opportune and comforting resurrection of Péguy and of Corneille, this vulgar display of sentimentality, this whole maudlin comedy surrounding the old fellow in his second childhood who imagines himself to be the Maid of Orleans. Do forgive me, but I find all that grotesque and hypocritical, and all I ask is that I be allowed to keep my distance from it (p. 44).

Jacques would give himself to no cause, let alone believe that any cause was worth dying for. Nevertheless, he would sometimes wonder if his being suspected of collaboration could have serious consequences for him at the Liberation. But the future would take care of itself. In the meantime, he was content to go on administering his father-in-law's industrial and real estate empire and making extra-marital conquests.

Madame Cécile Delahaye, widow of musician Charles Delahaye and owner of a no longer profit-producing little farm, was another Pétainist, though spiritism held her in its thrall more firmly than Pétainism. Consequently, while it was easy for Count de Balansun, who had long had a tender feeling for the sweet little lady, to tear a photo of the Marshal off the wall of her home, it would have been labor lost for him to have attempted to break her of her table-turning habit. A collaborationist she was not, unless showing a measure of maternal solicitude to, and sharing her record collection with, Rustiger—billeted in her home through no choice of hers— could be considered collaboration.

In Paris, however, Madame Delahaye's son Gérard had gravely compromised himself. His job, teaching bourgeois brats in a private school of the sixteenth *arrondissement,* and his courtship of Hélène de Balansun, who was working in a laboratory in the capital, still left him enough time to write a theatre column for *La Gerbe.* A mediocre fellow who nonetheless never deceived himself as to his shortcomings, he kept working into his column the kind of platitudes on French grandeur that the promoters of the New Order would have had the nation's citizens live by. Gérard had always suffered the consequences either of personal indecision or of making the wrong decision, but in the end he proved that his soul could triumph too. After giving up his post of part-time columnist, he joined the Paris underground for reasons having nothing to do with opportunism, and did so well before the clock struck eleven. Then, upon distinguishing himself in clandestine warfare, he signed up with the Free French for combat at the front.

Not to be outdone by her mistress in the practice of occultism, housemaid Berthe lived in the belief that Satan himself was bestowing nocturnal favors on her. When subsequently she was fired for her worsening perfomance as a domestic and for her growing insolence, Berthe took vengeance on her former employer by spreading lurid tales through the town about Cécile's bestowing like favors on her German tenant. Naturally, stupidity wed to hate can do a lot of damage, and it did in Berthe's case. Partly because the count had insulted her in connection with her professed concubinage with the devil and partly because of her ungovernable tongue, she familiarized Marguerite in detail with Francis's clandestine activities. Marguerite then instantly arranged a meeting between Berthe and Brackner, to whom the simple woman spilled everything, and from whom she even accepted a monetary reward. It did not matter that she shed a few tears in the course of the interview and that Madame Costellot sought and received Brackner's assurance that Francis would come to no harm. The boy's fate was sealed. *Nacht und Nebel* had come to little Saint-Clar.

The most conscious and the guiltiest of the story's collaborators is Merkel, a white-haired Frenchman with the face of «a learned Benedictine,» with a fondness for literature in general and the writings of the Marquis de Sade in particular. He heads a small unit of young thugs in the service of the Germans. In close association with their counterespionage services, Merkel—who was not a Clarois or even a native of the Southwest—and his gang were busying themselves with tracking down and «interrogating» resisters in order to break up their clandestine networks. Coordinated from Paris, their operations often took them deep into the provinces. Curtis doesn't tell the reader so, but the evidence points to their being under the command of the so-called French Gestapo of the Rue Lauriston in the Étoile sector, whose cruelty was well known to members of the capital's underground. Merkel is all brute. Ice water flows in his veins; his heart is of stone, and what he can least tolerate in his youthful acolytes is any sign of softness. We know little of his anterior life, yet it is evident that he is a small-time man who has suddenly found his place by doing dirty work for the Gestapo. Because he is a selfish opportunist? Or a mercenary? Or an ideological adherent? It would appear that he is all of these, but only to a slight degree. Above all, Merkel is a human monster whose thirst for sadistic thrills can best be assuaged by his striking fear into the hearts of the hunted and by inflicting pain on their bodies. As ill luck would have it, it was Merkel and his gang to whom was assigned the mission of drawing Francis and other schoolboy *Résistants* operating in the area into the German net.

Philippe Arréguy had become associated with their gang. Strikingly handsome, he was a gigolo and a first-class *crapule* whose maleficence could be excused in part because of the appalling standard of conduct provided him by his mother. Disappointment with his profits in the black market had prompted him to go to work for Merkel; he simply wasn't earning enough money to conduct effectively his courtship of Hélène de Balansun, ten years his senior, with a view to seducing her. And seduce her he does. It is a reluctant Philippe who is forced by Merkel to lay an ambush for Francis, his classmate and a friend of sorts. If next Philippe risks his life to save that of Francis, none of his actions before or after had been inspired by moral purpose. After Francis is shot to death by one of Merkel's young henchmen in the course of the escape attempt planned by Philippe, the latter flees to Paris and goes into hiding. There were other considerations, of course, but Philippe could be trusted to remain true to himself to the end. Hence, mid-August 1944 saw him pinning on an F.F.I. brassard and firing a pistol from behind the street barricades of an embattled Paris. Besides, he had always liked a good scrap. Then he joined the regular army—just in case. Young Arréguy was destined to offer up his life on the altar of the fatherland. However, his was hardly a hero's death. He was machine-gunned down by alert Germans in the Vosges when, against strict orders and all common sense, he went skiing down a slope facing their lines.

No force on earth could have kept Philippe's mother, Fernande, alive after his death. Her life would have been joyless without her Adonis-like son, for whom she had felt a more than maternal attraction; thus, she hurled herself into the waters of the Gave as soon as she learned of Philippe's passing (46). How fondly she used to recall her swinging years as a girl in her native Paris! How popular she had been there! Fernande had never taken to the stuffy bourgeois of her husband's home town, nor they to her. She shocked them no end with her crude manners and the obscenities which she spouted by the *kilo,* and she was too candid to have concealed her scorn for them. Partly because she was a sensual animal, but mostly because she had been dying of the boredom of living amidst the Clarois and at the side of her ox-like old husband, a traveling salesman of Singer sewing machines, she had been freely bestowing her favors on the French Justin and the German Werner. The occupation had not changed Fernande. Amoral she was, amoral she remained.

It was quite another matter with Hélène de Balansun, who had been working in a Paris laboratory during these years. Hélène had been a scoutmistress at sixteen and for years thereafter she had lived up to her image, that of a strait-laced, incorruptible amazon. For years Gérard Delahaye had carried a torch for the stiff beauty without ever managing

---

(46) In July 1940, art critic Carl Einstein, a German refugee and a nephew of Albert Einstein, committed suicide by drowning himself in the Gave.

to rise above the status of faithful friend. It will be recalled that Jean de Lavoncourt had committed suicide after learning that she had jilted him. Of all people it was the animalistic Philippe who was to seduce her—in the same brutal fashion in which before long he would abandon her. After that it was very easy for Jacques Costellot, who had long made her a high priority object of conquest, to set her up as his mistress in Paris. Of all the Clarois it was without question Hélène who had changed most during the occupation years.

When at long last the Liberation came to Saint-Clar, nobody shouted the order, «A chacun son Boche!» Nary a barricade was erected, nor a paving stone ripped out, nor a Molotov cocktail hurled. There didn't have to be. The Clarois merely awakened one fine August morning to discover that the Germans had departed during the night. The news having spread like wildfire, by eight o'clock a huge crowd had gathered in the square in front of the *mairie*. True, Saint-Clar had not had a liberation in the classic sense, yet there was quite enough for the Clarois to let steam off about. Accordingly, patriotic oratory and strains of the «Marseillaise» filled the air; inside of twenty minutes five thousand citizens were beribboned, and an Indian war dance was executed around a bonfire by the boys who had built it. Later there would be a parade of patriots whose standard-bearer would be a young pimp, the region's lowest scoundrel. And if to some observers it may have appeared that the celebration had run its course at noon, that was because the celebrators, respecters of ancient traditions, had taken time off to go home for lunch. But there were ominous signs too that, with the Germans gone, all manner of dire things could come to pass. In particular, the town's moneyed citizens and the bourgeoisie *en bloc* thought that they were reading such signs in the faces and voices of the proletarians of the poor districts. But, it may be asked, where were these good working-class people when the Germans were in control? Had not their comrades been the heart and soul of underground units in cities and towns across the land?

With the Liberation came the inevitable *épuration*—if it could so be termed. Hopes for an honest purge, if anyone had seriously entertained any, were immediately dashed. On this glorious day the self-proclaimed resisters and the scheming Darricades had the field all to themselves, and they had more than enough auxiliaries in the smugly hypocritical crowd surging before the town hall to cheer the purgers and jeer the purged. No *collabo* was to have his eyes gouged out, as had happened in the provincial town of Blémont in Marcel Aymé's novel on post-Liberation injustices and hypocrisies, *Uranus* (1948). Nor would anyone be shot in a cemetery or against a prison wall. But the sadistic instincts of the townfolk had to be satisfied, even if many of them had been oscillating between Pétainism and Gaullism according to how the winds of battle had been blowing. Moreover, they had already forgotten how passive their acceptance of the German yoke had been. So, a pair of syphilitic, tuberculosis-ridden prostitutes would be made to pay for their «collaboration» by being paraded through the streets in the nude, and a barber had mounted a platform in the square to crop the heads of other females who had disgraced themselves while their town was occupied by «the green vermin,» as Mauriac had labelled them.

But if Madame Coryse Salomé escaped arrest and the barber's shears, this was because it was rumored—and who would have been so rash as to try to prove the contrary—that the former mistress of the head of the *Kommandantur* had rendered important services to the Resistance forces. After all, is not the sacrifice of virtue on the altar of patriotism frequently the price war's heroines must pay to play the game successfully? Contrarily, drawing an unlucky number in the lottery was poor little Cécile Delahaye. Because the will of the angry mob had asserted itself, a vindictive housemaid's word could be believed and the spiritist would be exorcised in the cruel fashion of the turbulent hour. Her ignominy was by no means lesser that the count, in an extraordinary show of courage, had snatched her from the clutches of the barber after she had surrendered half of her silvery thatch. Berthe, for her part, was above suspicion. Never for a moment had the patriots bent on quickly administering long-delayed justice thought that there might be a need to settle a score with her. How were they to know, if only Marguerite Costellot knew, that with her connivance Berthe had betrayed Francis to Brackner? Furthermore, anybody as stupid as Berthe had to be judged innocuous.

There was no need for old Victor Lardenne to be paralyzed with fear, to pin an enormous Cross of Lorraine on his chest, and to applaud the *maquisards*. He was too rich, too in-fluential, and he hadn't really resisted the Resistance. Hence, there was no danger, after all, of his suffering the fate suffered by Mussolini on the Piazzale Loreto of Milan. Victor had also begun to pass the word that his son-in-law had given shelter to an English secret service agent in his home, right under Brackner's nose. Wearing a look of defiance and consumed by an anger he made no effort to conceal, Jacques had taken in the whole scene unmolested. However, his mother was not going to take any chances. As Marguerite saw it, a Saint-Clar in the spasms of Liberation was no place to be for a known collaborator with a handsome mop of hair. Therefore, accepting an industrialist friend's offer of help, she allowed herself to be whisked off in his limousine to a safer town. A practical woman, Marguerite planned to return as soon as cooler heads would again prevail. Finally, was it with a shaven head that Fernande Arréguy had plunged into the Gave? Nothing of the kind. Dragged down to the town hall for a shearing, Fernande had been quickly released by Darricade's new socialist and communist colleagues after she screamingly accused him of having engineered black market deals with her Werner by employing her as an intermediary.

In truth, it was not an impressive figure that Darricade personally and *Résistants* in general cut on Saint-Clar's day of Liberation. Sharing the spotlight with Darricade was Captain Figeac, a professional soldier who had entered the town late in the morning with two truckloads of his *maquisards*. Since, at the same time, this marks Figeac's entry into the story and since everything about him looks fake, the reader is obliged to surmise that he had joined Resistance ranks somewhere around a quarter to midnight; that he was one of the so-called «Naphtalines,» a name applied to those whose old army uniforms, hastily donned for the finale, still smelled of the mothballs used for their storage. What is known for certain, however, is that this graduate of Saint-Maixent had not felt the least bit comfortable with the *tutoyage* common to underground warriors and that he had been less than happy serving under the orders of a little Spaniard of twenty before the latter was captured and shot by the Germans. Above all, what emerges from the description of the day's events is a picture of Resistance grandstanding, its partisan divisions, and its utter incapacity to maintain even a semblance of order. While Figeac is not wanting in obnoxiousness, the villain of the piece is unmistakably Darricade, who deems it politically imprudent for him to so much as mention Francis's name in his speeches extolling the local heroes of the clandestine war, thus giving point to Alphonse Karr's *propos* that «In these things called wars, there is always less to complain about concerning those one kills than those for whom one gets oneself killed» (47).

---

(47) Norbert Guterman, comp., *A Book of French Quotations* (Garden City: Doubleday, 1963), p. 300.

Although Darricade fails to manipulate things political entirely to his satisfaction on the day of Liberation, it is apparent that he has thrust himself sufficiently to the fore to enable him to rule the roost for the foreseeable future. And it is no less apparent that if the likes of Darricade would be representing the Resistance on the political front in post-Liberation France, then no prospect but that of failure lay before those many underground warriors who had dreamt of national political renewal under their banner. All the greater was the scandal of the resisters' behavior on that day because, as the author emphasizes:

> Not a bridge had been blown up in the country side, not one tract had been distributed in the town, not one attempt had been made on the person of a single German noncom, not one train had been derailed. Who had resisted the Germans at Saint-Clar? Had Vichy not awarded a medal for civic merit to the town for its good behavior toward the troops of the occupation? (p. 353).

With due allowance made for the unadulterated patriotism and exemplary heroism of Francis, the Resistance as seen by us in this little corner of Southwestern France is a far cry from the heroic Resistance Joseph Kessel portrayed in his novel *L'Armée des ombres* (1944). Professedly, Kessel fashioned his story out of actual happenings involving real people. His angle of vision is very wide, with his clandestine combatants ranging all over metropolitan France, leaving and reentering it, etc. It may be, as claimed by the author, that everything in the book is true, yet the story rings false. Heroic exploits, hair-raising escapes, recitals of all but superhuman sacrifices, and the like succeed one another with a regularity which can only be accounted for by arbitrary selection. Further, the tone is highly lyrical; the accents, semi-hagiographical. As *bourrage de crâne,* as a wartime morale-builder, *L'Armée des ombres* may be justified. As an objective depiction of the French Resistance, it cannot—recognizing, of course, that the artist remains a free agent for whom creativity cannot be made the slave of historicity. To state the obvious, had Kessel's book appeared a few years later, it would surely have received a much milder reception from the same American and British critics who gave it glowing reviews in 1944.

Appearing a year after *L'Armée des ombres,* Roger Vailland's *Drôle de jeu,* though inspired by no corrective purpose, presents a picture of the Resistance shorn of glory and of glamor. There are no saints among even the most dedicated of Vailland's *Résistants,* and he unabashedly points to the cracks in the underground edifice. As the story unfolds, the reader gains the impression that a number of them are persisting in their danger-fraught work more out of habit than anything else. The book's protagonist, Marat, head of a Paris clandestine network, does resist out of conviction. Nonetheless, there is ample reason to believe that the excitement, the adventure of the underground fight would have been rather enough to have drawn him into it. Moreover, while it is indeed important to him that trains serving the enemy be derailed and that secret messages be safely carried to their destinations, he by no means forsakes the aesthetic, culinary, erotic, and drug-induced pleasures to which he has long been accustomed, just as he cannot abide the unwillingness of some of his comrades to follow suit. Temperamentally and philosophically a replica of the author himself, Marat is, then, a libertine for whom liberty counts, but not so much that the process of winning it should be allowed to interfere with the good life as he conceives it (48). Surely he would have laughed derisively

_____

(48) In his belief in the cause for which he is fighting, Marat

if somebody had nominated him for a Compagnon de la Libération award. Surely, too, Vailland fixed upon an apt title for his novel.

The picture of the Resistance drawn by Curtis in *Les Forêts de la nuit* is at the least as unflattering as Vailland's. Curtis satirizes endlessly and has abundant recourse to tongue-in-cheek commentary, to irony, caricature, and understatement, yet this picture emerges in sharp and clear outline. In the meantime, a reader who forgets that the artist need not be beholden to any cause and is subject to very different laws from those that govern the historian may view such a picture as a deformation of truth and a desecration of the memory of martyrs who, together with their surviving comrades, as Curtis himself affirms, «saved the honor of France and contributed to the final victory» (49). It is evidently in anticipation of precisely such criticism that the author utilized his preface to warn his readers against the temptation of looking for something in his novel which it is not intended to encompass, to wit, an exaltation of Resistance heroism or an all-inclusive, objective chronicle of the realities of 1940-1944 in France. At the same time, he reminded them politely that he considered it his prerogative as a novelist to select any themes that suited him and to color them at will. This is not to say that Curtis would have considered it within his rights to introduce a fourteen-year-old Resistance colonel into the action of his type of story, as Boris Vian had done in the case of his burlesque play *L'Équarrissage pour tous* (1946). By the same token, it would be rather beside the

---

is wholly unlike the unlovable Jean-Pierre Jerphanion, protagonist of Jules Romains' novel *Le Fils de Jerphanion* (Paris: Flammarion, 1956), who cannot forbear tarring with a heavy brush the Resistance of which he had been part, betraying Romains' own dim view of it.

(49) Curtis, «Avertissement,» *Les Forêts*, p. 7.

point to object that more Clarois should have been shown to be less lethargic and that more rutabaga should have been placed on their tables; that the seamy side of their behavior is too open to view, while their virtues are fogged over; that the German boot was not made heavy enough, since most Frenchmen suffered cruelly under the occupation and since the massacres of Oradour-sur-Glane, Asq, Tulle, and Saint-Genis-Laval were there to remind them of the cruelty of which their conquerors were capable.

What is plain is that Curtis had produced a novel which in its emphasis on the antiheroic went a long way toward debunking the legends and destroying the myths that a sizable body of propaganda-oriented French writers had, since the Liberation, been constructing around the German occupation and its aftermath. It is to his credit that he was already engaged at writing his novel in an hour when the passions inflamed by the events that had taken place in his country during the occupation and its bloody morrow were only beginning to subside; it is likewise to his credit that he reminded his compatriots—however obliquely and whatever his disclaimers—that their Resistance had indeed been the revolt of the few within the passivity of the many, and that not all the horrors perpetrated in France under the occupation wore a German label (50).

It would be going too far to pretend that Curtis had, in the case of *Les Forêts de la nuit,* authored a masterpiece. It is, nevertheless, a truly first-rate work which compels

---

(50) In his in-depth analysis of the aforementioned Marcel Ophuls film, Stanley Hoffman reminds us that the Resistance in France was hardly a mass movement, that less than 250,000 «membership cards» were given out by the Veterans' Administration after the war.» Hoffman, «In the Looking Glass,» Introduction to *The Sorrow and the Pity,* English translation of the filmscript of *Le Chagrin et la Pitié* (New York: Outerbridge and Lazard, 1972), xxii.

the reader's attention and reads well throughout. His book is palpably the product of an acute mind and of a richly cultured intelligence. The author, who was only thirty at the time of its publication, writes with zest and facility and is exceptionally adept at alternating an allusive style with a direct one. His dialogues are singularly lively; his narrative powers, striking. Each of his novel's episodes is inherently interesting and some are unusually absorbing. All are smoothly worked into the fabric of his novel. But it is satire that is Curtis's chief mark of distinction. Here he has few equals amongst the French writers of today.

Certainly the book was a very worthy Prix Goncourt awardee, and, in the writer's view, by far the best French work of fiction based on the German occupation of France. *Les Forêts de la nuit* is not, for all that, without some serious flaws. For a practicing lawyer the Count de Balansun is of a stupidity that is magnified beyond all credible proportion. Where he is concerned, it is as though the author were more interested in self-diversion than in representing a character of flesh and blood. Even the soul-wracking experience of losing his son fails to elevate him above the condition of a puppet on a string, and his on-the-spot transformation from integral *maréchaliste* to integral Gaullist is simply too much for the reader to accept. In like manner, it may be objected that Curtis has stopped short in preparing the ground psychologically for Hélène's metamorphosis from prude to debauchee. Finally, his portrayal of bourgeois characters in general, strikes one as being somewhat heavy-footed, a condition due in all probability to the importunities of the caricature of which he is visibly fond.

In his novel *Les Justes Causes* (1954), a tableau of France in the years 1944-1950, Curtis recounts the fortunes of four young Frenchmen during that period and returns to some of the themes with which he dealt in *Les Forêts de la nuit*.

The book opens with a distinctly ironic, low-key account of the last stages of the Liberation as witnessed mostly in a single unidentified quarter of Paris. There is no attempt on the part of the author to create an image of insurrectional heroism. Rather, the tone is one of deprecation. True, he does remind us that the crackle of firearms had been heard for a week and that blood had been shed, but the accent now is on people debating in a partisan spirit the question of who delivered the city from its oppressors, on the aesthetic and functional merits of various exotic-appearing street barricades, and on the persistence of heterogeneous «Eféfis» and their equally heterogeneous citizen supporters in manning battle stations at intersections where clearly no battle is in prospect. «It was,» Curtis writes, «in a climate of play-acting that the city was witnessing its liberation. The whole thing was reminiscent of a South American revolution, a pogrom, an enormous student fracas,» and whereas there were many reasons for joy, the citizenry exulted primarily because «on this evening History had come down into the streets and because each person had the feeling that he had gotten into the movie newsreels» (51). There is, in short, little here to suggest the frenzy and the throbbing excitement which characterized the preparation for and the arrival of Paris's day of glory and which were to be so joyously evoked by Larry Collins and Dominique Lapierre in their novel *Is Paris Burning?* (1965) and by Emmanuel d'Astier de la Vigerie, an important Resistance leader, in his book *De la chute à la libération de Paris* (1965). With due allowance made for the author's ironic intent, it is, nevertheless, as though his knowledge of the key roles played by General von Choltitz and by Swedish Consul General Nordling in facilitating the liberation of the city had damped his ardor.

---

(51) Curtis, *Les Justes Causes* (Paris: Julliard, 1954), p. 19.

The chief representative of the Resistance in *Les Justes Causes* is Odilon Bernard, a former Free French and *maquisard* lieutenant. Scion of a rich and well-connected Jewish family (Léon Blum is an old friend), son of a newspaper editor, he is now himself an editor—of *Horizons,* the leftist weekly founded by him. Not for anything would this mandarin of the Resistentialist intelligentsia have renounced the power and prestige that his crusading editorials and the success of his newspaper had brought him. Brimming over with vitality, charm, and intelligence, he contrives to lead a most extensive and complicated sex life—he has a veritable harem of females at his beck and call—while taking part in an interminable round of receptions and political conferences and attending to his journalistic duties. These involve not a little globe-trotting and the interviewing of the likes of Ho Chi Minh and Bao Daï. Lionized by many, hated by more, he emerges as too much the cynical exploiter of his Resistance record to reflect its glory and honor. In his editorials Bernard appears as the arch-apostle of *épuration,* crying for vengeance with a finality admitting of no charity. The reader does not have to be given to understand by Curtis that he does not regard Bernard, revelling in his new-found power and abetting the rot of *épuration* by his Jacobin severity, as a moral prototype of the *Résistant* combatant. All the same, it is interesting to hear the novelist spell out, as he finally and unmistakably does, albeit through the mouth of one of the story's wartime collaborators, the core of his position vis-à-vis the Resistance. He writes:

> The Resistance was repulsive to many Frenchmen because the visage with which it had appeared and had ruled unchecked in 1944 and 1945 was horrible ... But it was being forgotten that it had also worn the guileless visage of honesty, disinterestedness, and courage. In destiny's realm, a

Brutus, conspirators, and murderers can be found side by side. A measure of nobility and a measure of mediocrity were inextricably united in the Resist ance. With the purest of intentions, it had per- petrated, or allowed to be perpetrated, the most abject crimes. It numbered in its ranks far more hating Cassiuses and half-witted Cascas than upright Brutuses, but that is the usual proportion for any human enterprise. And the revulsion felt by so many Frenchmen for the Resistance strongly resem- bled that of the Roman people when Marc Antony would repeat his mocking leitmotif about «these very honorable men ...» (pp. 285-86).

The novel's other former *Résistant* is Huguenot François Donadieu, only in his mid-twenties at the end of the war. Fate had not been generous toward this young socialist. His actress wife had felt no qualms about entertaining Germans under the occupation, both in her country and theirs. Yet, this in itself is not what was to break up their marriage. Incompatibility had doomed it from the start. In addition, death had separated François from his little daughter. And he had had to eke out a meager living by doubling as a car salesman and cinema critic for Bernard's *Horizons*. It was at the latter's side that he had escaped to England and joined the Free French, to return later through the Pyrenees to wage war in the «army of shadows.» Patriotism, he allow- ed, had no part in his decision to flee France; he had done so only because he thought that he was subject to imminent conscription for labor in the German Todt organization. The strength of the engaging François lies in his fundamental decency and in his fidelity to even undeserving friends. His weakness had always been his tendency to get bogged down in his reveries and, oftentimes, to shirk the more strenuous of his obligations. In the end François, confessing to Bernard that political and social commitment had scant appeal for him, tells him that he has arrived at the conclusion that it was against his better judgment that he had decided to escape to England and to partake of what at the time struck him as being a «Malraux-like adventure.»

The youngest and the brashest of the quartet about whom the action of *Les Justes Causes* pivots is Thibault Fontanes. Only eighteen when he joined the Free French in Alsace in 1944, he is now seen in the role of neophyte novelist and journalistic polemicist. He offers his articles and commentaries to a variety of newspapers and receives a large quota of rejection slips because of his acerbic attacks on ex-*Résistants* holding the reins of post-Liberation power. As may be expected, Bernard is a favorite target of this darling of *épurés* and of all kinds of reactionaries. Thibault's reactionary sympathies notwithstanding, he cannot be enticed into becoming a member of any ultraconservative group—or of any other group for that matter—since for him truth is a many-sided thing and since this would mean surrendering what he most treasures, his independence of mind. Cocksure of the rightness of everything he does, he is not one to suffer fools. Nor is modesty his badge; he goes so far as to hand women who attract him his calling card, inscribed with the words «garçon d'avenir.»

The «just cause» for the story's Roland Oyarzun was collaboration with the German occupiers. Before the war he had been a muscular physical education instructor. Now he is a human wreck, physically and spiritually, and old before his time. He lives in poverty and in the fear that he will be done away with by the same elements who had him sentenced to a three-month term at Fresnes and to five years of national degradation. His had been a visceral hatred of Jews, *métèques,* Freemasons, communists, Gaullists, and other such «canaille»—of, therefore, the Hitler-concocted «super-dragon called the Judeo-Liberal-Stalin-Rothschild-World-

Conspiracy» to which Koestler satirically refers (52). The very mention of the name of Gide, «that ignoble perverter, that iconoclast, ... that gravedigger of Christianity, that foul degenerate, that accomplice of the 'Youpins' and of the Reds, that anti-colonialist,» was enough to make him jump to his feet (p. 128). Once the chief reactionary brawler among the students of the Latin Quarter, Roland had become a noisy Vichy propagandist and a supporter of Marcel Bucard and of his Franciste agitators. In fact, Curtis makes of this half-idiotic, singularly unamiable figure a caricature of a collaborator. His neuroses and his sullen masochism are destroying the lives of his wife and of his two very young daughters. His attempt to murder Bernard, judged by him to be responsible for his *milicien* brother-in-law's execution, aborts when his pistol jams. Ironically this violent anti-Semite eventually learns from his slatternly mother that his blood father was a Jew rather than the military officer whom he had admired. Utterly bored with his everyday life, he goes off, just when he is beginning to make an economic and moral comeback, to fight in Indochina, where he is killed in action. That Oyarzun is not at all proposed to the reader as a stereotype of a collaborator is further brought out in the lengthy discussions of collaboration and *épuration* in which the book's loquacious characters indulge.

Despite the fact that *Les Justes Causes* is a far from didactic work, Curtis does show his hand on the issues. The reaction to one of Bernard's articles, recorded here below, is that of François, yet recognizably his own also:

> The article was clumsy and dishonest because it failed to discriminate between persons who who had

---

(52) Arthur Koestler, *Scum of the Earth* (New York: Macmillan, 1941), p. 90.

dealt illicitly with the enemy, denounced compatriots, etc., and those who had gone no further than to consider the Marshal the legitimate head of the nation; between those very rare Nazified Frenchmen and the very numerous French *vichyssois*; between a young killer working for the Gestapo and a youth enrolled in the Legion Against Bolshevism. Bernard merged all the categories, put everything into the same bag, labelled «the traitors» (p. 193).

Elsewhere too the novelist is at pains to point up his conception of collaboration as a multiform, variegated thing, and to emphasize that there was a world of difference between, for example, the collaboration of a Jacques Doriot, more Hitlerian than were untold numbers of members of the Nazi party, and that of a Frenchman granting legitimacy a primacy it may not have deserved in the circumstances. Here Curtis is preaching the same line that was preached by Mauriac, who was deeply disappointed that the Resistance-established tribunals of the post-Liberation period gave no consideration to the fact that «collaboration with the occupier had been the official policy of the legal government of France—a government embodied in an illustrious marshal, recognized by the ambassadors of the entire world, including that of the United States and the Papal Nuncio» (53).

In opening to us the minds of Bernard, François, Thibault, and Roland, these four young men who had been caught up in the tempests of French history in the thirties and forties, and in concerning himself with their respective causes, Curtis provided us with a sort of sequel to *Les Forêts de la nuit*. Because at the same time *Les Justes Causes* was intended to be a broad synthesis of the French social, intellectual, and

---

(53) Mauriac, «Préface,» *Mémoires politiques*, p. 24.

political worlds of those years, its purely fictional content is appreciably lesser than that of *Les Forêts*. Therefore, in taking up once more the vexed problems born of the war, Curtis has had to give a rather full and wholly objective treatment to the issues on which he focussed in the earlier book. It will be recalled that, in the case of *Les Forêts,* Curtis emerges as a debunker, a demythologizer. And if more myths still had to be destroyed about the issues of collaboration with and resistance to the German occupier, Curtis, writing as both novelist and social historian, has done a thorough job of destroying them in *Les Justes Causes.* What is no myth, however, and what these two complementary works of fiction bring out most clearly, as not a few historical works have done, is that France was a terribly divided country under the German occupation and in the early post-World War II period—so divided that it is not an exaggeration to say that, in those fateful years, it was truly being ravaged by civil war.

Chapter IV

THE CONCENTRATIONARY WORLD OF
PIERRE GASCAR

Pierre Gascar is of that genus of writers, of which Barbusse, Remarque, Ludwig Renn, Richard Aldington, and Stephen Crane are prominent representatives, who achieve their highest flights under the crushing impact of war. In his case, however, it is war as witnessed for the most part from behind the pale of captivity—war no less total for all that. Taken prisoner by the Germans in 1940, Gascar made two unsuccessful attempts to escape. He was then moved to the distant prison camp of Rawa-Ruska, a few miles northeast of Lwow, in what was at that time a corner of the Polish province of Galicia. Before his collection of six lengthy short stories, *Les Bêtes,* and his novel, *Le Temps des morts,* combined, in 1953, to win him the Prix Goncourt and wide literary acclaim, the pseudonymous author Pierre Gascar had been much less known to the French public than was the reporter and literary critic of *France-Soir* writing under his true name, Pierre Fournier.

Jules Roy reminds us that Christ would have worn a yellow star in German-occupied territory and «would have died in an extermination camp» (1). Romain Gary informs

---

(1) Jules Roy, *Le Grand Naufrage* (Paris: Julliard, 1966), p. 232.

us that his father died in one of them, not from gas in its gas chamber but from fear, just as he was about to enter it (2). It is into the world in which this was possible that Gascar wishes to take his reader: the world of Hitler's «Final Solution,» of six million Jews clubbed, shot, gassed, or starved to death—the apocalyptic, the concentrationary world. In this world gone mad the meeting of the transport needs of beleaguered German armies was frequently jeopardized in order to guarantee that there would be no interruption in the flow of freight trains carrying Jewish men, women, and children to well-organized earthly hells rimmed by electrified barbed-wire fences and dedicated to their destruction. It is a world in which the gates of camps where millions perished bore such incriptions as «Arbeit macht frei» (Freedom through work), and «Jedem das Sein» (To each his own); where bands playing lively marches greeted deportees upon their arrival from the homes from which they had been torn and daily gave a musical send-off to *Kommandos* departing for work at dawn; where hangings were often staged with musical accompaniment; where, as if they could never bring themselves to believe it, the inmates were ritually reminded that «A concentration camp is not a sanatorium»; where they were sometimes treated to travelogue films, cabaret-style entertainment, and to soccer and boxing matches before they collapsed of fatigue and were hauled off to the gas chambers (3). It was a world ruled by SS men whose favorite words were *los, schnell,* and *schneller,* and who were always primed

---

(2) Romain Gary, *La Promesse de l'aube* (Paris: Gallimard, 1960), p. 105.

(3) Nerin E. Gun, a Turkish journalist who had been a prisoner at Dachau, speaks of the disappearance of the camp orchestra, which «for reasons never explained, had made a habit of playing «My Old Kentucky Home.» Gun, *The Day of the Americans* (New York: Fleet, 1966), p. 441.

to sic their sleek, pedigreed dogs at the cowering prisoners under the gaze of Hitlerian eagles (4). Knowing that in such a world a prisoner was doomed as soon as his spiritual resistance collapsed, on one occasion Louis Martin-Chauffier went on reciting verse from Virgil while being administered a brutal flogging—exemplifying the infinite resourcefulness of the human spirit in the face of disaster.

It is the world of Auschwitz-Birkenau (the latter's Polish name, Brzezinka, means «Birchgrove»), where the bodies of four million persons went up in the smoke of the crematoriums, smoke so foul-smelling that it emptied the ambient sky of birds. It is Auschwitz-Birkenau, with its shifts of clerks feverishly working around the clock to type out meticulous death reports on its millions of victims; where, on a railway siding, the direction in which an SS doctor's finger or walking stick pointed instantaneously determined whether a newly arrived deportee would at once be dispatched to his death or allowed a reprieve, until overwork and undernourishment, if not spiritual exhaustion, made a skeletal corpse of him; where, for purposes of camouflage, the death-dealing Cyclon B gas was delivered to the gas chambers in a car marked with the insignia of the International Red Cross; where, en route to these chambers, parents and grandparents would tickle the little children in their arms and recite nursery rhymes to them to give them a few last moments of earthly happiness; where many children carried their toys inside; where, in exceptionally cold weather, a handful of child-laborers, spared from death, were sometimes sent to the

---

(4) In his *Le Grand Voyage* (Paris: Gallimard, 1973), a novel on the concentrationary experience, an experience he had known intimately, Spanish-born former *Résistant* Jorge Semprún makes strikingly effective use of a gaze-of-Hitlerian-eagles motif. The sufferings of the inmates are made to appear all the more intense that they are ever being inflicted beneath the «stony» or «dead» gaze of haughty eagles with folded wings.

temporarily unused gas chambers or crematorium to warm themselves. A survivor of the dread place, S. B. Unsdorfer, sums it all up very simply. «Auschwitz became Jewry's cemetery, and the cattle wagons their cortege» (5), he writes. It is the world of Ubuesque Treblinka, the first mammoth death factory created by Himmler and his cohorts, where *Romeo and Juliet* was staged; Treblinka with its fake railroad station, installed to gull arrivals into believing that it was but a stop-off on their «resettlement» journey; where the road leading to the gas chambers was named Himmelstrasse (Road to Heaven); where, on the average, fifteen thousand people were killed daily, but whose functionaries once outdid themselves by gassing and cremating twenty-four thousand in a little more than six hours; and whose commandant, Franz Stangl, supervised the daily mass murdering, whip in hand and clad smartly if incongruously in a white riding jacket and riding breeches. It is the world of Buchenwald (Beechwood)—another name suggestive of sylvan isolation and peace—built around the oak in whose shade Goethe used to chat with Eckermann; Buchenwald, whose crematorium was inscribed with words exalting the purifying quality of fire; where during the torturous evening roll calls the enormous camp band, decked out in bright red uniforms, would play marches, waltzes, and other varieties of music «with enthusiasm, as though at a village sports day» (6); of Majdanek, where, on November 3, 1943, more than eighteen thousand Jews were machine-gunned to death; where, while 1,300,000 persons were being exterminated within its confines, «the slightest bookkeeping error sent everyone scurrying as if

---

(5) S. B. Unsdorfer, *The Yellow Star* (New York: Yoseloff, 1961), p. 14.

(6) Reported by Buchenwald *rescapé* Pierre d'Harcourt in *The Hidden Enemy* (New York: Scribner's, 1967), p. 105.

the fate of the Third Reich were at stake» (7); of Mauthausen, where murderous slave labor and disease once reduced poet-novelist Jean Cayrol to a skeleton weighing thirty kilograms; of Bergen-Belsen, ghoulishly called a «rest camp» by Nazi officialdom, where starvation, more than anything else, swept victims off to their final rest; of Lwow, where an SS guard was known to the prisoners as Tom Mix because he found sport in taking shots at them while riding about the camp on a horse; of Neuengamme, where the assembled prisoners were sometimes forced to sing during hangings; of Oranienburg, where a pretty bed of flowers framed the gallows; of Dachau, Ravensbruch, Belzec, Chelmno, Sobibor, and other dread places where human beings, descending to the level of beasts, treated other human beings worse than beasts (8).

Little wonder, then, that for concentrationary inmates sleep-induced nightmares were less frightening than the reality of their waking hours (9). Little wonder, too, that the ghosts of the surrealistic camps they survived haunts day and night the Elie Wiesels and the Jean Cayrols of the world. The «temps du mépris» confidently forecast by Malraux had indeed arrived. Reflecting on the ineffectuality of Western man's highly developed culture and centuries-old humanistic

---

(7) Alexander Donat, *The Holocaust Kingdom: A Memoir* (New York: Holt, Rinehart and Winston, 1963), p. 189.

(8) Less well known than a goodly number of the camps, Sobibor, in Southeastern Poland, was a death camp in the fullest sense of the term. «The chance of avoiding immediate death in the gas chamber [there],» Gerald Reitlinger stresses, «was not one in four, but less than one in forty.» *The Final Solution: The Attempt to Exterminate the Jews of Europe, 1939-1945* (London: Valentine, 1953), p. 337.

(9) Terrence Des Pres writes: «One survivor remarks that in camp he did not wake fellow prisoners when one of them was having a nightmare; he knew that no matter how bad the dream might be, reality was worse.» Des Pres, *The Survivor: An Anatomy of Life in the Death Camps* (New York: Oxford University Press, 1976), p. 75.

tradition in rendering him more humane, George Steiner notes: «We now know that a man can read Goethe or Rilke in the evening, that he can play Bach and Schubert, and go to his day's work at Auschwitz in the morning» (10). Steiner could have added that a man can, like Himmler, view as obscene the shooting of a deer and be the chief architect of mass murder, or that a man can have a special fondness for children and the paintings of Watteau and Fragonard and order such murder. The man was Hitler. But Hitler, for his part, never so much as set foot in a concentration camp.

With Gascar's *Les Bêtes* it is the nightmare world of Kafka born anew: strange, somber, mysterious, irrational, eternally menacing. The animals, swarming everywhere, quail helplessly before the onslaughts of their human tormentors. The latter, in their turn, fail not only to breach the curtain of incomprehension isolating the species but also the one that segregates them from their fellow creatures. And in the three most powerful stories, patently the product of an apocalyptic vision, a Kafkaesque dream-like haze envelops the impotent animals and anguished humans, overlying the world of reality and lending an air of timelessness to their tragic situation.

«Les Chevaux,» the book's opening selection, can readily be taken to be a strong indictment of war. Unnamed, unlocalized, and unrecognizable, the war in question is, at any rate, total. Peer, the protagonist, has been misplaced in a tiny unit charged with controlling a veritable sea of horses which for no apparent logical reason have been herded together at some remove from the fighting fronts. Disarmed by the indifference of the self-important army bureaucrats

---

(10) George Steiner, «Preface,» *Language and Silence: Essays on Language, Literature, and the Inhuman* (New York: Atheneum, 1967), ix.

above him and by the insensibility of his comrades in misfortune, agitated by his fear of the animals which press in on him from all sides as they gallop about in endless stampedes, the gentle Peer soon finds himself savagely beating the hunger-crazed, fear-paralyzed horses. Tottering on the brink of insanity, in the end Peer recoils with disgust from the suffering he has inflicted and performs a supreme act of liberation by allowing the whole equine horde to escape. His struggle with his conscience over, he deserts. War is ingeniously painted throughout as epic chaos and a *massacre des innocents*. News from the fronts is unvaryingly gloomy and the estate of the hungry, filthy, sorely neglected grooms—they receive too few rather than too many military orders—is scarcely happier than that of the animals which these humans assault with animal fury. Separated by an abyss of fear and hate, they are, where suffering is concerned, brothers under the skin.

War's horrors are again visited upon men and animals alike in «Les Bêtes,» a masterly contrived piece which gives its title to the volume. The animals are those of a circus that has been uprooted from its winter quarters; the men are Russian prisoners of war living in an adjoining barn. To stay alive, the Russians make dangerous forays into the countryside and bribe the German keeper of the animals out of most of the meat and bread intended for the menagerie, thus keeping it in a semi-perpetual hellish uproar that further widens the breach dividing the species. No fraternity of suffering is possible here, for the instinct of self-preservation is too potent in each, with the men initially manifesting fierce resentment over the animals' superior rations. The war-induced degradation of man becomes complete when the prisoners attempt to talk guards into an exchange of the beasts' meat supply for the corpses of two comrades, shot by the Germans when their thievery of potatoes is detected.

In a world gone mad, in a concentrationary world, humans thus become dehumanized, being reduced to life on an animal plane—to life as it was lived at Auschwitz. There, Elie Wiesel recalls, «A bit of bread was worth more than divine promises; a bowl of soup transformed a cultured individual into a savage beast» (11).

«Entre chiens et loups,» whose forty-seven pages make it the book's longest story, has as its setting a military kennel in the French zone of occupation of post-World War II Germany. Here, under simulated conditions of war, human targets, grotesquely clad in not entirely protective clothing, are pitted against dogs whose savagery is as nurtured as it is natural. The French officers on duty at the establishment talk of the next war with a matter-of-factness that cannot but imply its inevitability and proximity. What is more, Gascar would have us believe that the scourge is already loose. His hero, Franz, a Polish displaced person, underscores this by stubbornly refusing to escape from the dog arena into which, significantly, he had not been forced, assuming after his fashion «the duties of the human conscience.» He affirms:

> Every day I live the horror of our age, as yet a bloodless horror, while millions of human beings are casually falling asleep, with their inconsequential concerns and their trivial psychoses, while awaiting some general mobilization, or even some great deflagration, and are redrawing to their own scale a doubtless terrifying profile, but one which in no way resembles the face of the *Great Horror* —of night fallen over the earth, and which I, for my part, see penetrating the morning haze like another sun, when I am pulled about by the dogs

---

(11) Elie Wiesel, «Lectures,» *Entre deux soleils* (Paris: Éditions du Seuil, 1970), p. 72.

and run to escape them, when they catch hold of me again and I fall on the edge of that prophetic wood! (12).

In this «atmosphere of damnation» the camp commandant, who has few human feelings for his *hommes-mannequins,* becomes hysterical when Franz, in a sudden show of revolt, turns on the dogs with a savagery that had hitherto been their exclusive property. And when one of the military men is asked how he can manage to fall asleep amidst the infernal barking of the dogs, he explains that he does so by selecting a single bark out of the entire deafening chorus, then barking along with it until sleep is induced. Shades of Dachau's «dog cells,» where the inmates had to bark to receive the food being brought them. Shades, too, of other concentration camps with their transcendent ignominies, where men were intentionally confused with beasts and whose SS masters were not above indulging in the cruel refinement of addressing their dogs as «Menschen» in the presence of their slaves.

The book closes on an admonitory note, with Gascar emphasizing that the barrier separating man and beast has become exceedingly fragile. He writes: «At any moment, the beast can undergo a metamorphosis. We are at the frontier. We have the crazy horse, the rabid sheep, the trained rat, the intrepid bear: secondary states which open the animal hell to our gaze and where we discover anew, with a stunned sense of kinship, our own tortured face, as in a clawed mirror» (p. 204). That these lines were intended as a key to and a link with *Le Temps des morts* is plain, since in it the metamorphosis is complete. It is with the grim consequences of the brutalization of man that *Le Temps des morts* deals.

---

(12) Gascar, «Entre chiens et loups,» *Les Bêtes* (Paris: Gallimard, 1953), p. 186.

Gascar refers to the aforementioned Rawa-Ruska, the Brodno of his story, as a disciplinary camp. Its inmates, including about a thousand prisoners of war who, like Gascar, had been sent there after foiled attempts to escape from other camps, were not looked upon as subhumans. Neither did they wear zebra-striped prison pajamas twenty-four hours a day or live in the stench and shadow of the crematorium. The men, one gathers, were dying of malnutrition, of pestilence, of physical and spiritual exhaustion. All the same, they were dying naturally, if prematurely. The funerals given them were proper even to the point of the firing of volleys over their graves by German soldiers. Homesickness, weariness, and even idleness, the last an unknown malady in the *Konzentrationslager,* were weighing heavily upon the living. Yet, in contrast with the understandably meek compliance of the average concentrationary camp prisoner, whose masters were whip-bearing, jackbooted SS troopers and truncheon-bearing *Kapos,* the frustrated Frenchmen of Brodno were still plotting and attempting escape and seditiously chanting the «Marseillaise.» The story's setting is not, then, a concentration camp, though there can be no doubt that the novelist was bent on communicating the nightmarish characteristics of the forbidding world of such camps. Forbidding? To Jean Cayrol it is.

Cayrol underscores the virtually insuperable difficulties confronting those who would fashion fictional works out of the squalor and suffering of the concentration camps. «Picasso,» he asserts, «would have been the ideal painter to have set up an easel on the *Appell-Platz* of Mauthausen or of Buchenwald» (13). Or Bosch? Or Brueghel? Might not

---

(13) Jean Cayrol, «D'un romanesque concentrationnaire,» *Esprit,* Sept., 1949, p. 341. In this article he likened survivors of concentration camps to the biblical Lazarus, with the difference that his twentieth-century counterparts were condemned to grope about

practiced writers have done quite as well to have left to young Anne Frank in her family's Amsterdam hideaway the task of describing the terrors of life in a world ruled by the SS and the Gestapo? Would even a Dante or a Dostoyevsky have been equal to the challenge of incarnating the man-made hells of the concentrationary universe? Must, therefore, the literary creators abdicate before their supreme horrors, thus commissioning survivor writers of documentaries and of sociological treatises, the Bletons, Burneys, Donats, D'Harcourts, Kogons, Michelets, Roussets, and Undorfers, to grapple with what might well defy the powers of the artistic imagination? Ernst Wiechert, imprisoned in Buchenwald in 1938 by his own government, answers in the affirmative, since he speaks of «a vision of Hell, beyond the brush of the greatest etcher, because no human phantasy or even the dreams of a genius can measure up to this reality ...» (14) It is a noteworthy fact that a preponderance of critical sentiment supports Wiechert in the matter. Moreover, the novelists themselves imply concurrence, for all but a relative handful of them have kept the Hitlerian camps at arm's length.

Here an interesting case calls itself to mind. For his part, Auschwitz survivor Elie Wiesel—he became a prisoner there at fifteen—regards the death of a million children at the hands of Hitlerian disciples and, by extension, the concentrationary world as a whole, as lying beyond the limits of «the novelist's language, the historian's analysis, and the prophet's vision» (15). Further, he casts severe doubt on the ability of even survivors and eyewitnesses, himself included,

---

forever in utter solitude in a world from which their experience had hopelessly alienated them. The hell of Mauthausen has informed nearly all of Cayrol's writings since the war.

(14) Ernst Wiechert, *Forests of the Dead,* trans. Ursula Stechow (New York: Greenberg, 1947), p. 67.

(15) Wiesel, *op. cit.,* p. 74.

to transmit adequately their concentrationary experience in any written form. However, because he is intent on memorializing the holocaust of his people and on sounding the alarm on the deadly perils lying in its wake, he has even emerged as the holocaust's leading chronicler. Nor has he shunned the novel—the very short novel—as a medium for achieving his dual objective. His *La Nuit* (1958) is a novelistic portrayal of a child suffering the agonies of the damned at Auschwitz, Buchenwald, and points between. The child was himself. Fantasy is sharply curbed in this work of imaginative integrity and of great power, with the power due chiefly to the union of a lean, simple prose style with an underlying current of the sort of passion that only an overwhelming sense of outrage can beget. And when occasionally the passion rises to the surface, the tone is so sincere, the words so moving, that the message goes straight to the heart—as when he writes:

> Never shall I forget that night, the first night in camp, which has turned my life into one long night, seven times cursed and seven times sealed. Never shall I forget that smoke. Never shall I forget the little faces of the children, whose bodies I saw turned into wreaths of smoke beneath a silent blue sky.
> Never shall I forget those flames which consumed my faith forever.
> Never shall I forget that nocturnal silence which deprived me, for all eternity, of the desire to live. Never shall I forget those moments which murdered my God and my soul and turned my soul to dust. Never shall I forget these things, even if I am condemned to live as long as God Himself. Never (16).

_____

(16) Wiesel, «Night,» in *Night, Dawn, The Accident: Three Tales*, trans. Stella Rodway (New York: Hill and Wang, 1972), p. 43.

Among those undaunted souls who have striven to give fictional embodiment to the holocaust world were Erich Maria Remarque and Robert Merle. Their efforts deserve some examination because they direct attention to a number of what may be termed «laboratory» problems bound up with such writing.

Remarque, whose *All Quiet on the Western Front* (1929) was by far the most widely read novel on World War I, badly overreached himself when he turned his attention to the closed world of the concentration camps. His *Der Funke Leben* (1952) strikes one as being well-nigh everything that a fictional work on this resistant theme should not be. An endless parade of brutalities, the ghastliest that the warped mentalities of warped men can invent, passes before the gaze of the reader. Pistol blows between the eyes, kicks to prostrate bodies, and the tobacco juice spat on them compound the miseries of dysentery-ravaged prisoners upon whom press down the «greasy and sweetish vapors of the crematorium.» As in Rodin's bronze, «La Porte de l'enfer,» seemingly every form of spiritual and physical torture is given play. It is as though the author wished to catalogue all the barbaric violence done the human person in the camps and recorded in the numerous documentaries he manifestly studied. By persistently straining for dramatic effect Remarque stirs the sensibilities far beyond the point of gainful return. Greatly overworking his material and speaking *ad nauseam* of the unspeakable, he offends against the unwritten canon of discretion to which a work of this sort needs be subject. The human brutality on display simply overwhelms—nay, stupefies, the reader. And sharply outlined against this exorbitance is the poverty of psychology of the characters. This obtains especially with respect to the prisoners, lacking, as they do, the complex and unique differentness associated with them by Cayrol, who, it should be emphasized, esteems their inscrutability an immovable block in the path of those who, in their presumption—he believes— would portray the concentrationary world in works of fiction.

In Robert Merle's *La Mort est mon métier* (1952), termed a «fictive autobiography,» Rudolf Lang, the protagonist, traces his career as a Nazi, with strongest focus on that phase of it having to do with his activities as camp commandant of Auschwitz. Not a monster born of the novelist's imagination, he is, rather, patently and closely modeled after Rudolf Hoess, the camp's real-life commandant, a fact which, ironically, seems to have escaped the notice of the book's French reviewers. As such, Lang-Hoess was responsible for the deaths of approximately 2,500,000 persons, earning him the unenviable distinction of being the greatest murderer of modern times while in no way weakening his personal conviction that he was an ordinary, normal human being. In attempting to paint him against the background of the gas chambers and crematoria of the most massive death factory of them all, Merle has not feared to enter where few writers would tread, and this without his having had personal experience of concentrationary living. Be it said to his credit that, in the circumstances, the resultant work is decidedly more effective than most critics would have thought possible. The novelist does not aim to turn the stomach with unrelieved horrors, though horrors there are. His hero, in the manner of an industrial efficiency expert, speaks of «units» and «production»—the units are humans and the production concerns the rate of extermination and cremation—and he waxes enthusiastic over the technical perfection of his genocidal enterprise (17). He is an unquestioning, robot-like

---

(17) In his fictionalized documentary *Treblinka* (Paris: Fayard, 1966), Jean-François Steiner brings out what was by no means a fiction: that the stars of SS «technicians» rapidly rose or paled depending on the ingenuity they demonstrated in increasing the rate of extermination and cremation. A particularly brilliant

executant of all orders, the embodiment of the «Befehl ist Befehl» mentality. He is a bureaucratic servant gone mad, and it does not even occur to him that he is a branded criminal. Yet, a strain is put on the credulity only if the reader forgets that Lang's real-life prototype spoke and acted no differently (18). Nor, for that matter, did Adolf Eichmann, who took no small measure of pride in his achievement of hunting Jews out of virtually every corner of German-occupied Europe and of coordinating their transport to extermination camps—while professing no hatred for them. Finally, the book's unadorned, sober language appears to be well adapted to the portrayal of absolute evil, to the sacredness of the theme. Nevertheless, *La Mort est mon métier* leaves one dissatisfied. It is mutilated by the unseemly encroachment of fantasy on reality and by gratuitous literary artifice, of which a prime example would be the author's insistence on constantly injecting synthetic German flavoring of the *ja, nein, jawohl, Herrgott* variety. Above all, Merle's book lacks the intensity of mood and concentrated power needed to produce the fully damning indictment of a mentality and a system

---

stroke called for partying and drinking toasts to its originator. Best known to the inmates as «Lalka» (Polish for «Doll»), Kurt Franz, the camp's commandant, is labelled by Steiner as «the Stakhavonite of extermination» p. 200.

That Treblinka's technicians of death were second to none is certified by Simon Wiesenthal's statement that «of the 700,000 people known to have been taken there, about forty are now alive.» Wiesenthal, *The Murderers among Us* (New York: McGraw-Hill, 1967), p. 302.

(18) G. M. Gilbert, prison psychologist at the Nuremberg trial of Nazi war criminals, was told by Hoess: «We were all so trained to obey orders without even thinking that the thought of disobeying an order would simply never have occurred to anybody and somebody else would have done just as well if I hadn't ... Himmler was so strict about little things and executed SS men for such small offenses, that we naturally took it for granted that he was acting according to a strict code of honor.» Gilbert, *Nuremberg Diary* (New York: Farrar, Straus, & Co., 1947), p. 260.

which destroyed two-fifths of the world's Jews and a total of eleven million human beings (19).

Gascar obviously had an initial advantage in writing of a world he experienced in his own person, albeit outside the gates. In addition, because he was so positioned, he has had to trust to the magic of poetic suggestibility where others have in large part relied upon the elaborations of a grim realism. His oblique, insinuating approach served him well.

In *Le Temps des morts,* the German and Russian armies, locked in titanic combat, are so distant as to appear mythical, unreal. But neither distance nor the vast Volynian plain on which it lies can shield little Brodno from the onslaughts of total war. It has become a prison of no escape. Death —it is the story's haunting leitmotif— intrudes upon the vermin-covered, underfed and overcrowded Frenchmen behind barbed wire; death relentlessly stalks the village's Jews, marked for immolation with armlets surprinted with a blue star of David; and its Polish, Ukrainian, and Ruthenian inhabitants react as though they too were hedged in by it. Cosmic suffering has, then, been visited upon the tiny place, with the Jews the chief victims.

Gascar's is a highly exceptional gift for generating mood, for evoking atmosphere. He is a master at giving broad resonance to the naked word, to the isolated, seemingly insignificant act. The narrative is stark and the language fittingly laconic, if occasionally disfigured by an imagistic extravagance that savors of surrealism's automatic writing.

---

(19) As with Merle's work, so with Steiner's *Treblinka* insofar as the mixing of the factual with the fictional is concerned. Steiner too had to resort to heavy documentation, for neither had he been a concentrationary inmate. It is quite apparent that his by no means bad book is diminished by numerous contrived conversations between real and imaginary persons and—for the stubborn circumstances—by an excess of artistic arrangement. These strike the reader as impious.

An air of mystery shrouds the village and the surrounding countryside. The atmosphere is heavy with anxiety. Cowed peasants glide past the village cemetery as though in a trance. Patrols of the pro-German Ukrainian militia furtively slip through the shadowland of the forest in pursuit of partisans. From time to time a shot rends the augural silence, paralyzing men with fear. Earth and heavens take on subtle portents. Pointing to a sky empty of birds, a Jew laments: «It may well be that our hour has struck ... There are things written up there» (20). A virtual no-man's land comes into being as the villagers immure themselves within their homes. Dreaded SS men begin to appear in the area and before long unfamiliar trains begin to pass, slow-moving freights whose whistles are never sounded and whose cars are packed with shrieking and dying women and children en route to a nearby extermination camp. Then, quickly unladen of their human cargo, they shuttle back empty (21). The author, who continually employs counterpoint in contrasting the Arcadian peacefulness of the cemetery, where men leisurely transplant sod and water flowers, with the madness of the world without, again effectively resorts to it here, simultaneously detailing the appalling suffering of the doomed deportees entombed within the boxcars and the symbols of peace visible to those of them gazing out of the narrow open panels: luminous landscapes, trees, free men standing relaxedly in fields, and mechanical harvesters.

The Jewish citizenry of Brodno live in a veritable extramural concentrationary world, with obsessive fear, solitude,

---

(20) Gascar, *Le Temps des morts* (Paris: Gallimard, 1953), p. 94.
(21) Steiner describes the arrival of a passenger train at Treblinka whose «favored» passengers were German Jews: seriously disabled World War I veterans and/or holders of the Iron Cross, first class. «They died like the poor, but they had travelled like bourgeois,» he observes. *Treblinka,* p. 303.

and isolation destroying them morally before they too are routed out of their homes, herded together, and led off in somber processions to the trains that will carry them to physical destruction, victims of virulent racism (22). Terror-stricken, one of them had tried to avoid capture by living in a tree in the daytime and sleeping at night in whatever grave the French cemetery crew had freshly prepared. The others, in unconscious imitation of their brethren in all concentration camps, had sought to delay their fate by remaining as inconspicuous and as unseeing as possible. None evaded the dragnet. Reflecting on the large-scale violence, extortion, and murder that had accompanied German advances elsewhere in Europe and were presently accompaying them in the East, Gascar protests: «As the war moved away from us, it only removed the uncommonness of such things; the things themselves remained, the difference being that, no longer improvised, they were now assuming a workmanlike character: the ruins were handmade, homes became prisons, and murder was committed with advance notice» (23). But he cannot regard indignation and vituperation as worthy weapons, this

(22) In his *Histoire de la captivité des Français en Allemagne, 1939-1945* (Paris: Gallimard, 1967), Gascar pertinently recalls that the lives of French prisoners at Rawa-Ruska had as a backdrop the mammoth, systematic slaughter of East European Jews, in and outside the camps, and that the extermination camp of Belzec was close by. As bird's-eye witnesses of Nazi genocide these Frenchmen were shaken to the very depths of their souls and prompted to ponder endlessly on their own chances of survival. Portraying Rawa-Ruska as a microcosm of a Nazi-ruled world in language that echoes much of that of *Le Temps des morts*, Gascar speaks of its «fear-frozen landscapes, its citizens branded like cattle promised to the slaughterhouse, its trigger-happy SS patrols, its Ukrainian militiamen in black uniforms, and its convoys of weeping and moaning women and children en route to their death ...», p. 241.

(23) Gascar, *Le Temps des morts*, p. 65.

being about as plain-spoken language as any found in the book (24).

Appropriately, the camp's German soldiers are anything but replicas of such depraved brutes as Buchenwald's Master Sergeant Sommer. An ill-clad, ill-assorted lot, much like those often found in the backwash of battle, they are not, with perhaps one exception, Nazis *pur sang* . They mouth no praises of Hitlerism, shun all talk of the fighting fronts, and sometimes contravene orders by allowing the prisoners exceptional latitude of movement. Yet, conditioned by the dogma of the *Führerstaat* and forged in the fires of Nazi discipline, one of the two German soldiers having an important role in the action, a self-styled pacifiot and hardly the embodiment of cruelty, unhesitatingly shoots to death a Frenchman who ventures a dash for liberty. It is implied that he has done so quite as impersonally as his comrades, in undoubting compliance with their soldier's oath, were, with efficiency and dispatch, rounding up the area's Jews. The other, the Protestant pastor Ernst, is the story's voice of conscience. Like the Swabian military chaplain of Albrecht Goes's largely autobiographical novelette *Unruhige Nacht* (1950), he manages to preserve intact his own code of conduct, to rise superior to the circumstances. Like him, too, he is, first and foremost, the servant of all suffering humanity. This socialist and short-term veteran of a concentration camp regularly fraternizes with the French prisoners entrusted to him and contrives to bring spiritual aid and comfort to some Jewish girls engaged in the construction of a nearby road. Eventually, when his love for one of them is discovered, he is transferred to a disciplinary camp.

In general, *Le Temps des morts* eschews refinements and

---

(24) Twenty years after his liberation from Mauthausen, Paul Tillard re-created his concentrationary experience in his *Le Pain*

graphics, and is piously conceived. Some preciosity and over-wrought images do creep in, and the macabre, always a dangerous obstructant in works of this sort, does once impose itself, when the cemetery hands accidentally uncover a mass grave. For the most part, however, the reliance is upon a restrained poetic evocation. These factors, united with the becoming economy of words and simplicity of plot, the admirable consonance of mood and expression, the sustained emotion, and the deep if verbally restrained compassion, serve to make of *Le Temps des morts* the work of power and artistic integrity demanded by the subject. It may well be the most effective fictional portrayal of the concentrationary universe yet to have appeared in any language. Surely its position of preeminence in France cannot be challenged.

The one piece by Gascar related to war and the concentrationary world that clearly was not inspired by moral intent is the not at all short short story «Le Bonheur de Bolinka,» first published in the September 1953 issue of the *Revue de Paris*. The same work reappeared two years later under the title «Les Femmes» in a volume of four such stories bearing the same name (25). Set in a minuscule slave labor camp in Germany, the action revolves about the conniving of Ukrainian women inmates to obtain from time to time a few days of respite from their factory labors. Their strategy consists of clandestinely exchanging body lice, then turning them over to the camp's grumpy, demoralized German commandant as exempting evidence of infestation. Ultimately their subversion recoils upon themselves, for legions of lice overrun the barracks and nearly thwart a promised and desperately desired social gathering with male Russian slave

---

des temps maudits (Paris: Julliard, 1965) in simple, straightforward language, in large part allowing the grim facts to speak for themselves. However, in his case the scars of hate are plainly visible.

(25) Gascar, *Les Femmes* (Paris: Gallimard, 1965).

laborers in an adjacent compound. A gross, rough-hewn comic element ceaselessly disturbs this atmosphere of tragedy, further debilitating the slack narrative and converting «Le Bonheur de Bolinka» into the only artistic *malheur* amongst the works by Gascar bearing on the miseries spawned of war.

Looking back upon the war-associated stories of *Les Bêtes* and *Le Temps des morts,* one deduces that Gascar could not but have been aiming to shock the reader into a sense of moral outrage, to sound a mighty note of warning. The concentrationary world, he clearly predicates, lives on, if in shrunken proportions, since he finds an untamed beast lurking in every one of us. Like Elie Wiesel, like Simon Wiesenthal, that indefatigable hunter of Nazi war criminals, he is moved to action by his conviction that tomorrow's murderers are born today. At any moment, anywhere, Gascar suggests, mass exterminations could again be launched. But, he would place us on our guard and strike at our conscience while holding out no real hope of regeneration. He seems to see us all as hopelessly flawed, as infected with a malignant cancer of the soul—as potential accomplices in murder. And he finds no God to buttress us in our twilight struggle with other men and ourselves.

CHAPTER V

WINGED WARRIORS

Jules Roy and the Exupérian Heritage

Humiliated in 1940, France has taken pride in those of her sons who by their wartime deeds showed that they considered her worth fighting and dying for. Such a man was Antoine de Saint-Exupéry. It may be said that even though the god of war destroyed him, he smiled on him too, for if Saint-Exupéry's name and fame have had few parallels in twentieth-century France, this may be attributed in no small part to what war brought out of him.

Having declined the ease and security of a desk job to which his age entitled him, during the 1940 *débâcle* Saint-Exupéry made reconnaissance flights over the battle area in skies so full of enemy planes and flak that it took something of a miracle for an aviator to return safely to his base. Three years later his stubborn initiatives resulted in the waiving of military regulations to authorize his flying a 400 mile-per-hour P38 Lightning plane on reconnaissance missions, a quite remarkable development, since he was partly crippled by injuries suffered in earlier aviation accidents and of twice the age of the large majority of the pilots flying this aircraft. Not content to fly the specified maximum number of missions

— 215 —

reluctantly allocated him by the American Air Force under whose command his old reconnaissance group was then operating, he demanded and received permission to fly a few more. He perished on his ninth and presumably last allowable mission, a July 31, 1944 photographic reconnaissance over the Grenoble-Annecy area. Back at their Corsican base his fellow airmen, like their countrymen on the mainland, did not have to be reminded that not many men of their era could hold a greater claim to their admiration. He was lost without a trace, but much survived him, including, of course, his books. These had already secured for him a privileged place among the writers of his day.

One of these works was *Pilote de guerre* (1942). In it he compressed his experiences as a reconnaissance pilot during the 1940 collapse into a single symbolic flight to Arras at a time when «flight crews were being sacrificed like glasses of water poured onto a forest fire» (1). Everything about the mission defied logic because the rout was already so nearly complete that whatever military intelligence could have been collected would have been both useless and intransmissible. Telephone communications had been cut and the headquarters unit itself was on the move and in utter disarray. On the other hand, the comradeship of fighting men brooked no restraint, one's bonds to one's nation were all the more sacred when she lay prostrate, and a man's mettle can best be proven when conditions are worst. So, if the order for the mission was absurd, the mission itself was sacred and would have to be executed regardless of the cost in blood. All of this is articulated in the author's philosophic and moralistic musings, clothed in language of rare poetic beauty, and heightened by a note of tender warmth

---

(1) Antoine de Saint-Exupéry, *Pilote de guerre* (New York: Éditions de la Maison Française, 1942), p. 12.

and sincerity. And however obscene Saint-Exupéry would have reckoned the prospect of his emerging from the ruins of 1940 as a model of heroism and humanity, he does so emerge. As for the book itself, it has justly been placed on the highest shelf of the ever-growing library of fiction and documentaries on aerial warfare.

In the ranks of Frenchmen who found inspiration for books in the 1939-1945 war none more closely resembles Saint-Exupéry than does Jules Roy, author of more than thirty books and recipient in 1969 of France's Grand Prix des Lettres. Roy was born in Rovigo, Algeria, of humble parents whose own parents settled in that land in 1850. He received his early schooling, first at Staoueli, then at Aïn-Taya on the shores of the Mediterranean. At the age of eleven he entered a Lazarist seminary school in the suburbs of Algiers, more with the intention of being well taught than of initiating preparation for a priestly career. At twenty he was drafted into the army, where he answered a vocation begotten of a youthful but serious yearning to prove himself in combat, as his brothers had done in the Great War, and of his readings in Caesar, Montluc, Tolstoy, and Psichari.

Embracing military life wholeheartedly from the outset, Roy quickly rose to the rank of second lieutenant of infantry. During the inter-war years he did virtually all of his soldiering in France. History, he thought, was being slow about providing battles, and though a soldier through and through, in time he wearied of training cycles and of thankless expeditions to put down civil strife. In 1935, to counteract «the dull brew of peace,» he joined the air corps. The 1940 *débâcle* found him at Saint-Étienne-de-Saint-Geoirs (Isère), from which station he flew to Nîmes, to Perpignan, and finally to North Africa.

During the summer of that year he composed a series of poems later used by him as a device for making the acquaintance of Saint-Exupéry. These were combined to make up a slender volume which appeared in 1945 under the comprehensive title *Chants et prières pour les pilotes*. With these free verse poems—they are in reality prose only slightly transposed—Roy unselfconsciously celebrates France's war pilots in pious, tender accents reflective of deep inner feeling. He pledges fidelity to the fallen, appeals for divine protection for the living, who ask nothing better than the chance to avenge their departed comrades, and exalts them all for their abnegation and their pluck in the face of danger. He invokes God's pity for these winged warriors whose toils in the skies have, to his mind, been insufficiently understood. Innocent of prosodic intent, of meager poetic substance, his apostrophe-laden, rhetorical poems are redeemed by their freshness and spontaneity as well as by the honest ring of their message.

One turns to Roy's autobiographic essay *Le Métier des armes* (1948) for an account of his soldierly experience from the time of his return to Algeria until his arrival in England in late October, 1943, as a volunteer for duty in the Royal Air Force. Loyal to the Vichy government—he believed that it salvaged about as much as the circumstances allowed—for several years he commanded a reconnaissance squadron at Sétif. After the Allied invasion of North Africa in November 1942, he switched his allegiance to the Allies. First, owing to a shortage of planes and equipment, he was appointed commandant of a noncom training school. Then, restored to the air forces, he became deputy commander of a small bomber group, only to be thwarted again when it was dissolved, prompting his offer to serve in the then recruiting R.A.F. in any capacity whatsoever.

As his book clearly bears out, the author, neither a military opportunist nor a mercenary but rather a very conscientious soldier for whom discipline had the force of religion, wrestled hard if not long with his conscience before fixing upon a course of action on North Africa's D-Day. How, Roy asked himself, was he to act, he an aviator with a plane at hand and with an order ringing in his ears from a government endorsed by him to resist waves of men that were invading only to hasten the defeat of the same forces that had earlier crushed his countrymen? He spins and respins the threads of his argument through some ninety desultory pages. It nevertheless manages to hang together, and may be summarized as follows: Since an army's *raison d'être* is the defense of a nation's interests, the army is subordinate to the nation. Also, discipline is the backbone of the army, just as automatic obedience is the backbone of discipline. Hence, nothing can be in greater opposition to the efficiency of the army and therefore to the welfare of the nation than the soldier's arrogation of the right to exercise his own discretionary powers. But if the nation's first interest consists in getting itself out from under an oppressor's heel, can the army be acting in the nation's service if it seeks to prevent the same? Inasmuch as an affirmative answer is inadmissible, the soldier is left free to decide for himself where his duty lies, which duty will rest upon honor.

Many years later Roy further discussed his switch of allegiance in his *Le Grand Naufrage* (1966), a book mainly concerned with the trial of Marshal Pétain. For De Gaulle himself he was never to have as much affection as respect, yet he was only too happy to return to combat under the sign of the Cross of Lorraine that was painted on his Halifax bomber. Hindsight had convinced Roy that in 1940-1944 «Charles XI,» as he dubbed him, had shown himself to be a greater man than «Philippe VII.» Nothing, however, altered his conviction that, far form being a traitor, Pétain had been a shield for France in years when she also had need of a sword, and he remained persuaded that he himself had acted properly in serving the shield before enlisting in the service of the sword. But, for the courtiers at Vichy he had nothing but contempt.

The history of those and of later years would not be lacking in examples of the profound effects of the subversion of military discipline on the one hand and of its sustention on the other. Roy had himself more than once applauded De Gaulle's refusal, in June 1940, to lay down his arms, when instead he escaped to Britain to rally his compatriots to continue the fight. Conversely, in his book *J'accuse le général Massu* (1972), he vehemently denounced not only Massu but also other high-ranking officers for their dissidence in the late stages of the Algerian War, damning their refusal to obey orders as both dishonorable and entirely contrary to the national interest. And where the salutary breaching of the laws of discipline is concerned, he would not have had to be reminded of how much the face of history might have been changed if, like von Choltitz in August 1944, more German generals had allowed the dictates of their conscience to prevail over the oath of allegiance they had sworn to Hitler, and if Himmler («treuer Heinrich»), Adolf Eichmann, Rudolf Hoess, and other such literal-minded men in uniform could have perceived that disobedience is sometimes both the part of honor and the guarantor of a man's humanity.

Le Métier des armes also offers an excellent portrait of Jules Roy the soldier, who admits to having been strongly influenced by Renan's grandson, Ernest Psichari, and by Vigny, whose *Servitude et grandeur militaires* he had not read until 1942. Certainly he has much in common with each. Like Psichari, he is in his proper element in the army. Like him too, he loves to give orders, readily effaces himself before the demands of discipline, esteems soldiering in all its forms as an art, is sustained by his pride of accomplishment, and thrives on the army's Spartan exertions, its spit-and-polish, and its ceremonial. And is not, for example, this passage from *Le Métier des armes* pure Psichari?

> I believed that I was meant for great things. Whenever I would lead off a squad behind me, a feeling of rapture put rhythm into my strides, and the simple songs that rose from our ranks would billow in poetic swells. I dreamt that someday I would be able to impart my military ardor to larger numbers of men, and when I marched through villages on parade, I was as excited and as proud as if I were the parade leader of a victorious army (2).

What principally separates Roy from Psichari is that he, unlike the latter, makes no attempt to link soldiering with prayer and gives no spiritual connotations to military mystique.

A number of parallels in the lives of Vigny and Roy stand out. Both were at a very young age captivated by elders' tales of military prowess, devoured books exalting the military virtues, and lamented being born too late to participate in the glorious campaigns just terminated. In Vigny's case, Bourbon kings Louis XVIII and Charles X had sheathed the sword of Napoleon Bonaparte, so that the army had become for him a wooden horse inside of which he was suffocating, a «wooden horse that never opened in any Troy» (3). Both chose military careers drunk on dreams of future battles and considered themselves cheated because their dreams were not being fulfilled. Of cardinal significance in any comparison of the two men are their attitudes toward their own military careers in particular and their views on the profession of arms in general. In *Servitude et grandeur*

---

(2) Jules Roy, *Le Métier des armes* (Paris: Gallimard, 1948), p. 34.
(3) Alfred de Vigny, *Servitude et grandeur militaires*, ed. Gauthier Ferrières (Paris: Bibliothèque Larousse, n.d.), p. 107.

militaires, Vigny, who partook of army life for thirteen years, deplores having brought to soldiering a contemplative nature wholly unsuited to it and speaks of his «useless love of arms, the prime cause of one of the greatest disappointments of my life» (4). On the other hand, Roy, far from regarding his military career as a mistake, guilelessly writes, «My ambition is not to free myself from it but to draw myself nearer to it so as to find my strength in it» (5). He is very much the born soldier who needs the rigors of physical effort and the compulsions of discipline in order to fulfill himself.

Vigny and Roy alike see the soldier's true grandeur less in his courage or his endurance in battle than in his daily self-sacrifice, in his resignation and abnegation—the last a «heavier cross than that of a martyr» (6). Each regularly returns to the theme of the citizen's ingratitude in scorning in peacetime his wartime savior as a good-for-nothing idler who shakes off his lethargy from time to time by taking potshots at his rioting compatriots. And so long as parade exercises on the Champ-de-Mars were to exhaust the energies that Vigny would have conserved for the battle-field, he could not but equate soldiering with servitude, and soldiers with slaves. Though writing with profound reverence of the martyrs making up the army, the Romantic poet placed the soldierly life second only to capital punishment amongst the consummate relics of barbarism. Roy, for his part, does complain of overlong subjection to the blunting training chores of peacetime, but the army ever remains for him an object of love.

With nine months of unhurriedly scrupulous British training behind him, Jules Roy's thirst for combat was at

---

(4) *Ibid.,* p. 20.
(5) Roy, *Le Métier des armes,* p. 15.
(6) De Vigny, *Servitude et grandeur militaires,* p. 28.

last assuaged. Attached in the capacity of ship captain-bombardier to a French group flying with the R.A.F., he took part in thirty-seven missions over the Continent during a six-month span beginning on September 9, 1944. Out of this experience grew his two much acclaimed war books, *La Vallée heureuse,* winner of the Prix Renaudot for 1946, and *Retour de l'enfer* (1951).

The earlier book is aptly entitled, since the Ruhr Valley, destination of twenty of the author's war flights, had been ironically christened «Happy Valley» by R.A.F. pilots duly respectful of its formidable defenses. Perhaps best classified as a *récit,* its loose framework contains six episodes. One romantic interlude excepted, all revolve about bombing missions. Easily recognizable in Chevrier, the book's central character, is Roy himself, who probably assumed this guise with the aim of giving general extension to one man's experience. Apart from this fictive accretion and a few less obvious ones, *La Vallée heureuse* is rooted in lived reality. *Retour de l'enfer,* all fact, and made up of the jottings that Roy pencilled between murderous rounds of flights, briefings, and debriefings, betrays its spontaneity in clipped, unfurbished phrases which, together with the difference of form, most distinguish it from its predecessor. However, otherwise their similarity is such that they may be dealt with as a single unit.

Bomber warfare supplies much raw substance with which to hold the attention of the reader. Its tactical complexity, the omnipresent but not always visible dangers associated with it, and the fascinating code names sputtered out to crews over the inter-plane radio (Roy had to grapple with such cabalistic phrases as «big boys» and «lemon pie»), have a pulling power of their own. The works under discussion are, to be sure, rich in such substance. If, however, Roy's books on this form of combat are raised well above the level of the usual fare, this is because he is blessed with a sure eye, a sensitivity of spirit, and a gift for verbal expression. The reader soon acquires a due appreciation for the risks braved by these airborne technicians of warfare and is moved by the somber descriptiveness of many such passages as: «The wing circled about, emerged from the four winds in black swarms, fell into formation little by little and became an enormous, snarling beast that drew taut its limbs and pressed onward to do battle» (7).

Compelling as are his evocative powers, Roy's special domain is the psychological. It is because of his knack of seeing into the deeper recesses of the soul that he has been able to transform into uncommonly authoritative testimonies on war what could easily have remained bare chronicles. Bomber warfare was to Jules Roy a revelation and a bitter disappointment. He had been thirsting for the man-to-man combat in which French captains from Bayard to Marin la Meslée had distinguished themselves, but his R.A.F. assignment ruled out that possibility. Of what account, he time and again intimated, was individual initiative when the precondition of a successful mission was everyone's unquestioning execution of the minutest orders laid down by the briefing officer? Of what importance judgment balances when Bomber Command, sometimes weeks in advance, had established for one's Halifax a rigid itinerary, situating it in space to the mile and minute? How was a man to measure his courage, strength, and skill if his weapons consisted of maps, compasses, levers, and push buttons? Where the flush of victory for a warrior lost in the anonymity of a thousand crews swept along in a vast bomber stream? Where the adventure? Where the luster, the romance, if there were no liberated women to be kissed? Scarcely surprising is it, then, that the author should suggest

---

(7) Jules Roy, *La Vallée heureuse* (Paris: Gallimard, 1946), p. 53.

the joylessness of his work by comparing himself to a miner routinely descending into the pit. This «industrial war,» these factory-like airdromes with their wheels grinding day and night, depressed him no end.

And poisoning all was the fear that gnawed relentlessly at these «angels of death»: fear of crashes and collisions, of ack-ack, of winds that push the aircraft off course; fear nourished by harsh statistics and by visions of flaming bombers. Fear accompanies them into their planes, into their Nissen huts, into the English villages. Even while fishing on the banks of a little stream they cannot entirely divest themselves of it. They are taut, frugal of words at the take off, nervous and short-tempered during the away flight, but loosen up a good deal once the bombs have been released, and remain fairly calm on the homeward run. If, back on terra firma, they at all indulge a sense of victory, it is because of the satisfaction of knowing that they had not flinched over the target; because, too, the law of averages had once more failed to catch up with them. They neither strut nor swagger. Yes, they do visit the local pubs, give an occasional party, do cut a caper now and then. For the most part, however, they are sober-minded, pensive, and introspective. They find little to laugh about in war. That their temperamental kinship with their English-speaking R.A.F. brothers is scant, Roy is well aware. One of the characters of *Retour de l'enfer* explains this by pointing out that, with an average age of thirty, French crews were generally eight years older than their Anglo-Saxon counterparts (8). In this connection one does well to recall that Roy himself was thirty-eight when flying out of his Elvington (Yorkshire) base. To add that the dominant note of these two war books is one of gloom is to state the quite obvious. Finally,

---

(8) Jules Roy, *Retour de l'enfer* (Paris: Gallimard, 1952), p. 101.

15

in his successful attempt to convey to the spectator the impact of this horrendous business upon the souls of the actors, the author is ably served not only by his strict candor but also, and especially, by a style whose unpretentious sobriety he adapts with equal facility to meditative meanderings, the flow of narrative, and the painting of frescoes.

It is, of course, common knowledge that combat soon rid bomber personnel of any air force, Allied or enemy, of any illusions they may have had about the allure of «the wild blue yonder»; that, furthermore, these busy technicians, charged with the execution of highly complex and dangerous missions, did not usually worry overmuch about their obliteration of lives of innocent civilians merged in an impersonal, invisible mass thousands of feet below. There is no evidence that Roy looked at the matter much differently. But if the night missions in which he took part over the heavily defended industrial heart of Europe did leave him with some spiritual scars, he was at least spared the sight of the holocausts of fire-bombed Hamburg (July 25-August 3, 1943)—«Operation Gomorrha»—and of Dresden (February 13-14, 1945); of Dresden in particular, where P.O.W. Kurt Vonnegut, Jr., was put to work as a «corpse miner» extricating from the devastated city's rubble the bodies of some of the 135,000 persons killed by R.A.F. and Eighth Air Force raids in a time span of twelve hours and fifteen minutes, an event which made of him a confirmed pacifist and has haunted his consciousness ever since. Surely Roy's gloom could only have deepened if he, like some bomber crews, had had occasion to see the glare from the Mardi Gras (February 13) and Ash Wednesday-Saint Valentine's Day (February 14) fire-bombing of Dresden for as long as thirty minutes after passing over the city (9). We cannot tell from Roy's writings

(9) Reported in David Irving, *The Destruction of Dresden* (New

how he felt about those controversial raids, since he does not comment on them. What we do know is that no doubts assailed him with respect to the legitimacy of the type of warfare in which he was engaged, and there is ample reason for believing that he was fortified in his work by his recollection of what Luftwaffe bombings had done to Warsaw, Rotterdam, London, and Coventry before Allied bombs began to rain on «Festung Europa.»

Clearly the bomber plane was not fulfilling the role that Victor Hugo, extraordinary prophet that he often was, had foreseen for the airplane. Eighty years earlier, in the poem «Plein ciel» of his *La Légende des siècles,* Hugo had predicted the advent of the airplane and had conferred the name «aeroscaphe» on it. Where he erred, however, was in his further prediction that this «august plow of the clouds,» this «floating Louvre» would so acquaint man with man that all frontiers would thereby be obliterated and, with them, the law of blood and iron. What the great poet had failed to envision was the possibility that one day enormous flotillas of flying boats would be streaming high over national boundaries, laden with bomb-loads capable of obliterating whole cities in a day or night.

Neither through his own lips nor through those of his comrades does Roy indulge in grand talk about patriotism. But his Chevrier sorely misses France—so much so that the reader cannot help wondering if there is not a bit of pose in his relative insensitivity to the beauties of the English countryside as well as in his abuse of the leitmotif word «exil»—and Chevrier is grateful for the chance to finally

York: Holt, Rinehart and Winston, 1963), p. 146. A pilot who participated in the Dresden bombing states: «At 20,000 feet we could see details in the unearthly blaze that had never been visible before; for the first time in many operations I felt sorry for the population below» p. 142.

commune with compatriots heroically resisting the occupiers when a mission over the Nord has him dropping bombs on railroad facilities. Agonizing as his daily task is, he affirms without resort to declamation that he is satisfied that in the manner most suited to him he is helping to ensure the future liberty of France and of the world. Nazis he hates as the enemies of humanity, but he manifests a brotherly sympathy for German combatants exposed to the same dangers as himself. But to all heavy talk about the war he clearly prefers the absorption of a detective story.

Roy's *Comme un mauvais ange* (1947) may be classified as an extended meditation on man's conquest of the air. Recollecting wistfully the good old days when, suspended in the atmosphere in a little plane, he could lazily sort out the landmarks of the Algerian farm on which he grew up, his spirit is darkened by the thought that war had made the airplane the symbol of man's sometimes diabolic genius. The same stars whose matchless beauty once dazzled the aviator have become but beacons on his route to battle; whereas men used to fly to achieve a leisurely self-revelation, they now are swiftly dispatched into the skies to demolish whole cities. Roy, who believes humans too cursed with a faculty for forgetting their own worst calamities to warrant any great optimism in regard to war abolishment, then goes on to predict that pilots will yield to robots in wars to come. In spite of all, he contends that wars are bound to end someday, since the immensity of the suffering engendered of each of them can only serve to bring about the eventual reconciliation of nations.

The title of Roy's *Passion de Saint-Exupéry* (1951) implies the measure of the spiritual affinity he feels vis-à-vis the deceased poet-hero. A work of unabashed glorification, it was yet another contribution to the secular canonization of «St.-Ex.» Roy, who enjoyed but five fleeting contacts with

Saint-Exupéry, all at the Laghouat, Algeria, airfield, brings to light nothing of note about the man himself or his message. He panegyrizes him as an *engagé* and as the greatest of the age's *chevaliers*. Careful to emphasize that as an ex-participant in bomber warfare he does not himself qualify as a *chevalier,* he is of the opinion that the species is now extinct everywhere save in tanks and in fighter or reconnaissance planes. These were the Galahads, Lancelots, and Tristrams of the new age. That he secretly envies the Hillarys and the Clostermanns who could charge off to clean, direct, individual battle on the wings of their sleek Spitfires and Typhoons is obvious.

A too visible schematism and, for him, an uncharacteristically rigid style make of Roy's three-act play, *Beau Sang* (1952), a middling production. Be that as it may, it commands attention to the extent that it further illuminates this man in arms. In true Exupérian fashion, the conflict here is between discipline and laxity, between duty and temptation. The protagonist is Pierre d'Aumont, a soldier-monk bound by vows of poverty, chastity, and obedience. The action takes place in 1307, immediately after Philippe le Bel has ordered the disbandment of the Knights Templar. Wounded by the king's men tracking him down, a Templar veteran of Crusade fighting takes refuge in a château. Just when he is on the verge of succumbing to the charms of one of the two women shielding him, a younger Templar arrives and proceeds to reimpress him with the singleness of his sworn devotion. Inasmuch as the soldiers peopling Roy's earlier war books have either no interest in women or only a very ephemeral one, it is pretty much in the natural order of things that D'Aumont should elect to return to his closed life of battle and prayer. For having disgraced his order he willingly submits to a whipping by the younger man, who is his hierarchal inferior, and to his decree that he no more carry into combat the gonfalon of the Templars, as he had been privileged to do for a score of years.

But all walls are breached sooner or later. Suffering from battle fatigue, the navigator protagonist of Roy's novelette *Le Navigateur* (1954) was to find solace and a little peace in the arms of a young Englishwoman. Also, an airman in a second novelette, *La Femme infidèle* (1955), was to violate an unwritten law of comradeship by seducing a mate's wife. Here, however, we are back to the Roy of the old dispensation. The book's moral: women and airplanes, equally tyrannous of attention, simply do not mix. The adulteress, Hélène Ferrer, had betrayed her flyer husband because he had betrayed her with his passion for his *métier*.

It is in their stances on current affairs that Roy and Saint-Exupéry most part company. For all his commitment to man and to justice, Saint-Exupéry scrupulously maintained political and ideological neutrality in speech and in print, often exasperating his friends by his refusal—usually in the name of human reconciliation—to give public voice to his sympathies. And who but he could, as an eyewitness reporter on events of the Spanish Civil War, so describe them that it was not at all easy for his readers to distinguish loyalists from revolutionaries? Who but he could have urged them to «forget the Sudetenland for a few hours» in writing October 1938 articles for *Paris-Soir* on the Czechoslovakian crisis? (10).

Not Roy, to be sure. Again and again in his books, articles, and public pronouncements he has not only made his views known on issues of the day but he has fought assiduously in the public arena to defend justice wherever it was threatened—whether in the streets and courthouses

---

(10) See Jean-Louis Major's *Saint-Exupéry: l'écriture et la pensée* (Ottawa: Éditions de l'Université d'Ottawa, 1968), pp. 221-24.

of Paris, the jungles of Indochina, or the mountains of Algeria. So strong were Roy's objections to the type of war his country had been waging in Indochina, of which he had been a reportorial witness for three months, that he resigned his commission as a colonel, thus terminating his twenty-five year career in the French military. And there are more than intimations of his sentiments on colonialism and its abuses in the six volumes of his cyclic novel *Les Chevaux du soleil* (1967-1975). In it the lives of generations of *pied noir* and Moslem characters evolve against the background of French Algeria throughout its entire 1830-1962 history.

There is, then, good reason to regard this disciple of Saint-Exupéry as his most worthy successor. That is not to suggest, however, that Roy is the artistic equal of the man commonly referred to as «the Conrad of the air.» In point of intellectual breadth, of philosophic depth, their works are hardly comparable. Chevrier is no Rivière, and Roy himself is neither the engaging moralist nor the exquisite poet that his predecessor was, even if he can make his readers feel the throb of battle in the skies, give graphic representation to the sinister beauty of aerial armadas in night flight, and do much else with uncommon artistry.

The Almost Incredible Pierre Clostermann

It is Pierre Clostermann who most merits title as spokesman for France's fighter pilots of the Second World War. He had fought under French colors in the Royal Air Force's Fighter Command, as had Pierre Mendès-France and semi-legendary figures René Mouchotte and Max Guedj. But Mendès-France had not seen enough action to garner many combat laurels and Mouchotte and Guedj had been killed. Also killed in action was Marin La Meslée, premier ace of the French Air Force, later the Free French Air Force. Published posthumously in 1950, *Les Carnets de René Mouchotte* made dull reading. Of substance this war diary had more than enough, but its flat style, its want of emotional content, and Mouchotte's extreme reserve regarding his own accomplishments were not calculated to attract a large number of readers. On the other hand, the combination of Clostermann's immense war-won fame and his lively war book, *Le Grand Cirque* (1948), had plenty to attract them, and did.

While Clostermann's reputation as the Guynemer of World War II needed no reinforcement, his book surely did not detract from it. Like such war books as Wouk's *The Caine Mutiny* and Monsarrat's *The Cruel Sea, Le Grand Cirque* well exemplifies the ability of the reading public to make up its own mind. And if these other two works received no better than a mixed press, Clostermann's fared even worse, drawing only a minimun of comment from the professional critics, and that of a decidedly lukewarm sort. This could not, however, keep it from becoming a best-seller almost overnight and from registering sales of 527,000 copies in France alone in the seven years following its appearance (11).

The only child of Alsatian diplomat Jacques Clostermann and of a Lorrainese, Pierre was born on February 28, 1921, in Curitiba, Brazil. At that time his father was serving as France's Consul General at Rio de Janeiro. The future war hero acquired his early education at a private school in Boulogne-sur-Seine, making annual crossings to Brazil in the summer. In June 1940 he interrupted his research in aeronautics at the Ryan Aeronautical Company in San Diego, California, to go to England. Meanwhile, his father was making his way to Brazzaville in French Equatorial Africa to join a unit of the Free French Forces. The year 1942 was

---

(11) See «Les Plus Forts Tirages de l'édition française depuis dix ans,» *Les Nouvelles Littéraires,* April 7, 1955, pp. 1, 4.

to see Clostermann abandon the studies in political science that he had undertaken at Oxford to enlist in the R.A.F. Already a licensed pilot with five years' flying experience, he nonetheless underwent the R.A.F.'s characteristically long and meticulous training before being assigned to Fighter Squadron 341 of the celebrated Alsace Group commanded by René Mouchotte. Late in the year this group was attached to the R.A.F.'s élite Biggin Hill Squadron. The challenge was implicit. Clostermann more than met it.

As a fighting airman he was the very personification of *furia francese*. His accomplishments as a pilot of Spitfires and Tempests read like fiction and his personal legend continued to grow apace. By V-E Day «Clo-Clo,» as he was incongruously called by his R.A.F. mates, had flown 420 missions, during which he confirmedly shot down 33 enemy planes and scored 12 «probables.» He was credited with damaging or destroying another 30, as well as some 72 locomotives, 225 trucks, 5 tanks, 2 torpedo boats, and one submarine. While engaged in all this frenetic fighting he suffered only minor injuries. Promoted to squadron commander in early 1945, no mean honor for a foreigner, he was demobilized in August of the same year. The most decorated French flyer of World War II, ace of France's aces in the war, and a *Grand Officier de la Légion d'Honneur,* his highest wartime rank, unbelievable as it must seem, was that of lieutenant (12). This slight he blames not on the R.A.F. but rather on the indifference of the French chair-borne superiors concerned. But lest there be any misapprehension, it should be noted that he was no greedy collector of trophies, medals, citations, and promotions, as his glorious German

(12) Clostermann is today a lieutenant-colonel in the reserve of the French Air Force.

and French World War I antecedents, Baron Manfred von Richthofen and René Fonck, had been.

The war over, this indomitable warrior decided to channel his natural combativity into the political arena. In 1946 he was elected deputy from the Bas-Rhin to the National Constituent Assembly, becoming, at twenty-five, its youngest member. An ardent Gaullist, he piled victory on victory at the ballot box until he resigned his office in September 1969. In 1955 French gunmen made an attempt upon the life of Clostermann, a strong backer of Moroccan Sultan Ben Yussef, who had been deposed two years earlier (13). As an officer in the reserve of the Armée de l'Air he saw flight duty in Algeria in 1956-57. In addition, he has occupied a number of key posts related to national defense, has pursued an independent career as an engineer and test pilot, and has served on the boards of a number of large industrial corporations. Although he had quite enough to keep him busy during those years, he managed to write two more war books: *Feux du ciel* (1951), a history in the form of *récits* of the air war of 1939-45, and *Appui-feu sur l'oued Hallâïl* (1960), in which he described the Algerian War as seen by him from the air.

In his preface to *Le Grand Cirque* Clostermann discloses that, initially, much of its content was intended for just two readers, his mother and father. But unable, owing to military censorship and mailing restrictions, to familiarize his parents adequately with the life that he might lose as a fighter pilot, he undertook to keep a day-to-day record of it in a thick Air Ministry notebook. He had, it is not to be wondered at, filled three such notebooks before leaving uniform. Because this miraculous survivor subsequently came to feel honor-

---

(13) See Alexander Werth, *The Strange History of Pierre Mendès-France and the Great Conflict over French North Africa* (London: Barrie Books, 1957), p. 211.

bound to communicate, both directly and inferentially, the heroic deeds of his many deceased flying compatriots to their families, as well as to help rekindle in Frenchmen the flame of national pride and faith, he pared down his notes, strung them together, and published them as *Le Grand Cirque*.

Few readers will support the author's contention that his book depicts the typical military experience of Free French pilots. Certainly there was a sameness about their daily lives, with their alternation of monotonous waiting in dispersal and of the bustle of combat; certainly too, those who lived long enough could, like Clostermann, tell of bolted lunches, screaming dogfights, hit-and-run raids, solo prowls in the sky, train strafing, bomber escorts, and uneventful patrol flying. However, the difference, which obviously lies in the measure of Clostermann's achievement, doubtless had no small part in making *Le Grand Cirque* a phenomenal sales success. For how many pilots could tell of singlehandedly shooting down three planes and damaging two in forty minutes, or claim four planes shot down and a submarine run aground in a day?

Understandably, then, in reducing for publication the mass of his wartime jottings, he has for the most part retained the more interesting and exciting episodes of his combat career. Nevertheless, the choice of these was not made with a view to self-dramatization, since some of the missions described focus exclusively upon the feats of his mates and in others he emerges as less a hero than a goat. The resultant work is exceedingly difficult to classify. It might best be viewed as both a war diary and logbook if the definition of each is stretched to the limit. The difficulty is that only a tenth of his 420 official sorties enter the picture, a goodly proportion of them only incidentally, and less than two-thirds are dated, with the intervals varying from a day to weeks and even months.

It is, of course, a truism that, whatever the appeal of a book's subject matter, it is the manner of its presentation that counts in the long run. Stated otherwise, *Le Grand Cirque* would have gone the way of countless other war books had not Clostermann had a knack for conveying his dramatic experiences to the reader. His narrative, aside from some long passages that supply historical perspective to blocks of entries, passages admittedly composed long after the fact, wears an air of staccato spontaneity. The writing is matter-of-fact and unpretentious but rarely ungainly. Swift, elliptic inter-plane dialogues, in English, seasoned with colorful R.A.F. jargon, are fused in with rough, unpolished descriptive tracts. Episodes reappear in the book with the same freshness and formlessness with which they were scribbled down on the spot. The mood of the moment is caught and the reader is made to feel like an eyewitness of this war without quarter.

Pressing on with his descriptions of epic battles, of planes whirling about the sky in hot pursuit of one another, Clostermann gives evidence of being so concerned with accurately setting down the swift succession of his thoughts and emotions that any consideration of literary effect is strictly secondary. He is quite content to compare parachutes in descent with puffs of smoke, and the debris of shot-up planes with falling leaves, and to speak of Focke-Wulfs «flitting about like huge moths.» The goggled enemy pilot glimpsed at close range reminds him of a weird-looking insect, and as he dives into a dense concentration of enemy planes, with their «radial engines, yellow bellies, black crosses, and clipped wings beating the air like fins,» he has the impression of «diving into an aquarium of demented fish.» His visual imagination does occasionally summon forth such ornate miniatures as this: «Air duels: the graceful arabesques of a dance by silvery mosquitoes—diaphanous white lace of vapor trails—Focke-Wulfs gliding like toys in the infinite sky» (14). On the whole, though, he seldom resorts to colored writing, so that it strikes the reader that he has, as is his claim, done little dressing up of his actual wartime entries. Much of his book's charm is engendered precisely of this lack of finish, of this rough-edged spontaneity.

Despite its graphic richness and all the excitement underlying its narrative, *Le Grand Cirque* would seem to owe its popularity chiefly to its value as a human document. But in order to discover the personality behind these pages one cannot, as in reading the accounts of aerial warfare by Saint-Exupéry or Jules Roy, look to a store of philosophic reflection. Perhaps because of Clostermann's considerably younger age, perhaps also because he is by nature less introspective, and unquestionably because he had less time on his hands and a dissimilar objective in writing, the reader must find Clostermann the man within the terse comments that he injects into his primarily descriptive narrative. These are not few.

He writes without guile, holding back neither the good nor the bad about himself. If he sometimes tells of his calm in the thick of action, far more often he mentions a racing heartbeat, an outpouring of sweat, and the nausea of fear clutching at his throat. He will credit himself with a sound tactical maneuver, inveigh against himself for an imprudent one. Never after describing his exultation on the separate occasions of his first engagement with the enemy and of his first victory over him does he record his heroism with the faintest suggestion of heroics. His survival he attributes to the smiles of fortune, and he generously draws attention to Max Guedj, accounted by him the French Air Force's greatest World War II hero.

---

(14) Pierre Clostermann, *Le Grand Cirque* (Paris: Flammarion, 1948), p. 213.

As a class, war aces are not remarkable for their self-effacement. The glory-hungry Richthofen knew the value of a good press and acted accordingly. Fonck had much to brag about and bragged monumentally. Charles Nungesser was as cocky as he was courageous. Certainly Goering, who scored twenty-two victories during the First World War, did not then or ever believe that meek shall inherit the earth. Contrariwise, in his modesty Clostermann does not seek but incontestably merits a place at the side of Mouchotte, La Meslée, and—from the 1914-18 war—Guynemer and the Royal Flying Corps' Albert Ball and Edward Mannock.

Without his saying so in so many words, Clostermann did enjoy aerial combat. In fact, it is obvious that at times he found it breathtakingly exciting. In the air he never ran from a fight, however numerous the attackers; on the ground he invariably felt balked to learn that he had not been listed for what promised to be a challenging mission. One can sense in him a Fabrice del Dongo, an Alban de Bricoule, or a Henry Fleming—a youthful adventurer eager to rise to the occasion, to meet the supreme test, to measure his strength in the face of danger and death. And not until the closing months of hostilities, when the concentration of German flak had been so greatly increased as to largely nullify the factors of human skill and courage, did he grouse about the endless grind of fighting. This master of aerial tactics loved to match wits with the enemy, was quick to diagnose his blunders, and, after outmaneuvering him, to swoop in for the kill.

For Clostermann planes are obsessively fascinating. He takes an even livelier interest in them than is indigenous to the war pilot species. Ordinarily he dwells briefly on their distinguishing characteristics and gives revealing sidelights on their performance under battle conditions. From time to time, however, a page begins to take on the aspect of a manual on planes or on flight. He recognizes in a flash the make of the German plane attacking his own and is not infrequently awed by its symmetric beauty. About his own craft, faithful ally in his daily gambles with death, he speaks most lovingly. Witness this sad parting on the eve of Clostermann's demobilization in late August, 1945:

> I wanted to take «Le Grand Charles» for the trip to the Schleswig headquarters ... With it I climbed very high into the cloudless sky, because only there could I say goodbye to it.
> Together we rocketed upward one last time, straight toward the sun. We made a loop—two, perhaps—and a few very slow, fiddle-faddle, tender rolls, so that I might carry off in my fingers the vibration of its obedient and flexible wings.
> And I wept in its tight cockpit, like I shall never again weep as long as I live, when I felt the cement of the runway brush its wheels and when, with a great twist of my wrist, I settled it on the earth like a cut flower.
> As always, I carefully cleared its engine; one by one I switched off the contacts, then the landing lights; I removed the shoulder straps and the wires which had been binding me to it like a child to its mother. And when my pilots and my mechanics, who had been awaiting me, saw my sob-shaken lowered head and shoulders, they understood, and silently moved off to the dispersal area (15).

By and large Clostermann sees his war in the context of the mission at hand: its relative importance, its dangers, and its lessons. Now and then, nevertheless, he extends his gaze

---

(15) *Ibid.*, pp. 265-66.
Saint-Exupéry too speaks of a mother-infant relationship between pilot and plane: «... It is the plane that nourishes me.... Suckled by the plane itself, I feel a sort of filial tenderness for it. A sort of nursling tenderness.» *Pilote de guerre*, p. 45.

to embrace the overall strategic picture, as when he writes of the Normandy landings, the Rundstedt offensive, and the Remagen bridgehead operation. But his primary concern is with the scope and nature of the involvement of aerial forces in these battles. His remarks on Luftwaffe pilots and techniques are as illuminating as they are apposite, and he is intent upon disabusing his readers as to the validity of statistics published by public-opinion conscious Allied press services in the wake of great aerial engagements. He does not, as Saint-Exupéry did, resolutely search out the moral significance of his participation, merely resting content in the knowledge that he was doing the right thing at the right time. Having witnessed, as few have, human capacity for self-annihilation, was Clostermann, therefore, to feel that man had at last been rendered wise as to his unwisdom? Alas, this moving conclusion to *Le Grand Cirque* would seem to bear out the contrary:

> The Great Circus departed.
> The public was satisfied. The program was rather heavy, the actors were not too bad, and the lions devoured the trainer.
> It will be spoken about casually for a few more days. And even when all will be forgotten—the brass bands, the fireworks and the beautiful uniforms—there will remain on the village square the sawdust halo of the riding track and the peg holes.
> The rain and the short memory of men will quickly obliterate the traces (16).

One is left with the impression that this French fighter pilot regards his German counterparts less as enemies in a more usual sense than as adversaries in a deadly game, all of whom

---

(16) *Le Grand Cirque*, p. 282.

deserve respect by the very fact of their willingness to play at it; adversaries, furthermore, to whom esteem is due in proportion to the degree of demonstrated valor. In referring to them he employs no epithet more abusive than the almost universal «Boche,» and that without emotion. There is, to be sure, nothing very exceptional about looking at it this way, inasmuch as fighter pilots, with few exceptions, have always been inclined to regard themselves as a breed apart, having their own mystique, their own code of honor, their own rules of war and standards of gallantry. And if they have taken delight in their special mode of warfare, this is because they have indeed seen themselves as the last remnants of the age of chivalry, as knights in twentieth-century armor. Here is how one of their number, Cecil Lewis, who served as a Royal Flying Corps pilot throughout the Great War, describes it: «It was like the lists of the Middle Ages, the only sphere where a man saw his enemy and faced him in mortal combat, the only sphere where there was still chivalry and honour. If you won, it was your own bravery and skill; if you lost, it was because you had met a better man» (17). How different was their lot from that of infantrymen, pawns in the grip of forces beyond their control, who could at any moment be impersonally blasted to bits by an artillery shell or a bomb! And if the *poilus,* Tommies, and dogfaces could sympathize with their opposite numbers, brothers in the great fraternity of human suffering, in no way was theirs a sporting fraternity. In contrast, Clostermann,

---

(17) Cecil Lewis, *Sagittarius Rising* (n.p.: Giniger, 1936), p. 45. Cf. «... In a Spitfire we're back to war as it ought to be—if you can talk about war as it ought to be. Back to individual combat, to self-reliance, total responsibility for one's own fate. One either kills or is killed; and it's damn exciting.» Richard Hillary, *Falling through Space* (New York: Reynal and Hitchcock, 1942), p. 124.

16

speaking for himself and his comrades, shows us how a good soldier-aviator is supposed to behave when, toward the war's end, he learns of the death in action of one of the Luftwaffe's greatest heroes, twenty-two-year-old Lieutenant Colonel Walter Novotny. In a passage deploring the inhumanity of some of the duties a fighting airman is called upon to perform, he writes:

> Our revenge today is in saluting a brave enemy who has just died, in proclaiming that Novotny is ours, that he is of our orbit, one to which we admit neither ideologies, nor hatreds, nor frontiers. This type of camaraderie has nothing to do with patriotism, democracy, Nazism or humanity. On this evening all of these lads understand this instinctively. And if there be any souls who merely shrug their shoulders over this, that is because they cannot know—they aren't fighter pilots (18).

In sharp contrast with such chivalrous sentiments are the author's unmincing remarks in scattered passages of *Feux du ciel* on Wehrmacht and SS atrocities in wartime.

The reader would search in vain the pages of *Le Grand Cirque* for any literary play with patriotics. It is readily discernible that Clostermann believes only in a patriotism articulated in action, for he relies upon words only long enough to pay warm tribute to the patriotism and deeds of his fellow French airmen or to vent in caustic language his feelings about those apathetic Frenchmen who make light of their flying compatriots' sacrifices. His castigation of them, little need to add, implies the bitterness of his sentiments on the wartime conduct of the Bonnards, Célines, Darnands, and Doriots. In this connection it should be pointed out that upon being grounded on account of combat fatigue in

---

(18)   Clostermann, *Le Grand Cirque,* p. 214.

July 1944, Clostermann was assigned to the French Air Ministry in Paris, but feeling estranged in a headquarters atmosphere, with its sedentary combatants and its bureaucratic zealotry, he effected a return to active operations in December.

Le Grand Cirque sheds little light on the off-duty lives of R.A.F. pilots. The uninitiated reader will learn, but will almost have to read between the lines to do so, that these airmen ordinarily kill time pipe-smoking, listening to the radio, playing cards, and drinking at the mess bar; that, too, a unit's morale can always be accurately gauged by the volume of noise generated and drink consumed there. They are given to levity and buffoonery and inclined rather often to seek reprieve from vocational tension in the arms of the fair sex or in hard drinking at the nearest Red Lion or Black Horse. Clostermann himself appears to have been immune to the charms of village queens and of Piccadilly's temptresses alike. The favorite recreation of this young hero, who strikes the reader as being in some ways mature far beyond his years, seems to have been talking shop: planes, armaments, tactics, and combat experiences.

For four years Clostermann had been mining numberless official Allied military documents and privately published works in Europe and America in the preparation of his *Feux du ciel*. The nine *récits* comprising the book have been molded from the substance of this mass. Actuated by the will to win over self and by an inflexible sense of duty, the book's heroes, French, American, Canadian, Polish, German, and Japanese aviators, carry on in the face of ridiculous odds. What we have is a *tour d'horizon* of human bravery. Whereas such conspicuous personalities as Beurling and Guedj are shown fighting lionheartedly, the emphasis is not on glorification, since it is clearly brought out that, immeasurably more than the sensational feats of arms of some, it is the valor and dedication of the many, irrespective of their national origin and the causes for which they were fighting, that should compel our attention. While highlighting a number of examples of virtual miracles accomplished by greatly outnumbered Allied aviators in the war's early years, Clostermann, without going into the question at length or in depth, sharply criticizes the Armistice-induced neutralization of French naval and air forces. His talent for vivid description and for sustaining a narrative again impresses. And he cannot be said to have laid on the colors too thickly, ever a pitfall in this type of writing. For all that, the emotional impact of the true episodes recounted by him —true except for the words and reactions that he has had to lend to historically identifiable men, in most cases en route to flaming deaths— is slight. He is, to be sure, extraordinarily conversant with what he is writing about, yet the reader cannot help but be prejudicially aware of the synthetic aspect of the method.

Nor does Clostermann's *Appui-feu sur l'oued Hallaïl* (1960) approach the standard of *Le Grand Cirque*. It could scarcely have been otherwise, since the raw material at his disposal was much more meager. To begin with, in Algeria he could fight no duels in skies in which no enemy planes were flying, although there was no lack of antiaircraft and machine-gun fire. Besides, while piloting a jet was not without its attractions, having to do blind strafing and to bomb mountain villages to rubble was. For such work he had no stomach whatsoever. So it was only after he requested and effected a transfer to duty as an aerial observer and liaison flyer that his spirits rose.

In any case, without giving us another *Le Grand Cirque*, Clostermann again shows himself to be a writer of the first water on combat aviation, one who at the same time shuns false heroics and political and philosophical excursions. It matters not that the author appears in the pages of the book as Commandant Jacques Dorval, nor even that Clostermann has Dorval die on a lonely plateau after his plane is shot up by the *fellagha,* because the disguise is transparent. All too evident is the younger Clostermann's love of adventure in the skies, of the smell of oil and leather, and of the fraternity of winged warriors, however much Dorval may complain that advancing age, desert heat, and the unclean aspects of the warfare witnessed by him are exacting an exorbitant tribute from him. Finally, where identities are concerned, the book's many glossy photographs, in which the uniformed author figures prominently, tell their own revealing tale.

In summary, Clostermann's story is chiefly that of a boy who fought a man's war superlatively and portrayed it ably. He has not written deathless literature and as a writer on aviation he cannot be raised to the plane occupied by a Saint-Exupéry or a Malraux. But his subject was the realization of the human spirit in some of the most defiant circumstances imaginable, and he brought to it a verve, candor, integrity, and an untutored artistry which coalesced to do it justice and himself honor. Would it be fair to ask for more?

Chapter VI

FRENCH WRITERS LOOK AT «THE DIRTY WAR»

With the fall of the great fortified camp of Dien Bien Phu on May 7, 1954, France suffered one of the most ignominious defeats in her entire history. On that evening it was Berlioz' «Requiem» that was played by the nation's radio stations—not the «Marseillaise,» the «Marche lorraine,» the «Chant du départ,» or other stirring martial airs. Despite the numerical superiority of the French Expeditionary Force; despite direction by the élite of her generals and, at a lower level, by many hundreds of Saint-Cyrians; despite the expenditure of nearly twelve billion dollars by herself and her noncombatant but heavily involved American ally, she had gone down to defeat—defeat at the hand of an essentially peasant army without planes or tanks or warships and commanded by a professor of history turned general. As though this were not shattering enough to national pride, it was, as the late eminent student of the war, Bernard Fall, reminds us, the first time since the British defeat at Yorktown in 1781 that a colonial power had been bested in the field by one of its *protégés* (1). David had again slain Goliath.

---

(1) Bernard Fall, *Le Viet-Minh* (Paris: Armand Colin, 1960), p. 221.

A «sale guerre,» French communists promptly dubbed it and millions of Frenchmen of various political stripes would later call it—and such a war it was. Savagely fought, for eight years, over enormous expanses of the most treacherous terrain imaginable, at home it was, until the last few years, half ignored by a largely indifferent, ill-informed public, and only halfheartedly and inconsistently promoted by a government which stubbornly persisted in terming it a «policing operation» or a «pacification» and which was weary of its crippling drain on the national budget (2). But there were those who were not in the least indifferent and who actively opposed the war. Leftists and liberals sustained a loud chorus of protest against the continuation of hostilities. Antiwar demonstrations were not uncommon, war matériel was regularly sabotaged, and strikes and riots in French ports, while relatively few and not sustained for long, provided abundant grist for antiwar propaganda mills. The sentencing in 1952 of the young naval officer Henri Martin to five years of solitary confinement for authoring antiwar tracts and distributing them at the naval arsenal of Toulon brought Sartre, Hervé Bazin, Jean-Marie Domenach, Francis Jeanson, Michel Leiris, Jacques Prévert, Vercors, and other well-known writers running to his defense and demanding his reprieve and rehabilitation in their jointly authored volume L'Affaire Henri Martin (1953). It mattered little that the book, whose chief polemicist and forceful commentator was Sartre, appeared

---

(2) In his war diary La Naissance des mercenaires (Paris: Arthaud, 1970), published long after the conflict, paratroop captain Albert Merglen recorded bitterly that but 58 of 620 deputies had been present at the National Assembly on December 19, 1952, for an important debate on the critical Indochinese situation. January 17, 1953, p. 180.

For Merglen, the war was an utter waste. Analogizing in the manner of Churchill and in Churchillian cadences, he protested: «Never was more asked of an army for fewer reasons and fewer results» p. 259.

shortly after Martin was reprieved, since, as much as anything else, it was a collection of bitterly antiwar pieces that drew yet more attention to the crisis of conscience that a large segment of the nation was undergoing. Finally, from the beginning of the war to the end, the existentialist review *Les Temps Modernes* sustained a barrage of criticism against French promoters of it.

In contrast, Viet Minh fighters and their civilian supporters regarded the conflict as a sacred war, a war for independence, and prosecuted it in the spirit of monolithic solidarity which President Ho Chi Minh and General Vo nguyen Giap considered indispensable to victory. And when it all ended, seven and a half years later, 92,000 officers and men of the French Expeditionary Force were dead, and Cao Bang, Lang Son, and Dien Bien Phu were being written into French history books as crushing defeats.

Works of fiction and documentaries by French writers on the French Indochinese War have been comparatively few, a fact that can readily be understood in light of the small percentage of combatants from metropolitan France. Significantly, only slightly more than thirty per cent of the garrison that had defended Dien Bien Phu were French nationals. Nonetheless, these works shed a great deal of light on the war itself and on the thinking of the men who fought it. With this in mind and with an eye to weighing their value as literature, let us look into their pages.

High grade fiction on the Indochinese conflict has been of scant output. One of the better novels based on it, *La 317ᵉ Section,* by Dien Bien Phu veteran Pierre Schoendoerffer, a paratrooper sergeant who had gone to Indochina as an army cameraman, provided the scenario for a much commended war movie of the same name, directed by Schoendoerffer himself. In his novel he describes vividly but without sensationalism the tribulations and gradual destruction by the Viet Minh of a column of loyalist Laotians commanded by four Europeans on a week-long forced march through a steamy jungle. Schoendoerffer's characters grouse like warriors in the flesh and are as foulmouthed. Like them too, they all but completely avoid verbalizing their thoughts on the war in which they are caught up. Instead, they doggedly carry on in spite of their hopeless isolation from the world without, in spite of futility and frustration and the seeming pointlessness of it all. The novelist hardly wastes a word in faithfully recreating the atmosphere of jungle war, of war fought on a small scale, the while making effective use of such character stereotypes as a pea-green lieutenant fresh out of Saint-Cyr and of an old, battle-hardened adjutant for whom war is an exalting *métier*. Only a few gratuitously macabre scenes, reminiscent of Barbusse at his worst, prevent this story from being a work of total integrity.

A first novel, Laurent La Praye's *La Trompette des anges* (1956), scarcely identifies itself as such. Art in the rough —yet no less effective art—propped by an unmistakable narrative talent and by keen psychological insights, marks the book. With a sure hand La Praye sketches the colorful portraits of four officers and a noncom engulfed by the vortex of war. Sated with the monotony of his daily living, Gérard, a young French doctor and the novel's central figure, comes to Indochina to test his strength on the anvil of war. Test it he does, but not for long, since he is trapped and killed in a Viet ambush just three days after his arrival in the Far East. Before he dies, however, he has ample time to observe how variously those about him have adjusted or failed to adjust to the war which hedges them in on all sides and is devouring them all. Moreover, having been unable to adjust to one another, they have condemned themselves to a solitude of the soul that erodes them quite as effectively as does the military enemy.

In the central episode of Michel Tauriac's novel *Le Trou* (1955), French armored troops are heavily engaged by the Viet Minh after villagers in league with it have prepared the ground for a sneak attack on them. The book's youthful author succeeds in making the reader see the war as it was and the warriors as they were. Himself a veteran of the conflict, Tauriac portrays it without political bias or preconceived notions. He is at his best when he eulogizes his former comrades in arms or when he directs shafts at the home front. His fair-mindedness, rare powers of observation, profound sensitivity, and the impressive flexibility of his style serve him well.

René Hardy's *Le Fer de Dieu* (1953) is perhaps the best of the numerous novels for whose action the war merely supplies a background. Hardy, who was not an eyewitness in Indochina, describes the herculean efforts of a former international revolutionary newly arrived in Indochina first to find, then to effect a reconciliation with his brother, a Benedictine monk. Danger lurks at every turn of the road, everybody mistrusts everybody else, and mystery shrouds everything as gunrunners ply their sordid trade and as men of ideals combat moral rot as relentlessly as they combat the enemy in the field. Though occasionally marred by heavy melodramatic accents, Hardy's absorbing novel of adventure is more than a little reminiscent of the novels of Malraux in its action and in its preoccupation with man's solitude, his struggle to give meaning to his life through personal heroism, and his helplessness in the face of death.

Although not any of the six installments of Jean Hougron's cycle *La Nuit indochinoise* may be classified as a war novel, the action of three of them, *Tu récolteras la tempête* (1951), *Soleil au ventre* (1952), and *Mort en fraude* (1953), is tightly interwoven with the war. Hougron's tough-talking, danger-loving, swashbuckling, sensual heroes thrive in the kind of moral climate the war affords them. They drive convoys through Viet-infested jungles, track down racketeers or are themselves tracked down by them, and wrestle against Viet Minh terror tactics in the villages and cities. In the end all but a few of them succumb to the general decay. The author, who, amongst other things, was a teacher, trucker, and beer merchant in Indochina from 1946 to 1951, narrates his stories with exceptional force, in spite of the unevenness of his obviously hurried writing.

Bearing the clear stamp of a communist propaganda mill are Pierre Courtade's *La Rivière noire* (1953), Georges-Henri Guiraud's *Aux frontières de l'enfer* (1956), and Raymond Barkan's *Les Naufragés de l'occident* (1958), all novels. The stentorian voices and rhetorical outbursts that have destroyed countless works of propagandistic fiction are not the most debilitating element here. Nevertheless, the propaganda again undoes the art and, with some variations, the pattern is consistent. Talk still smothers dramatic tension, the characters are plainly labeled symbols, and the pages are crammed with doctrinal clichés. The French soldier is either ox-witted, or naïve, or confused, or a drunkard, or bestiality incarnate, or all of these. He either receives no letters from home or letters which scold him for doing the wrong thing in the wrong place, or inform him that he has fallen victim to cuckoldry. While French commanders may only be guilty of poor judgment, French politicians must without exception be stupid and cynical. French-authored atrocities are always marvels of grotesque ingenuity and all German Legionnaires have innocent blood on their hands from World War II days. French casualties are invariably heavy and corpses have to be in an advanced state of putrefaction. In contrast, Viet Minh fighting men are well-nigh *sans peur* and *sans reproche,* and their civilian supporters are the very embodiment of cheerful sacrifice. Both, in company with their Russian and Chinese brothers, are riding on a tidal wave of victory en route to blissful tomorrows.

Probably the most striking of the numerous documentaries on the French Indochinese War are *L'Enlisement* (1963), *L'Humiliation* (1965), and *L'Aventure* (1967), the three volumes of Lucien Bodard's series *La Guerre d'Indochine*. This prestigious *France-Soir* reporter not only «was there» but also knew just about everybody who was anybody, in and out of uniform, in the underworld and above ground. Bodard deftly sketches pen portraits of them while painting in darkest hues a teeming Saigon which he damns as unfeeling and rotten to the bones. *L'Enlisement* movingly portrays the predicament of a modern army bogged down in swamp and jungle and engaged in a no-holds-barred struggle against incredibly determined guerrilla forces. In *L'Humiliation,* the author, along with much else, anatomizes for pages on end the problem born of the overvaluation of the piaster and of the resultant repatriation of profits, pointing up its colossal dimensions while building a veritable sociological treatise around the countless actors playing shoddy roles in this shoddy drama. Bodard observes: «In Indochina, there are mercenaries of war and mercenaries of the piaster. Some men are there because they like battle. Others because they like the piaster» (3). The adventure of the 800-page *L'Aventure* was the one lived by General—posthumously Marshal— Jean De Lattre de Tassigny. Bodard's great verbosity notwithstanding, he draws a masterly portrait of the charismatic leader who had been dispatched to Indochina in December 1950 to try to stem the Viet Minh tide. A man whose vaulting ambition and leonine pride were matched by his iron determination and well-developed sense of showmanship,

---

(3) Lucien Bodard, *L'Humiliation* (Paris: Gallimard, 1965), p. 150.

he had promptly promised to bring «victory on a silver platter» (4). And, so that his own triumphs and those of his troops would be properly appreciated, he surrounded himself with a second army, that of reporters, cameramen, and divers other publicists, civilian and military, whom he courted unashamedly and prodded endlessly at mammoth press conferences, at table— everywhere. For a time it appeared that De Lattre would be as good as his word. Infused with a new fighting spirit, his troops, only a few weeks after he had taken over the supreme command, had defeated Giap's divisions in a pitched battle at Vinh Yen, thus halting the enemy advance on Hanoi. The cape had not been rounded, however. It soon dawned on De Lattre that Giap's disciplined, fanaticized army of shadows had only scattered, burying itself in the wilderness, and that it would thereafter avoid large-scale battle in open country, the only type of battle for which his training and experience had prepared him. The puzzled De Lattre's fame, power, and glory could not at this time alleviate his brooding anxiety, since he felt the ground of Indochina slipping out from under his feet. And there were too many signs of impending disaster by the time of his death, of cancer, in January 1952, to allow for renewed optimism. «Le Roi Jean» had not, as he had boasted, saved Indochina and Asia at Vinh Yen, the place he liked to refer to as his «yellow Marne.»

No writer more passionately concerned himself with the piaster racket, the biggest of the many rackets that flourished during the war, than Jacques Despuech. Wounded in Indochinese combat in 1947, this veteran of World War II and ex-prisoner of the Gestapo returned to the Far East in 1949 to work as a civilian employee of the Exchange Control

---

(4) Cited by Bodard, *L'Aventure* (Paris: Gallimard, 1967), p. 119.

Office. Because he was stirred to the depths by the scandalous transfer of funds to Europe and elsewhere that he saw effected there, he accepted a bid from the French Army intelligence services to double as an agent in ferreting out major offenders and in tracing out their worldwide networks of operation. His sleuthing produced a mine of evidence. In his *Le Trafic des piastres* (1953), he did not hesitate to name names while describing in detail the mechanics of the outrageous transfer of funds. For patriotically flirting with death for four years he was rewarded by being fired from his civil service job abroad and by being forced into costly litigation at home. It was doubtless to forestall more of the latter that Despucch used only imaginary names in the book's anguished sequel, *Missions inutiles à Saïgon* (1955).

Anne-Marie, Béatrice, Claudine, and Éliane were not to be immortalized by French veterans of the war as were the Madelons and the Lili Marlenes of other wars, for these euphonious names are not those of idealized females peopling soldiers' dreams. They are, rather, the code names of some of the chief fortified hill positions associated with the 56-day nightmare that was Dien Bien Phu. Giap, the legendary Viet Minh commander in chief, saw the battle as a Valmy, for he had no difficulty recalling that Valmy had been the first victory of Revolutionary France over a European coalition. Jules Roy devoted a 600-page documentary to the war's disastrous finale. In his *La Bataille de Dien Bien Phu* (1963), Roy stops short of agreeing with Clemenceau's dictum that «war is too important a business to be left to the generals.» But pillory them he does: Colonel Christian de Castries, commander of the Dien Bien Phu garrison; General René Cogny, commander of land forces in the Tonkin Delta; and, above all, General Henri de Navarre, stoutest champion of the plan to draw the Viet Minh out of the jungle and into the *cuvette*. Harried French airmen, endlessly flying in support of it, preferred to call it a «pot de chambre» (5). True, Roy does not lay all the blame at the door of the generals, since for him the biggest villains of the piece were an insensitive French public and an unthinking French government; true, he dwells on some of their virtues, yet he constantly holds up to ridicule their errors of judgment and the pettier aspects of their characters—this with a petulance and a fury that diminish the value of a documentary otherwise distinguished by its painstaking scholarship.

For his part, Jean Pouget, former aide-de-camp of General Navarre, indulges in neither emotionalism nor recrimination in his book *Nous étions à Dien-Bien-Phu* (1964). To him all the defenders of the ill-fated bastion are heroes. Whereas Roy is especially harsh on Navarre and Cogny for their bickering and their mutual mistrust, Pouget takes pains not to besmirch their military honor—or anyone else's for that matter. And he emphasizes to those many critics, Roy included, who, with the benefit of hindsight, were to cry: «Mais qu'allaient-ils faire dans cette cuvette?»—that, advantageously placed as he was to see and hear, he knew of no visiting dignitary, civilian or military, who believed that the garrison's defenders were doomed because they were situated at the bottom of a natural basin—an astonishing observation,

---

(5) On a visit to Dien Bien Phu, aptly described by him as a «prefabricated battlefield,» *Le Monde* correspondent Robert Guillain felt like a caged, throughly observed animal. He compared it to an immense stadium whose stepped rows of seats were occupied by the Viet Minh, and to a «gigantic, complicated trap ... more densely inhabited than an anthill.» Guillain, *La Fin des illusions: Notes sur l'Indochine (Février-Juin 1950)* (Paris: Centre d'Études de Politique Étrangère, 1954), p. 11.

Guillain's pessimism deepened. Seven weeks before the fall of Dien Bien Phu, he grimly reflected on the unparalleled situation of this «underground army ... in its upside-down fortress» in the mountains, «this jungle Verdun created smack in the middle of enemy territory» and connected with friendly bases by nothing but a 300-kilometer aerial road, p. 47.

to say the least, particularly in light of the fact that this basin was close to the Chinese border and but a few miles from the Laos frontier (6).

Written in a patriotic vein, Major Paul Grauwin's *J'étais médecin à Dien-Bien-Phu* (1954) chants the praises of the defenders of the *cuvette* while singling out for special tribute the thousands of men in all branches of the service who, without the benefit of paratroop training, volunteered at the eleventh hour to be dropped into the besieged camp. He reminds his readers that the war dead included three generals' sons: Lieutenants de Lattre, Leclerc, and Préau (7). A strong patriotic note is likewise sounded in Roy's *reportage, La Bataille dans la rizière* (1953), with the author repeatedly referring to the French Expeditionary Force as the «armée de la croisade.» It also echoes through Georges-Léon Descamps' halting novel *Broussards d'Indochine* (1953) and Pierre Richard's diary *Cinq Ans prisonnier des Viets* (1964). Richard blends Christian fervor with soldiering after the manner of Psichari and Péguy, but lacks their force. These patriotic accents notwithstanding, nowhere in the works under study is it a case of anyone's caring, *à la* Péguy, to lay down his life on the altar of the «terre charnelle.» There were *purs,* of course, but none so pure as Péguy. Nor was it likely

---

(6) Roy reveals that, on an unspecified future date, Pierre de Chevigné, France's Minister of Defense at the time of the battle, pointed out that this was the first time since the Roland of the epic poem *La Chanson de Roland* fought at Roncevaux that foot soldiers had to labor under the grievous handicap of being positioned in «such a gorge.» *La Bataille de Dien Bien Phu* (Paris: Julliard, 1963), p. 164.

(7) All three were graduates of Saint-Cyr. Of the French Army's 92,000 war dead, 800 were Saint-Cyrians. Paul-Marie de La Gorce, who has supplied these figures, estimates that, for seven years, one French officer fell each day in Indochinese combat. De La Gorce, *La République et son armée* (Paris: Fayard, 1963), p. 469.

17

that there could have been in a war that remained undeclared; in an army with merely a small fraction of its personnel from mainland France, the rest being racially variegated Foreign Legionnaires, Algerians, Senegalese, and Vietnamese (about a third of the garrison defending Dien Bien Phu were Germans, according to Alexander Werth) (8); in an army whose fighting men represented seventeen nationalities—a greater number than that comprising the racially heterogeneous army with which Napoleon had invaded Russia; in a war which was so unpopular in France that it was not until the final year of hostilities that any prominent French politician dared risk advocating the use of French conscripts; in a war which was not being fought in defense of the fatherland and prompted no rush to the colors by Frenchmen of any age. How far removed this army was from the French Army of 1871, symbol of national unity in a dark hour and acclaimed by Maurras as «the queen of France»!

The consciousness that they were fighting for the independence of their homeland was for the great mass of Viet Minh soldiers all the motivation they needed. Their adversaries are, on the other hand, represented as being unmotivated or diversely motivated. Some had simply seen themselves shipped off to the Far East upon joining the army to find release from the boredom of everyday living, or had signed up in order to see the world, or had even done so in a moment of pique or dejection—as men have done from time immemorial. Others, adventurers at heart, had sought out combat for its thrills, excitement, and the opportunity to transcend themselves in a supreme moment of truth. Whereas probably none of them were unmindful of the fact that the

---

(8) Alexander Werth, *France, 1940-1955,* with a Foreword by G. D. H. Cole (New York: Henry Holt and Co., 1965), p. 671.

struggle was in substantial part bound up with the issue of communism versus democracy, few gave more than fleeting attention to its ideological aspects. Commenting on the ideological illiteracy of his comrades in arms, Philippe de Pirey, author of the documentary *Opération gâchis* (1953), who admits having sought adventure, and adventure alone, in volunteering at nineteen for paratrooper commando duty, writes, «They only knew that they were to do battle against communism, but were ignorant of what it was really all about, and gave as much of a damn about it as about their first pair of dungarees» (9). For most of these professional soldiers it suffices that duty has called them there, as it might have called them anywhere. This is not, however, an acceptable justification in the eyes of Valion, the protagonist of Roy's play *Le Fleuve rouge* (1947). A humane and idealistic commanding officer, he, like the other heroes of the author's numerous war books, is at once a man of action and of thought. Like them also, he must ceaselessly search out the meaning of his acts and is never unhappier than when he is unable to resolve his doubts. He is as impressed by the courage, faith, and determination of the enemy as he is depressed by the callousness of the fatherland, shabby war profiteering, and the willingness of his comrades to have recourse to torture tactics. Ultimately he cracks under the strain born of his failure to answer his own questions on the war that he has been conscientiously fighting.

It may be recalled that, conversely, the equally idealistic Alden Pyle, crew-cut young protagonist of Graham Greene's *The Quiet American* (1965), ends up at the bottom of a river for thinking he knew what the French Indochinese War was all about and for his stalwart faith in his own capacity to

---

(9) Philippe de Pirey, *Opération gâchis* (Paris: La Table Ronde, 1953), p. 29.

change things. Full of good intentions and of bookish knowledge, but wholly lacking in an awareness of the complexity of the war situation, he undertakes to fight both communism and French colonialism by creating a «Third Force» while working as a secret agent of the United States Economic Mission in Saigon. When the bungling of this Boston-bred, Harvard-educated crusader with a «wide campus gaze» results in the death of over fifty innocent civilians, and promises more of the same, Fowler, a British reporter friend of his, arranges to have him done away with by Viet Minh agents. «God save us always from the innocent and the good,» he remarks, probably echoing the novelist's own sentiments.

The communist apologists are not alone in paying tribute to the courage and commitment of the Viet Minh warriors. Numerous are the lines of praise by Frenchmen in the tenor of Marshal De Lattre's avowal to the *bacheliers* of the Lycée Chasselou-Laubat in Saigon on July 11, 1951, to wit: «There are over there [with the Viet Minh] people who are fighting well for a bad cause» (10). Writer after writer dwells on the heroism of Viet soldiers, some of whom, called «volunteers for death,» would, in order to breach important defenses, rush up against them with heavy loads of explosives on their backs. In addition to such direct praise there is, by implication, the highest tribute possible in the striking fact that nowhere do any of these authors disparage in the slightest the fighting qualities of these little men who, with slogans such as «a grain of rice is worth a drop of blood» ringing in their ears, having a thousand times wished Ho Chi Minh «a thousand years,» and having formulated their joint resolutions, would then hurl themselves into battle to the accompaniment of bugles and of their own shouts. De Pirey makes the significant point that, in spite of the French Army's massive

---

(10) Cited by Fall, *Le Viet-Minh*, p. 182.

dissemination of handbills over the battle areas encouraging desertion by enemy troops and promising good treatment as P.W.'s to bearers of them, he, a veteran combatant, saw nary a one present himself.

«Insects,» «ants,» «termites»—these are the descriptives applied scornfully but with grudging admiration by the non-communist writers to the Viet Minh fighters and to their swarms of coolies, porters, and diverse other auxiliaries. Fiercely indoctrinated, these meticulous, assiduous, persistent, seemingly indefatigable men and women perform their functions, however arduous or perilous, with the efficiency of machines. One of the warriors in Jean Lartéguy's *Les Centurions* (1960), a novel mainly concerned with France's war in Algeria, likens them to student drudges who «by dint of sheer hard work and tenacity gather in all the prizes at the year's end» (11). The better to impress an unconditional loyalty upon them, the Viet Minh high command had made abundant use of the old communist technique of auto-criticism, a feature of interminable series of open meetings maintained at every level. Here miscreants who had made the mistake of forgetting that they were robots first and individualists never, would publicly and with all the scrupulosity of the most fervent of penitents confess serious transgressions against the war effort and petty misdemeanors alike. And should a deviant perchance be tempted to cover up his offense, the system required, under stern penalty, that any of his comrades having knowledge of it lay it bare.

Great prominence is given the role of the political commissar. Present in prison camp, in bivouac, in the brush, and on the field of strife, he tirelessly explicates, predicates, stimulates. Above exclusively military officers in authority,

---

(11) Jean Lartéguy, *Les Centurions* (Paris: Presses de la Cité, 1960), p. 114.

but ever acting in close concert with them, he has the primary responsibility for the conduct of operations, and his number multiplies when a battle is in progress. Seemingly insulated against fear and conflicts of conscience, he glides behind the warriors, whispering or shouting encouragement, reminding them of the objectives of the battle, drumbeating into their ears the slogan especially adopted for it, and in general seeing to it that they perform their duties like the automatons they are supposed to be.

Also constantly claiming the attention of the reader of these works of fiction and documentaries is the exceedingly high incidence of witness to the organizational efficiency of the Viet Minh. The documentaries in particular bear out that, in the waging of political, economic, and sociological war the French Army simply was no match for it. Indeed it appears that no detail was overlooked by the Viet Minh high command. There was even a Viet equivalent of a Tokyo Rose or of an Axis Sally to feed propaganda over the air waves to French units between interludes of music, predecessor of the Hanoi Hannah whom American G.I.'s were to come to know in Vietnam. And it is brought out in Ngo-Van-Chiêu's *Journal d'un combattant Viet-Minh* (1955) that Giap's forces were not without a special services branch which made it possible for the attackers of Dien Bien Phu to enjoy movies between rounds of battle. Feeling helpless before their operational efficiency, one of Lartéguy's warriors laments: «They are like worms; you cut them in two and you think you're finished with them, but all you've done is double their number, each of the sections having assumed an autonomous life» (12). To this the awed Descamps adds his own analogy and lament: «The Viet Minh is like a cloud. You

---

(12) *Ibid.*, p. 63.

turn your back on it and it envelops you. You run up against it and it gives way, scatters, and blurs» (13). Truly the Viet Minh was making good Ho Chi Minh's boast that the Viet Minh tiger would not allow the French elephant the merest respite at any time, anywhere.

That troops of the «Army of the French Union» fighting in Indochina merited a red badge of courage is underscored by the abundance of tributes paid them by writers of every political stripe. That they were not soldier-saints is no less clear. Official policy, as laid down by Generals Leclerc, Chanson, and others, called for «correct» behavior toward the native population and for the avoidance of counter-terror tactics. But, in the face of the enemy's fanaticism and the reign of terror established by him, combatants on the French side matched terror with terror and resorted to torture in order to force confessions and gather intelligence, a fact to which the books of De Pirey, Hougron, Roy, and Schoendoerffer amply attest (14). Indeed, the sundry atrocities depicted by De Pirey are reminiscent of the scenes of horror that fill the plates of Goya's *Los Desastres de la guerra* and, to state the obvious, show warriors of the French Expeditionary Force in a very poor light. The sentiments of chivalry and magnanimity that countless combatants of many wars have shown their foes, looked upon by them as fellow sufferers and victims, appear to have had little place in this dehumanizing war. *Furor bellicus* had implanted a burning hatred in the combatants' souls, had poisoned them beyond redemption. The law of the talion had replaced civilized rules of warfare.

Whatever their allegiance, these writers are of one voice

---

(13) Georges-Léon Descamps, *Broussards d'Indochine* (Paris: Julliard, 1953), p. 84.

(14) Schoendoerffer's sympathetic portrayal of American troops in Vietnam in his documentary film *The Anderson Platoon* (1967), termed by him «a visual combat diary,» was acclaimed a masterpiece on both sides of the Atlantic.

in heaping scorn on the home front, separated from the battle front by better than eight thousand miles. What Roy laments as a «monstrous national indifference» to the war, the majority of the other writers view as downright hostility, making it plain at the same time that such hostility was the prime factor in demoralizing troops fighting desperately against Viet Minh forces whose solidarity with their civilian supporters graphically exemplified Clausewitz's concept of the nation-in-arms and of total war, and who had learned well Mao Tse-tung's first lesson, on the need for a guerrilla warrior to live amidst the population like a fish lives in water. Tauriac, La Praye, and Lartéguy focus on the complete divorcement of the soldier from the civilian, with Lartéguy betraying a burning hatred for his *concitoyens,* whom he accuses of having cast adrift the defenders of their interests. «They had been abandoned,» he protests, «like those suddenly useless mercenaries that Carthage had put to death so that she would no longer have to pay their salaries» (15). Lartéguy's paratrooper veterans of Dien Bien Phu and of Viet Minh prison camps return to Paris only to become social castaways, since they can no longer bring themselves to accept the values of the milieus of which they had been part. Turning their backs on the greed, hypocrisy, and political confusion which they judge to be ruling the day, these disillusioned warriors soon band together and go off to join battle with the F.L.N. in Algeria.

Comradeship is in none of the fictional works in question what it was in Remarque's celebrated *All Quiet on the Western Front* and in innumerable other war novels. Nonetheless, in varying degrees the theme of comradeship courses through all of them. It is not the wordy, brothers-all camaraderie glorified in the books of Kipling; it is rather, save in the

_____
(15) *Les Centurions,* p. 167.

cases of Tauriac and Roy, unpretentious and unarticulated. It suffices that these fighters find strength in the knowledge that they share the same anguish and bitterness, confront the same dangers, and can count on one another in an hour of crisis. When, on the other hand, a major in Roy's *Le Fleuve rouge* intermittently speaks in sentimental accents on the need for friendship, his words somehow sound hollow, as though he were clumsily debasing the fraternity of arms. Nor do these warriors seem to want to become deeply attached to one another, realizing as they do that death intervenes all too quickly to separate them. Besides, the dead are soon forgotten when the combatants must incessantly busy themselves scrutinizing every bush and branch, fighting off insects, and pulling leeches off their sweaty bodies.

Tender, romantic love finds no suitable climate for flowering in this ugly war. Viewing both serious amorous concerns and the gratification of physical passion as threats to single-minded devotion to duty, the Viet Minh command had proscribed sentimental and sensual involvement by its combatants. It apparently succeeded brilliantly in its objective. In contrast with Viet Minh soldiers, called «asexual» by Lartéguy, the French Army's fighters are portrayed as anything but chaste Hannibals. Moreover, the grim here-and-now seems to have absorbed them so entirely that, unlike the soldiers populating works of fiction dealing with World Wars I and II, they rarely direct their thoughts back to women on the home front.

That humor has an all but magical effect in relieving the fears and tensions of warfare is, of course, commonly known, and common is the soldier who has frequent recourse to his sense of humor as a safeguard against despondency. Yet humor is nearly completely absent from all but two of the fictional works studied, namely, La Praye's *La Trompette des anges* and Lartéguy's *Les Centurions*. Could it be that, in their desire to portray a horrible war with a proper degree of horror, these writers thought it morally indefensible to dwell on the comic? It is also worth noting that, whatever their political or ideological orientation, all these authors portray the Viet Minh soldier as a sober, deadly serious type. One is therefore tempted to conclude that the free and easy exercise of a sense of humor by a Viet Minh fighter would have been regarded by his commanders as subversive of the war effort.

Rare are the «big» battle scenes in these books, since the war dealt with in them was, except for Dien Bien Phu, devoid of large, full-scale battles. With the front nowhere and everywhere, with the enemy invisible but ubiquitous, with the fighting apt to erupt in any place at any time, this was essentially a war of patrols, ambushes, shadowy movements, and of hit-and-run tactics, a war with which a Hugo or a Zola, those painters of broad, populous military frescoes, would scarcely have been at home. Nor, for that matter, would a Theodor Plievier, in his fascination with large-scale tactical maneuver. It was, these writers everywhere remind us, a struggle of unmatched fierceness, waged mostly at night, in rugged mountains, dense jungles, infested marshes, and in an ocean of rice paddies; amidst squalor, filth, and disease; under a blazing tropical sun and in an eternity of monsoon rain. It was a lawless, nameless, faceless war with no room for romanticization or for romantics in uniform of the Ambrose Bierce and T. E. Lawrence breed. It was, finally, a war generative of unutterable suffering, suffering fairly crying out for the testimony of a Duhamel and deserving of his tender *sympathie,* the word being understood here in its etymological sense. In modest measure it did find such witness and fraternal understanding in Paul Grauwin, surgeon at Dien Bien Phu, and in Jules Roy, a reportorial observer of the «sale guerre.»

CHAPTER VII

ALGERIA: THE TORTURED CONSCIENCE

It began on November 1, All Saints' Day, 1954, only three months and four days after France's Indochinese War had ended, and was usually referred to as «the insurrection,» or «the state of siege,» or «the events,» or «the pacification,» or «operations for the maintenance of order,» or a «police action to restore order.» In an uninspired moment André François-Poncet, France's astute former ambassador to Nazi Germany and to Fascist Italy, defended the French effort against its detractors by emphasizing, amongst other things, that the nation's traffic fatalities outnumbered those her army —generally referred to as «the forces of order»—was suffering in Algeria. His calculations were correct, though he could not have been expected to foresee in 1956 that the Algerian War —for it was a war—would last for seven and a half years and that, before it would end, more than a million French soldiers would participate as «restorers of order,» about a million Algerian Moslems would die war-associated deaths, two million others would become displaced persons, and, finally, in Algeria, as in Civil War Spain, almost every family, European or Moslem, would count one or more war dead (1). In addition,

_____

(1) Since there had been no official declaration of war by

so violent were the political passions unleashed by the war that the Fourth French Republic would fall victim to it, and the same coalition of pro-French Algeria colonels, *colons,* and politicians primarily responsible for bringing General de Gaulle back to the helm of the ship of state in 1958 would come dangerously close to scuttling it three years later, with some of them now calling him whom they had looked to as the man of the hour «Père-la-Défaite» in unsubtle contrast with the «Père-la-Victoire» eponym bestowed on Clemenceau in more glorious days. For this group the Mediterranean did indeed divide France the way the Seine divides Paris, as their leader, General Raoul Salan, was wont to consider it. No longer the silent servant of politicians, the army, «La Grande Muette,» now hurled itself into the political arena, determined to destroy the influence of those whom it blamed for its plight. At one point Algeria's most illustrious son, Albert Camus, saw fit to remind his audience that not all French Algerians carried riding whips and were cigar-smoking, Cadillac-driving plutocrats. At a late hour in the war the children of Algiers' desperate ultras were chorusing «Death to the Archbishop» in the streets because Archbishop Duval, head of the Algerian Church, had been an outspoken critic of brutal police and military tactics, and on the eve of the armistice the battle cry of massacring European residents of Oran was «Vive la mort!»

When peace finally came and an independent Algeria was created, «présence française» in Algeria was little more than a memory, since all but a handful of Europeans had opted for the suitcase when warned that the alternatives were «the suitcase or the coffin,» and such French Algerian towns as Bossuet, Corneille, Lamartine, Renan, Mirabeau,

---

the French government, not a single Croix de guerre was awarded for bravery in action.

Maréchal Foch, and Maginot were given the names of Moslem national idols. On the other hand, Algiers came to have a John F. Kennedy Square, a token of Algerian Algeria's appreciation for the June 2, 1957 speech the then Senator Kennedy had delivered in the United States Senate in which he had criticized the French repression and come out for negotiation. Gone was the Algeria which, as prominent leftist leader François Mitterrand emphasized, could, in association with Tunisia and Morocco, have become a French California if French administrations had not been neglecting these countries for scores of years (2). But the passions generated by the war were not to subside at all rapidly. Four years later, extremist opponents of an Algerian Algeria reacted to the staging of Jean Genet's *Les Paravents,* a play only indirectly concerned with the Algerian War and colonial domination, by releasing rats and hurling acid and bombs into the government-subsidized Théâtre de France during one of the performances. The play had appeared in print in 1959, yet, quite understandably, nobody undertook to put it on during the remaining years of the conflict.

Actually, the largest French army that had ever crossed an ocean had won a military victory, since F.L.N. (Front de Libération Nationale) forces in the field had been contained and not an inch of territory had been surrendered to the enemy. But because the minds of the Moslem Algerians had not been conquered, the revolution went on and the war was lost—morally, politically, and economically. While dwelling on the folly and futility of some army methods of pacification, Louis Martin-Chauffier put it most aptly. «Nero kept on embracing Britannicus, but could not succeed in

(2) François Mitterrand, *Aux frontières de l'Union Française: Indochine-Tunisie* (Paris: Julliard, 1963), p. 24.

suffocating him» (3), he remarked. Mauriac, reflecting on the army's predicament, observed, «What is the good of being a lion when the gnat goes on harassing it and making fun of it?» (4).

It was a singularly complex, a truly Sisyphean war, one that would have tried the patience of saints. The French soldier was expected to be at one and the same time a destroyer of villages and a rebuilder of them, a killer of men and a conqueror of men's souls, a warrior and a pacificator —a tall order, to be sure. As Philippe Héduy, a veteran of the Algerian conflict and one of the authors figuring in this study, pointed out, on one day he would come bringing bonbons and medicine to Moslem villagers and, on the next, he would be back with a list of suspects in his pocket and a grenade in his hand, for daytime allies would all too often become murderous enemies in the black of night. Determined, capable practitioners of psychological, sociological, and economic warfare— *bonnes à tout faire,* they often called themselves—would as often as not see the fruits of months of hard effort destroyed by the momentary hotheadedness of a handful of their comrades in arms or by the brutal acts of unauthorized vigilante squads of European settlers who respected no law save the law of the talion. It was a war without front or rear or rules. Its only rememberable battle was the Battle of Algiers, which raged between January and October, 1957, in which General Massu's paratroopers were pitted against the terrorist networks of the Algiers underground, and the only notable «battle» line was the electrified Morice Line erected by the French along the border of Tunisia

(3) Louis Martin-Chauffier, *Algérie An VII* (Paris: Julliard, 1961), p. 45.

(4) Mauriac, *Le Nouveau Bloc-Notes: 1958-1960* (Paris: Flammarion, 1961), Sept. 9, 1960, p. 366.

to shut off the flow of supplies and troops from that country (5). It was a war in which *fellagha* militants slit the throats of *attentiste* compatriots to muster full support and in which Moslem combatants on the French side were often obliged to turn in their weapons between missions.

Vigny would have found much servitude and no grandeur in it; Montherlant's Alban de Bricoule, avid seeker of combat thrills, would probably have been sorely disappointed by it, and it would have been unthinkable for a novelist to have attempted to foist upon the reading public 1954 or 1955 models of the *poilus* of René Benjamin, joyously departing for combat with the sprightly lyrics of «La Madelon» on their lips and with flowers in their gun barrels. Very early in the war the multi-talented Boris Vian was frustrated at every turn in his attempt to popularize his own pacifist song «Le Déserteur,» finding it well-nigh impossible to cope with boycotting by the media and with the hostile demonstrations his singing tours touched off. Only after its lyrics were substantially altered did «Le Déserteur» become a popular success (6). It would have required much straining for Maurice Barrès, champion of war as a generator of national energy, to accommodate his theory to this war. Its victims were as various as his grandson, Captain Claude Barrès, who had revelled in fighting France's ill-starred wars since the

---

(5) With the 1966 film *The Battle of Algiers*, an Algerian and Italian co-production, director Gillo Pontecorvo, using non-professional actors, brilliantly recaptured the intensity of the struggle within the city. He invested it with such a convincing realism that it can easily be mistaken for a documentary. Not until 1970 was the film shown in France. Even then its opening had been delayed because of threats of violence, of bombings, and of reprisals against the families of the owners of the cinemas that had booked it.

(6) Without being identified as his creation, Vian's song in its English translation, featuring the voices of Peter, Paul, and Mary, became a hit tune in the U.S. during the Vietnam War.

age of fifteen, and well-known Berber writer Mouloud Feraoun, as sincere a friend as France had had in Algeria, thoughtlessly gunned down by O.A.S. (Organisation de l'Armée Secrète) killers a few days before the cease-fire (7). There would have been no place in it for a twenticth-century Maréchal de Saxe, chivalrously bidding the enemy to open the firing, and there was no place in it for General Paris de la Bollardière, who created a sensation by resigning his command in Algeria in protest against a style of repression that clashed violently with his concept of soldierly honor. This direct descendant of three generations of professional soldiers had been a commander of airborne troops in Indochina after seeing action on a number of fronts during the Second World War as a regular and as a *Résistant*. On the intellectual scene, philosopher Maurice Merleau-Ponty, he too an above-ground and underground combatant of the 1939-45 war, dramatized his outrage over a war which he accounted a spreading cancer by turning in to the government his red ribbon of the Legion of Honor.

Again the French Army, haunted by the specter of 1940 and embittered by a growing succession of defeats and humiliations for which it was as much the scapegoat as anything else, had been given the thankless assignment of putting down what most termed a colonial rebellion, although Algeria was a dependency rather than a colony of France. And surely the army was not to be helped by the Pilate-like gesture of Robert Lacoste, Resident Minister for Algeria, who in January 1957 turned over to Massu's Tenth Paratrooper Division responsibility for all police and security measures with the immediate

---

(7) Feraoun's posthumous *Journal 1955-1962* (Paris: Éditions du Seuil, 1962) gives a moving account of the spiritual struggle and ultimate failure of this fair-minded, tenderhearted Moslem intellectual to rise above the hatred which both *fellagha* and French brutality were burning into his soul.

commission to «rid Algiers of its pox,» to blot out terrorism in the city «by any means.» Then, as the *paras* and other army units turned more and more to torture as a means of gathering intelligence in the cities and in the *bled,* and as the repression of a harassed, frustrated army grew more and more inhumane, a barrage of criticism descended upon the army as well as upon the French government and the colonial administration. In the minds of millions the image of the beleaguered French soldier in Algeria was now that of a *militaire-flic.*

However, there had been criticism almost from the beginning, not only because of the government's decision to pursue what to many promised to be another needless colonial war but also because the particularly dirty character of the fighting could not for long be concealed from public view. Hence, the title of the November 1955 issue of the liberal Catholic monthly *Esprit,* «Arrêtons la guerre d'Algérie,» even at that early hour reflected the views of no mean segment of the French public. A few years later leftist writer Daniel Anselme's novelette *La Permission* (1957) focussed sharply on the wide gulf separating French combatants from a citizenry seemingly incapable of understanding their lot or appreciating their sacrifices in a war that repelled many while leaving others callously indifferent. On furlough in Paris, the book's trio of war-weary enlisted men suffocate in the capital's business-and-pleasure-as-usual atmosphere and find it impossible to communicate with the civilian population, who either scornfully ignore them in the streets or subject them to their scornful glances. Nevertheless, more than any other factor, it was the widespread use of torture by police and army interrogators in North Africa that stirred up the press and the intellectual community. O.A.S. *plastiqueurs* repaid the candor of *L'Express, Le Monde, France-Soir,* and *France-Observateur* on torture and on diverse sins of the repression by bombing the offices of these newspapers. *France-Soir* was given a double treatment, since a plastic bomb was also exploded in the Saint-Cloud home of its editor, Pierre Lazareff. Commando squads of ultras often assaulted individuals selling *Témoignage Chrétien* in front of churches, and Georges Suffert, its plain-spoken young editor, was for a short spell a kidnap victim. *France-Observateur, Les Temps Modernes, La Croix,* and, of course, *Esprit,* were also high on the dishonor list of military and civilian extremists and saw a number of their issues confiscated. Nor did it matter that their editors could be as critical of rebel terrorism as of French wrongdoing: witness the case of Jean-Marie Domenach, *Esprit*'s crusading editor, who stigmatized as a «Lidice» and an «Oradour» the slaying by maquis forces of three hundred of their compatriots at Melouza (8). As in the case of *L'Homme Enchaîné* of World War I years, the argument here was that the public display of holes in the army fabric was damaging to army morale. But, for the editors of these publications honor required that the honor of the blameless in uniform be upheld by identifying the blameworthy.

Of the better known French intellectuals none took a more extreme position on the war than did philosopher Francis Jeanson, a prominent disciple of Sartre. The concluding words of *L'Algérie hors la loi* (1955), which he co-authored with his wife, were, «Let us work to liberate France» (9). His own response to his appeal drew him deeply into pro-F.L.N. activity, for he took to organizing a clandestine support network, an undertaking that landed him in jail. The stormy trial of the Jeanson network took place

---

(8) Jean-Marie Domenach, «Les Enchères de la terreur,» *Esprit,* July, 1957, p. 105.

(9) Colette and Francis Jeanson, *L'Algérie hors la loi* (Paris: Éditions du Seuil, 1955), p. 274.

before a Paris military tribunal from September 6 to October 1, 1960, and opened many eyes to the breadth of the opposition to the war in the worlds of letters and of the performing arts. Before the end of hostilities even Brigitte Bardot earned herself a spot on O.A.S. reprisal rosters, a condition which she seems to have supported with exemplary calm. A second well-known actress who aroused the ire of the O.A.S. for her free-spoken opposition to the war was Simone Signoret.

On the very eve of the trial's inaugural session an open letter entitled «Déclaration sur le droit à l'insoumission dans la guerre d'Algérie» appeared in the press. Commonly known as the «Manifeste des 121» after the number of its original signatories, all intellectuals, (several dozen names were added subsequently), it proclaimed both the right of French conscripts to evade military service in Algeria and the legitimacy of French citizens' aiding the F.L.N. Among the signing writers were Georges Auclair, Simone de Beauvoir, Jean-Louis Bory, Claude Lanzmann, Maurice Pons, Alain Robbe-Grillet, Claude Roy, Françoise Sagan, Nathalie Sarraute, Claude Simon, Vercors, and ethnologist Claude Lévi-Strauss. Quite predictably, the manifesto exploded like dynamite in the already charged atmosphere.

To their credit, a large number of French writers were to record, individually and collectively, strong «Nous accusons...» in reaction to torture and brutal repressive acts by Frenchmen in uniform and to the sanctioning of such tactics by military and civil officials alike. In the finest tradition of French humanism they were to lash out at those who were bringing discredit upon the nation that had written the Declaration of the Rights of Man. Especially galling to them was the fact that torture, which Montaigne and Montesquieu had so roundly condemned and which Louis XIV had officially abolished, was tacitly being authorized, as, they readily recalled,

Himmler had authorized it in 1942 in an effort to demolish the expanding networks of the French Resistance. Though, unlike the Gestapo, the French Army ran no school on torture, a December 18, 1959 article in *Témoignage Chrétien* revealed that, at the training camp for subversive warfare at Philippe-ville, systematic instruction was being given on «humane» techniques for conducting torture. Irony supreme—the camp bore the name Jeanne d'Arc!

To Sartre, arch enemy of colonialism, it was a colonial war, therefore a criminal one. If he cast his full support to the rebels, this was because he firmly believed that not only they but the French people as well had to be worked free of the colonial yoke. In his deep detestation of the war Existentialism's high priest, accompanied by its high priestess, Simone de Beauvoir, carried his antiwar crusade as far as Brazil, where he had gone to serve as spokesman for French opponents of the war. Understandably, French recourse to torture and to «pacificatory» acts of violence placed in his hands a powerful antiwar weapon, as the pages of *Les Temps Modernes* of those years fully bear out. It was to be expected that Sartre, who loathed Nazism and all its works and who never wearied of giving critical attention to such works, would raise a storm of protest upon learning that some of his fellow countrymen were torturing and employing Nazi-like methods of repression in North Africa. The horror was, as George Steiner put it, in a somewhat different context, that «ten years after the Gestapo quit Paris, the countrymen of Voltaire were torturing Algerians and each other in some of the police cellars» (10). And if Frantz von Gerlach, the protagonist of Sartre's play *Les Séquestrés d'Altona*, staged in 1959 and 1960, suffers the torments of hell and is driven

---

(10) George Steiner, «Preface,» *Language and Silence* (New York: Atheneum, 1967), ix.

to madness, this is because he cannot conjure away memories of the torture and other atrocities he committed as a German officer in Russia during the Second World War. Sartre strongly suggested that such conduct on the part of Frenchmen in Algeria might well lead to similar personal disaster for them. At the same time, his multiplying examples to illustrate that torture was «neither civilian, nor military, nor specifically French» (11), a manifest truth that is also highlighted by Alec Mellor in his important study, *La Torture* (1961), by no means implied that he considered the guilty any less guilty thereby. Moreover, he saw little to distinguish the guilt of the torturers from that of uncounted French civilian «bourreaux,» made so, he affirmed, by their refusal, like the Germans of yesteryear vis-à-vis Dachau and Buchenwald, to believe and to denounce what they had not seen with their own eyes. Quick to focus on French offenses, Sartre did not, on the other hand, take a dim view of F.L.N. terrorism. Given his almost fanatical support of the rebel cause and his longstanding acceptance of terror as both a sort of cement binding together colonial peoples bent on liberation and as a liberating sword for them, his position on the matter surprised no one. Sartre's manifold activities in opposition to the war so violently agitated forces opposed to Algerian independence that on one occasion thousands of war veterans marched down the Champs-Élysées shouting «Shoot Sartre,» and on another his apartment was reduced to rubble by an exploded bomb (12).

Similarly, a plastic device was detonated on a ground floor windowsill of the fashionable Boulogne home in which

---

(11) Jean-Paul Sartre, *Situations, V: Colonialisme et néo-colonialisme* (Paris: Gallimard, 1960), p. 80.

(12) An early target of O.A.S. *plastiqueurs* was the Nîmes office of the brother of General Salan, Dr. Georges Salan, an advocate of Algerian independence.

Malraux lived. The glass it shattered badly disfigured the four-year-old daughter of its owner. Malraux, who occupied the floor above, was not at home at the time. As De Gaulle's close adviser and Minister of Cultural Affairs he had steadfastly supported the president's Algerian policy and strategy, and with characteristic flair he had rushed to the Ministry of the Interior to seek arms and recruit men for the defense of Paris during the Algiers revolt of army ultras in April 1961. Anathema to rightist extremists, he had also fallen out of grace with leftist intellectuals for his failure to address himself resolutely to the issue of torture and for his support of press censorship in the context of the war in North Africa. As they saw it, this former revolutionary and indefatigable servant of liberty had badly demeaned himself. Initially they had entertained high hopes that he would exert his influence to blot out what had become institutionalized military torture in Algeria, for he had co-sponsored with Roger Martin du Gard, Mauriac, and Sartre an April 1958 anti-torture manifesto, and had, shortly after his return to office with De Gaulle in June of the same year, invited three Nobel Prize winners —Camus, Roger Martin du Gard, and Mauriac—to organize a commission to examine the torture problem *in situ*. He could not be blamed, though, if Mauriac, for his part, declined the invitation and the commission died aborning. As the war dragged on, Malraux did, however, lay himself open to the blame of anti-torture crusaders by almost entirely steering clear of the torture issue within metropolitan France, dwelling on it only when circumstances forced him to do so in the course of public appearances in South America, Mexico, the Sahara territory, India, and the United States, in 1958-1962.

Simone de Beauvoir's views on the war fully coincided with those of Sartre, and she was to be seen at his side wherever the action happened to be. Her diary *La Force des choses* (1963) abounds in references which testify both to her stoic acceptance of the very real dangers to which Sartre and she had been exposing themselves and to the scope and intensity of her involvement with the Algerian issues. During those years this ardent champion of existential commitment made her most distinctive personal contribution by lending the prestige of her name and her vigorous support to the defense, initiated by lawyer Gisèle Halimi, of Djamila Boupacha, an arrested Moslem F.L.N. underground liaison agent who had suffered indescribably cruel torture at the hands of paratrooper interrogators. In a 1962 book with the victim's name as its title and a sketch of her by Picasso on its cover, the crusading pair, reinforcing their own criticisms with those expressed in letters in it by Jules Roy, Françoise Sagan, Françoise Mallet-Joris, and others, fixed blame on the torturers and floodlit the extent to which French justice in Algeria had become the corrupt handmaiden of an army whose political power had grown to ominous proportions. An earlier *cause célèbre* that had similarly rallied French intellectuals to it had to do with the alleged torturing and fatal strangling by paratroopers of Maurice Audin, a young communist lecturer in mathematics on the staff of the University of Algiers. The Comité Maurice Audin organized at that time rapidly developed into an anti-torture propaganda group which, according to Pierre Vidal-Naquet, numbered «literally thousands of members of the teaching profession in Paris and in the provinces» (13). So bitter was Simone de Beauvoir about French misconduct in the war that she was even prepared to confess, «Today the sight of French uniforms makes me shudder as much as the swastikas of bygone years ... Yes, I was living in an occupied city (Paris), and I hated the

---

(13) Pierre Vidal-Naquet, *Torture: Cancer of Democracy*, trans. Barry Richard (Baltimore: Penguin Books, 1963), p. 142.

occupiers more intensely than those of the 40's because of all the ties I had to them» (14).

As is commonly known, once the war broke out, Camus wrote a good deal less on it than might properly have been expected of Algeria's most famous son, especially in light of the strong public positions he had earlier assumed on Algerian ills and of his twenty-year campaign in behalf of French-Algerian rapprochement. Deciding in 1958 to rest his case on what he had up to that time written on the situation in his native land—after, however, making it plain that he rejected all consideration of negotiation with the F.L.N. prior to successful pacification—he settled himself in a position independent of both extreme camps and announced that he would no longer engage in polemics that could only serve to harden the contending camps in their positions and to divide the French yet more severely. He did indeed remain above the battle, leaving to others the responsibility of deciding on which side the preponderance of guilt lay—an unusual stance for the former *Résistant* and editor of *Combat,* for him who was among the first to denounce Franco and the repression of the Hungarian Revolution in 1956, and who had seldom failed to assume the front rank in the unending fight against man's inhumanity to man. That he had lost none of his passion for justice or his compassion for suffering men, there can be no question. That the left in particular viewed his conduct as unbecoming that of a responsible artist in society is evident from the avalanche of criticism it loosed against him, just as it had done in 1957 when Camus answered an Algerian student's question on his silence on French employment of torture in the war by declaring, in substance, that if he had to make a choice between justice and his mother

_____
(14) Simone de Beauvoir, *La Force des choses* (Paris: Gallimard, 1963), p. 407.

(who was still living in Algeria), he would choose his mother. To Mauriac this was an unsatisfactory answer, so he was quick to point out to his fellow humanitarian that «any injustice to men, committed in the name of France, crushes France, our mother» (15). Nevertheless, on atrocities Camus' message is crystal-clear. In his *Actuelles III* (1958), to which one must turn to get at the core of his thinking on the war, he warned that torture could only bring in its wake nihilism, the law of the jungle, the demoralization—in its etymological sense—of France, and the abandonment of Algeria. But terrorism, striking blindly at the innocent, was no less blameworthy and disfigured any cause. Perpetual seeker after truth that he was, it was natural that Camus should have condemned the deceit of both right and left: that of the right in approving «in the name of French honor, what was most contrary to it,» no doubt the criminal acts of police and army personnel; that of the left in excusing «in the name of justice, what was an insult to true justice» (16). For all that, there were those who looked for better from him. In his fine study *Albert Camus 1913-1960* (1961), Philip Thody, referring to the criticism by leftist writer Roger Stéphane of Camus' verbal abstention in 1957, at a time when the scandal of torture was jolting the conscience of the nation, gave voice to the reasoning of those many persons who would have been pleased to see this noble spirit break his silence. Thody wrote, «An outright condemnation of the use of torture by the French army in Algeria, at the very moment when the attention of the whole civilized world was focussed on the latest winner of the Nobel Prize, could have made an immense

---

(15) Mauriac, *Le Nouveau Bloc-Notes: 1958-1960*, Feb. 23, 1958, p. 29.
(16) Camus, *Actuelles III: Chronique algérienne* (Paris: Gallimard, 1958), p. 19.

contribution towards the disappearance of a practice which, Camus later recognized, did more harm to France's cause than a hundred armed enemy bands» (17). It is in much less measured accents that Simone de Beauvoir was to speak of Camus' self-imposed silence, even in the hours immediately following his sudden death. At that time her reactions were unmistakably those of a woman shocked and aggrieved—such, however, at the passing of the man who had been a beloved companion in «the years of hope» rather than «this just man without justice» whom, she emphasized, she had banished from her heart «when he gave his consent to the crimes of France» (18).

Dedicated to his deceased friend and *pied noir* compatriot, Camus, Jules Roy's documentary *La Guerre d'Algérie* (1960) was doubtless intended more to prick the conscience of the French than to bring forth new information on the war. Roy is particularly severe on the army's D.O.P. (Détachements Opérationnels de Protection) branch, basically a secret service unit, for whom torture had become a standard practice. True, he decries F.L.N. terrorism, but, like Sartre, he keeps on reiterating that it was the sole instrument available to the badly outnumbered rebels, a posture hardly calculated to increase his popularity with some elements of the army in which he had been a career officer. Roy's volume *Autour du drame* (1961) brings together articles written by him for *Le Monde* and *L'Express,* all but one in 1960 and 1961. Urging relentlessly that the guns be silenced and the daggers sheathed, he gloomily if realistically concludes that only a halt in the fighting could remove the cankers of torture and terrorism.

---

(17) Philip Thody, *Albert Camus 1913-1960* (London: Hamish Hamilton, 1961), p. 210.
(18) Simone de Beauvoir, *La Force des choses,* p. 508.

Reemerging in the arena after—very untypically— remaining silent on the Indochinese War, was François Mauriac, whose militancy dated back to the 1935 invasion of Abyssinia by Mussolini's troops. «Abomination,» «disease,» «cancer,» «the last swallow of poison»—these are some of the descriptives Mauriac scattered through his «Bloc-Notes» column in speaking of the war, a war whose earmark was, he never wearied of repeating, a relentlessly escalating *pourrissement*. He had from the outset declared himself emphatically on the side of Algerian independence. In addition, and no less significantly, his Christian conscience agonized over the fearful moral consequences that the plunging of untold numbers of French youths into this sort of war would have on an entire generation of Frenchmen, and he was withering in his criticism of the O.A.S. colonels and their political supporters («our Francos,» he called them), sowers of hatred that would make future reconciliation of the warring races infinitely more difficult. Small wonder, then, that an attempt was made to blow up Mauriac's country home at Malagar. Torture, which came under his journalistic fire as early as January 1955, he tirelessly denounced, warning that there could be no accommodation with it, for, «To present the crimes of the adversary as attenuating circumstances is to plead guilty» (19). Yet, despite this, despite too his crying shame upon the Mollets and the Lacostes, branded by him as abettors of torture, in the later years of the conflict he was to arrive at the pessimistic if realistic conclusion that torture was an inevitable excrescence of a war featuring terrorism and counterterrorism which only the end of hostilities could remove—a conviction shared by Sartre, Jules Roy, and Domenach. Here, as ever, his hopes rested on De Gaulle. Interestingly enough,

---

(19) Mauriac, *Bloc-Notes 1952-1957* (Paris: Flammarion, 1958), Dec. 19, 1957, p. 393.

however, after the return to power of his political idol, he wrote much less on torture, a change that did not escape the notice of either his detractors or his admirers.

The wrestling of the Christian conscience with torture is of central importance in the novel *Les Murmures de la guerre* (1961) by French Jewish writer Roger Ikor. With his writings the French reading public chiefly associates a fascinating portrayal of the efforts of Eastern European Jews to integrate themselves in a French environment. In *Les Murmures de la guerre,* the tensions are generated by problems of adjustment of another sort. They have to do with the refusal of a captain and a sergeant to sanction the policies of their colonel on the gathering of evidence. For the colonel there is no problem: the prisoner is on hand, the information must be had, the end justifies the means, and the means are undeniably efficacious. Besides, he does see to it that the conducting of what he likes to refer to as «reinforced interrogations» is entrusted only to proper officer types with no penchant for sadistic pleasure. And once the untidy business is over with, the colonel is not above serving champagne to particularly brave but cooperative victims. Against the dictates of his conscience, the captain, who is heavily imbued with Catholic and military traditions, does, once, obey the colonel's order to extract the necessary information, whatever the cost. The experience crushes him. Moreover, recognizing that divine law admits of no compromise, he resolves never again to torture, as he puts it, his one true master by inflicting torture on a fellow creature of God, whereupon he resigns from the army and enters a religious order. When the sergeant, who has long suspected the colonel of utilizing torture as a military instrument, has his suspicions confirmed, he too takes a stand in conscience. He requests and obtains reassignment to a combat unit in the *bled,* leaving the obliging colonel unencumbered of nice but naïve fellows whose moral scruples can only impede military efficiency.

Commandant Jean de Larsan, whom the portrait in Catholic writer Pierre-Henri Simon's *Portrait d'un officier* (1958) concerns, is another who finds his way out of the impasse at which he has arrived by resigning from the army in which he had been pursuing a career for twenty years. The hero of this *récit*—it is essentially an extended dialogue, and a *récit* in name only—is a patriot and Christian of the Péguy stripe whose concept of soldiering is radically out of keeping with much of what he has been witnessing in Algeria. Having first begun to search his heart with respect to his military vocation while engaged in the dirty fighting of the war in Indochina, he now reaches the breaking point, mainly because of his conviction that a Christian officer in the service of a civilized nation can have no truck with torture or with brutal methods of repression, no matter how vicious the deeds of the enemy may be. Yes, his own hands remain clean until the end, but he wearily observes, «It isn't easy to live a Cornelian life in the century of Kafka» (20).

Published a year earlier, Simon's *Contre la torture* is, as its title implies, an anti-torture tract, one of the more resounding ones of early date. While analyzing the causes and tracing the epidemic spread of this disease in the present century, the author points to a reported case of torture by the French military on Christmas Day, 1955, as a mirror of the failure of the sons of a Christian nation to hear the voice of the Beatitudes. Simon owns that guerrilla wars of liberation are *a priori* generative of unlimited violence and that the enemy combatants in this one were not «disciples of Gandhi,» yet he sternly warns that there is always a boundary line

---

(20) Pierre-Henri Simon, *Portrait d'un officier* (Paris: Éditions du Seuil, 1958), p. 170.

«between licit violence and criminal brutality» (21). The book's force derives mainly from its large block of extracts from anonymous witnesses' letters and from war diaries. Insofar as conveying a message is concerned, the horrors nakedly related in them suffice unto themselves.

Like Ikor's captain and Simon's major, Roland Guérin, the protagonist of Gilbert Cesbron's novel, *Entre chiens et loups* (1962), quits the fight in Algeria when he can no longer ignore the promptings of his Christian conscience. For him it is a matter of refusing to be a party any longer to the indiscriminate violence of combat, of an unwillingness to sacrifice human dignity on the altar of military advantage.

As a portrayal of the spiritual suffering of a devoutly Christian soldier trapped in a war in which the precepts of both Christianity and Islam were being massively ignored, the minuscule *Dossier Jean Muller* (1957) has incomparably more power than the fictional representations of it by Ikor, Simon, and Cesbron. This pamphlet is constituted of damning excerpts from letters written by Muller to friends at a time when he was participating in the «peacemaking» operations he describes in revealing detail. Fortified by his invincible belief in the essential worth of all men and in their right to uniform justice, Muller, together with some of his comrades in arms, rose superior to the tragic circumstances, but he gave his life in a war in which not a few of those at whose side he fought were less receptive to the teachings of Christ than to those of Clausewitz, father of the doctrine that war is an act of violence that knows no limits.

---

(21) Simon, *Contre la torture* (Paris: Éditions du Seuil, 1957), p. 67.

Georges Bernanos, who was appalled at the brutalities he witnessed on Majorca during the Spanish Civil War, was of the view that unlimited violence is equally unavoidable in a civil war. He wrote: «You don't depart for a civil war with lawyers, judges, and the codes of examining magistrates in your baggage vans ...»

Writing with the fire of an apostle and bringing to bear his conspicuous talent for argumentation, in his *Algérie An VII* (1961), Louis Martin-Chauffier rejected, one by one, the rationalizations with which the proponents of torture were seeking to justify its use. To those who maintained that public denunciation could not but sully the honor of the army, he answered that the torturers could not be expected to cease and desist so long as their crimes were being covered up by silence. Thus, though anxious lest he convey the impression that De Gaulle, whom he greatly admired, approved of such a degrading practice, he made no attempt to hide his profound disillusionment over the French president's failure to stay the hands of the torturers. Martin-Chauffier, it should be mentioned, had in early 1957 gone to Algeria as a member of an international committee of five former concentration camp inmates that had been charged with the duty of investigating conditions in detention camps for Moslem nationalists.

The only other French member of the committee was Germaine Tillion, head of the Department of Social Sciences at the Sorbonne and distinguished authority on North African ethnography. Her book *L'Algérie en 1957* (1957) was a rigorously but not at all coldly scientific study of the economic ills that were besetting the country in which she had spent seven years and which she dearly loved. In it she appealed for the immediate undertaking of what she termed a «Defense and Restoration of Men» in the form of a gigantic economic reform for Algeria which, amongst other things, would demand on the part of France alone a capital expenditure of no less than five billion dollars in the space of five years —a not unreasonable sum in light of the fact that the French

---

and, «You don't wage civil war with white gloves. Terror is its law and you know it.» *Les Grands Cimetières sous la lune* (Paris: Plon, 1938), pp. 183, 187-88.

government ultimately spent twelve billion dollars on the war. The thesis of Professor Tillion's later and lesser known work, *Les Ennemis complémentaires* (1960), is precisely that suggested by its title. While her accents are always measured and her tone dignified, there is no mistaking the fact that she, a victim of torture under the German occupation, was grievously pained by the interminable cycle of torture and terror marking the war she execrated. Against these twin scourges she had been fighting ceaselessly, a truth to which she does not seek to draw attention. And it is only very briefly that she dwells on her historically confirmed and much lauded personal intervention with rebel leader Saadi Yacef in an effort to halt terrorist attacks on the European population of Algeria in the summer of 1957.

Louis Salvaing, hero of Vladimir Pozner's *récit* «Les Étangs de Fontargente,» survives a long term of service in Algeria. However, the memory of a *massacre des innocents* in which he had been forced to take part while in uniform so obsesses him that he shoots himself to death. Pozner, who was seriously injured in a late-hour O.A.S. bomb explosion, has built a moving story around Salvaing's case of conscience, one which would have been yet more effective were it not for his clumsy attempt to make political capital of it. As is the case with the other five shorter stories comprising *Le Lieu du supplice* (1959), the volume of which it is part, its communist crusading is altogether too visible. The emphasis is on military servitude, with the machine totally crushing the individual, as well as on making an ugly war appear that much uglier: the home front is *that* demoralized, French settlers are *that* heartless, contact with opposing forces is *that* frequent, danger is *that* omnipresent, summer's heat and winter's cold are *that* extreme, and, of course, the mail always arrives late. Remorse similarly gnaws at the conscience of the returnee hero of André Stil's novel *Nous nous aimerons demain* (1958), whose haunting recollections of French atrocities in North Africa have left him an inadaptable human wreck (22). Because Stil was at the time editor of *L'Humanité*, it may be superfluous to add that here too the crusading is against more than military atrocities alone.

In their impact—psychological, moral, and historical— the aforementioned works are not at all comparable to Henri Alleg's *La Question*. When this documentary of only 112 small pages appeared in early 1958, it raised a storm whose thunder roll was to echo far beyond the frontiers of France. Now, for the first time, one who had himself suffered the indignities of military torture in Algeria had described—and in vivid detail—the whole sordid business. Moreover, the French government's ill-advised, botched efforts to ban the book, after 66,000 copies had been sold, served only to magnify the scandal. Alleg, French editor of the ultraleftist newspaper *Alger Républicain* and a central committeeman of the Algerian Communist Party, had been seized as an undercover agent of the F.L.N. Well-connected as he was, he could have supplied his captors with a storehouse of invaluable information. But attempts at bribery, threats, blows, kicks, injections of truth serum, instruments of torture, and the entire gamut of demonic psychological tricks known to the para-torturers of the notorious El Biar torture center in Algiers could not unseal his lips. Outraged he was, to be sure, and all the more so that he was but one of the numerous victims whose cries of anguish reverberated through the corridors of the building. None would have been surprised had he surrendered to hate and vituperation. That he did not do so is both a credit to his humanity and an asset to his

---

(22) A novel of recent date, Bernard Clavel's *Le Silence des armes* (1974), portrays another human being wrecked in spirit by his haunting visions of torture and of other atrocities committed

témoignage. La Question is, as a matter of fact, something of a miracle of disciplined writing. Its lines are lean; its language, bare; its tone, restrained. It is no less devastating an indictment for all that.

In his slightly fictionalized documentary *Lieutenant en Algérie* (1957), a work of uncommon distinction, Jacques Servan-Schreiber, already then one of France's most influential journalists, holds nothing back on French brutality in the area in which he saw action, just as he held nothing back thereon in the columns of *L'Express*. Yet, whereas he, like Mauriac, was convinced that France could lose her soul in Algeria by exposing hundreds of thousands of young Frenchmen to inhumane methods of pacification, making racists and moral washouts of them, his condemnation of French military misconduct is less voiced than insinuated. And it is possible to read a hint on the need for understanding into some of his lines, especially in light of the fact that no sooner would the author's Black Commando unit achieve a little hard-earned progress in its effort to regain the loyalty of terror-frozen Arab villagers than F.L.N. activists would bring off a bloody coup, swiftly to be answered in kind by irate French soldiers, some of whom, to begin with, shared the opinion of some of their commanders that «You don't win wars by turning the other cheek.»

There were those too who, though anti-torture, were quite tolerant of the use of violent military methods of repression in the field and impatient with critics of the military, even of uniformed torturers. Philippe Héduy, author of a diffuse *journal de route* entitled *Au lieutenant des*

---

by French troops during the Algerian War. Its hero, the son of a pacifist nurtured on readings of Romain Rolland, Giono, Tolstoy, and Gandhi, refuses to return to combat after coming to his Jura home on convalescent leave and is killed by local forces of order during a shoot-out.

Taglaïts (1960), abhorred torture and discouraged recourse to it by others, but he bemoans what he terms «the magnificent isolation» of the army: loved by none, criticized by all, it was, he insists, continually being bidden by rich French colonists to strike ever harder with the same hand that forces at home were tying to its back. Héduy launches a scathing attack on all those elements that he holds responsible for preventing a victory which, he is certain, could have been won, an attack to which he time and again returns throughout the book. These were many: the French government, which, in his view, was conducting a «war from the fingertips,» «the France of Pilate, which no longer wanted to assume responsibility,» the «suburbanite priests,» «the ill-engaged writers,» the «drawing room Muscovites,» the committees formed to defend «those bomb-throwing Joans of Arc,» and so on; in sum, all the «French *fellagha*.» This is the lament of one who, without envisaging the war as a struggle between the Cross and the Crescent, as did former rightist premier Georges Bidault, shared Bidault's and General Juin's stubborn determination to hold on to French Algeria at any cost. So much did the preservation of French *présence* in North Africa—in the fullest sense of the term—mean to Héduy that, in late 1961, when De Gaulle was busily liquidating the influence of the *jusqu'au-boutistes,* he was arrested for taking part in a plot to assassinate the president.

In his *Guerre sans visage* (1961), orientalist and sociologist Paul Mus, here publisher and commentator of his son's wartime letters from Algeria, assigns the bulk of the blame for the lack of popular support of the war to politicians and to the press. Whereas in the main he writes in the dispassionate vein that characterizes the writing of scientists and at no time betrays his emotion over the death in combat of his only son, paratrooper lieutenant Émile Mus, he makes no effort to hide his feelings whenever he dwells on the disaffection of the

French soldier through the indifferent and loose-ended promotion of the war. Just as he cannot abide the deception of equating the fighting of a war with «operations for the maintenance of order,» so he cannot stomach the relegation of news of twenty French deaths in combat action «to five lines on page four» of the newspaper, wedged between splashes on movie stars and items on the latest exploits of the *blousons noirs*. And Professor Mus, who had served as a paratroop captain during the French Indochinese War and whose writing on that war heavily underscored his thesis that French solidarity should have been determinedly pursued as a *sine qua non* for victory over a foe animated by a potent sense of national unity, now inveighs against those who, in the name of national unity, were doing their utmost to cover up the abuses of recalcitrant French colonialist and military elements and to undermine the efforts of others toward ensuring the future reconciliation of present adversaries.

In his military diary *Nous avons pacifié Tazalt* (1957), paratrooper officer Jean-Yves Alquier reserves his heaviest blows for intellectuals critical of methods resorted to by French troops in the repression, pointing out at the same time that the mighty efforts of his unit to reestablish friendly relations with the Moslem population were constantly being nullified because of the ability of twenty throat-cutting rebel terrorists to intimidate a country district numbering 25,000 inhabitants, with the reader finding himself forced to conclude that, the book's title to the contrary, Tazalt had not really been pacified and that the entire French pacification effort was doomed to failure.

The win-at-any-cost hard-liners found a most enthusiastic and influential spokesman—influential because his books sell so well—in journalist-novelist Jean Lartéguy, who had fought in the Korean War as a paratrooper in a French battalion. Haunted by the twin ghosts of the 1940 *débâcle* and of

Indochina, none were more determined not to be robbed of victory than the group of paratrooper veterans about whom revolves the action of Lartéguy's novel *Les Centurions* (1960), of which ultimately over a million copies were sold in France and abroad. To these embittered veterans of Dien Bien Phu a moral victory is no victory at all and, since in their lexicon military defeat would be defined as the crime of crimes, they can hardly wait to apply in another guerrilla war the hard lessons taught them by their communist conquerors in Asia, lessons now being applied against them by thousands of Algerians who had seen action there on their side. Under the aegis of their brash, jaunty, myth-building leader, Colonel Raspéguy, they mold a mixture of ragtag reservists and of the dregs of various paratrooper units into the toughest *para* regiment in North Africa. Their aim is to build a revolutionary army to fight a revolutionary type of war, an army of «non-communist communists,» since, as Raspéguy stresses, military history contains no example of a regular army's winning over a well-organized guerrilla. Algeria will be lost, of course, but Raspéguy's regiment meets all of its challenges, supplementing its rough and ready fighting spirit with unhesitating reliance on summary justice, exemplary reprisals, and—yes—torture. What matter if parliamentary bleeding hearts and hierarchical superiors be shocked by the methods, so long as rebel networks are undone, the *djebels* are pacified, and it is again safe to walk in the streets of Algiers? Torture, kill, ravage—but win—and if you are so foolish as to want to ask yourselves any questions, do so later: this is the utilitarian philosophy Raspéguy inculcates in his fighting men (23).

No such utilitarian extremist is the colonel-protagonist

---

(23) Lartéguy's novel provided the scenario for the Hollywood-produced film *Lost Command* (1966), with Anthony Quinn playing the lead role.

of rightist writer Jean Brune's gargantuan novel *Cette Haine qui ressemble à l'amour* (1961). This far more sensitive individual feels acute pangs of conscience. Yet, with him too pragmatism eventually rules over principle, and he too comes to justify torture on the grounds of military necessity. Similarly, in his much lauded first novel *La Grotte* (1961), Colonel Georges Buis, who experienced the war in his own person, depicts the central character, aging Major Enrico, as a man of principle and purpose. Here again principle becomes subordinate to purpose, however, with Enrico turning a blind eye in the direction of the warriors under his command when passion or, he implies, practicality, causes them to forsake their humanity.

There was, then, no solid front by French writers in the campaign waged against torture and the excesses of the repression. There could not have been. Passions ran too high, loyalties were too fierce, and the war was too complex. At the same time, as has been seen, the motivations of some of the crusaders were not wholly unadulterated. And if no French Kiplings were to glorify the Algerian War, this was because it was too dirty an affair to bear glorification. Here one can readily assent to the judgment of Geoffrey Bocca, who writes: «Few modern wars have been uglier and dirtier than the Algerian war. It had about it a sordid unnaturalness, like abortion. It pitted comrade against comrade, forced one to hate opponents one would have preferred to admire and compelled soldiers to assume attitudes repugnant to them. It resembled the mythical succubus, the female demon suposed to haunt the sleep of mortal men and sap their virility, the feminine counterpart of the incubus, which ravished mortal women while they slept and was responsible for the birth of demons, witches and deformed children» (24). If, finally,

---

(24) Geoffrey Bocca, *The Secret Army* (Englewood Cliffs, N.J.: Prentice-Hall, 1968), p. 152.

for the French the war's chief legacy was a sea of bitterness and a further divided citizenry, it did, nevertheless, again demonstrate that large numbers of French men and women of letters ever stand ready to raise their banners and their voices against those who would degrade humanity and themselves.

SELECTED BIBLIOGRAPHY

Adam, Paul. *La Littérature et la guerre.* Paris: Crès, 1916.

Aldridge, John W. *After the Lost Generation: A Critical Study of the Writers of Two World Wars.* New York: McGraw-Hill, 1951.

Alvarez, A. «The Literature of the Holocaust,» *Commentary,* November 1964, pp. 65-69.

Bergonzi, Bernard. *Heroes' Twilight: A Study of the Literature of the Great War.* London: Constable, 1965.

Bieber, Konrad F. *L'Allemagne vue par les écrivains de la Résistance française.* Genève: Droz, and Lille: Giard, 1954.

Bonneville, Georges. *Prophètes et témoins de l'Europe: Essai sur l'idée d'Europe dans la littérature française de 1914 à nos jours.* Leiden: Synthoff, 1961.

Brée, Germaine, and Bernauer, George. *Defeat and Beyond: An Anthology of French Wartime Writing, 1940-1945.* New York: Pantheon, 1970.

Cayrol, Jean. «D'un romanesque concentrationnaire,» *Esprit,* September 1949, pp. 340-57.

Cooperman, Stanley. *World War I and the American Novel.* Baltimore: The Johns Hopkins Press, 1967.

Cru, Jean Norton. *Du Témoignage.* Paris: N.R.F., 1930.

Cru, Jean Norton. *Témoins: Essai d'analyse et de critique des souvenirs de combattants édités en français de 1915 à 1928.* Paris: Les Étincelles, 1929.

Debû-Bridel, Jacques (ed.). *La Résistance intellectuelle: Textes et témoignages réunis et présentés par J. Debû-Bridel.* Paris: Julliard, 1970.

Falls, Cyril. *War Books: A Critical Guide.* London: Peter Davies, 1930.

Field, Frank. *Three French Writers and the Great War: Studies in the Rise of Communism and Fascism.* Cambridge: Cambridge University Press, 1975.

Fussell, Paul. *The Great War and Modern Memory.* New York and London: Oxford Univrsity Press, 1975.

Gibson, Robert. «The First World War and the Literary Consciousness,» in John Cruickshank (ed.), *French Literature and its*

Background, Vol. 6, *The Twentieth Century*. London: Oxford University Press, 1970, pp. 55-72.

Goldberger, Avril. *Visions of a New Hero: The Heroic Life according to André Malraux and earlier advocates of human grandeur*. Paris: Minard, 1965.

Gray, J. Glenn. *The Warriors: Reflections on Men in Battle*. New York: Harcourt, Brace, 1959.

John, S. B. «Vichy France, 1940-1944: The Literary Image,» in John Cruickshank (ed.), *French Literature and its Background*, Vol. 6, *The Twentieth Century*. London: Oxford University Press, 1970, pp. 205-25.

Klein, Holger (ed.). *The First World War in Fiction: A Collection of Critical Essays*. London: Macmillan, 1976.

Langer, Lawrence L. *The Holocaust and the Literary Imagination*. New Haven and London: Yale University Press, 1975.

Miller, Wayne C. *An Armed America, its Face in Fiction: A History of the American Military Novel*. New York: New York University Press, 1970.

Parrot, Louis. *L'Intelligence en guerre: Panorama de la pensée française dans la clandestinité*. Paris: La Jeune Parque, 1945.

Pfeiler, William K. *War and the German Mind: The Testimony of Men of Fiction Who Fought at the Front*. New York: Columbia University Press, 1941.

Rabaut, Jean. *L'Antimilitarisme en France, 1810-1975*. Paris: Hachette, 1975.

Remenyi, Joseph. «The Psychology of War Literature,» *The Sewanee Review*, winter, 1944, pp. 137-47.

Rieuneau, Maurice. *Guerre et Révolution dans le roman français de 1919 à 1939*. Paris: Klincksieck, 1974.

Seghers, Pierre. *La Résistance et ses poètes (France 1940-1945)*. Paris: Éditions Seghers, 1974.

Steiner, George. *Language and Silence: Essays on Language, Literature, and the Inhuman*. New York: Atheneum, 1967.

Stromberg, Ronald N. «The Intellectuals and the Coming of War in 1914,» *Journal of European Studies*, June 1973, pp. 109-22.

Tison-Braun, Micheline. *La Crise de l'humanisme. Le Conflit de l'individu et de la société dans la littérature française moderne*, Vol. II, 1914-1939. Paris: Nizet, 1967.

INDEX

A

Abellio, Raymond (pseud. of Jean Georges Soulès), 155.
Abetz, Otto, 53, 155.
Abraham, Pierre, 78n.
Actuelles: Chroniques 1944-1948 (Camus), 162.
Actuelles III: Chroniques algériennes (Camus), 281.
Adam, Georges, 158.
Adam, Paul, 19.
Addams, Jane, 66.
«Adieu du cavalier, L'» (Apollinaire), 24.
Adorable Clio (Giraudoux), 26-28.
Affaire Henri Martin, L' (Sartre et al.), 248-249.
Agamemnon, 46.
Alain (pseud. of Émile Chartier), 24n, 48-50, 103, 107.
Alain-Fournier (pseud. of Henri Fournier), 1, 9.
A la recherche du temps perdu (Proust), 2, 4.
Albert Camus 1913-1960 (Thody), 281.
Aldington, Richard, 88, 193.
Alexander the Great, 44.
Algérie An VII (Martin-Chauffier), 270n, 287.
Algérie en 1957, L' (Tillion), 287-288.
Algérie hors la loi, L' (F. and C. Jeanson), 274.

«À l'Italie» (Apollinaire), 23.
Alleg, Henri, 289-290.
All Quiet on the Western Front (Remarque), 44, 89-90, 205, 264.
Alquier, Jean-Yves, 292.
Ame enchantée, L' (Rolland), 75-77.
Amouroux, Henri, 138n, 148.
Anatole France à la Béchellerie (Le Goff), 17-18.
Anderson Platoon, The Schoendoerffer), 263n.
Andrey, Prince (in *War and Peace*), 130.
Angell, Norman, 66.
Année des vaincus, L' (Chamson), 124.
Annette (in *L'Ame enchantée*), 75-76.
Annonciatrice, L' (Rolland), 76-77.
Annunzio, Gabriele d', 19, 31, 46.
Anouilh, Jean, 161-162.
Anselme, Daniel, 273.
Antimémoires, I (Malraux), 157n.
Antoine (in *Les Thibault*), 96, 97, 102, 103-106.
Apollinaire, Guillaume (pseud. of Wilhelm - Apollinaris Kostrowitsky), 1, 2, 22-25.
Appui-feu sur l'oued Hallaïl (Clostermann), 234, 244-245.
Aragon, Louis, 157.
Arc, Jeanne d', 37, 146, 172, 276.
Arcos, René, 48.
Ardagh, John, 115n.

— 299 —

Argenson, Le Marquis d', 147n.
«Argent, L'» (Péguy), 39.
«Argent suite, L'» (Péguy), 39.
Aristophanes, 43.
Aristotle, 44.
Armée des ombres, L' (Kessel), 150, 181-182.
Aron, Robert, 160.
Arréguy, Fernande (in *Les Forêts de la nuit*), 163, 169, 176, 179-180.
Arréguy, Philippe (in *Les Forêts de la nuit*), 163, 175-176, 177.
Assia (in *L'Annonciatrice*), 77.
Astier de la Vigerie, Emmanuel d', 186.
Attila, 67, 142.
Auberge de l'abîme, L' (Chamson), 123-124.
Au Bon Beurre (Dutourd), 138n.
Auclair, Georges, 275.
Au-dessus de la Mêlée (Rolland), 61-68, 70, 94.
Audin, Maurice, 279.
«Au général de Gaulle» (Claudel), 147.
Au lieutenant des Taglaïts (Héduy), 290-291.
Aumont, Pierre d' (in *Beau Sang*), 229-230.
Autour de la caserne (Bonnetain), 13.
Autour du drame (Roy), 282.
Aux frontières de l'enfer (Guiraud), 252.
Aveline, Claude, 158.
Aventure, L' (Bodard), 253-254.
Aymé, Marcel, 155, 178.

B

Bach, Johann Sebastian, 198.
Bagatelles pour un massacre (Céline), 152.
Bâillon dénoué, Le (Mauriac), 141.
Bainville, Jacques, 171.
Balansun, Émilie de (in *Les Forêts de la nuit*), 163.
Balansun, Francis de (in *Les Forêts de la nuit*), 163-164, 165, 166, 167, 168, 171, 174, 175, 179, 180.
Balansun, Hélène de (in *Les Forêts de la nuit*), 163, 173, 175, 176-177, 185.
Balansun, Comte Pierre de (in *Les Forêts de la nuit*), 163, 166-167, 173, 179, 185.
Ball, Albert, 238.
Bancquart, Marie-Claire, 17n.
Barbusse, Henri, 68, 74, 77, 79-83, 85-94, 109, 127, 193, 250.
Bardot, Brigitte, 275.
Barkan, Raymond, 252.
Barrès, Claude, 271.
Barrès, Maurice, 16, 19, 31, 51, 56, 64-65, 83, 271.
Bataille, Henri, 80.
Bataille dans la rizière, La (Roy), 257.
Bataille de Dien Bien Phu, La (Roy), 255-256.
Bataille du silence, La (Vercors), 169n.
Battle of Algiers, The (Pontecorvo), 271n.
Bayard, Chevalier de (Pierre Terrail), 224.
Bazin, Hervé, 158, 248.
Bazin, René, 83.
Beau Sang (Roy), 229-230.
Beauvoir, Simone de, 142n, 157, 169, 275, 276, 278-280, 282.
Beaux Draps, Les (Céline), 152.
Beckett, Samuel, 158.
Beethoven, Ludwig van, 6, 59, 155.
Benda, Julien, 47n, 158.
Benjamin, René, 83, 155, 271.
Benoit, Pierre, 155.
Béraud, Henri, 155, 161.
Bereire (in *Lectures pour une ombre*), 28.
Berger, Marcel, 48.
Bergson, Henri, 64, 144n.
Berlioz, Hector, 247.
Bernanos, Georges, 88, 149, 160, 286n.
Bernard, Jean-Marc, 1.
Bernard, Odilon (in *Les Justes Causes*), 187, 188, 189, 190-191.

Bernardin de Saint-Pierre, Jacques Henri, 72.
Berthe (in *Les Forêts de la nuit*), 163, 173-174, 179.
Bêtes, Les (Gascar), 193, 198-201.
«Bêtes, Les» (Gascar), 199-200.
Beurling, George, 243.
Bidault, Georges, 291.
Bieber, Konrad, 140n.
Bierce, Ambrose, 266.
Binard, Pierre, 158.
Blanzat, Jean, 158.
Bleton, Pierre, 203.
Bloch, Jean Richard, 105n.
Bloch, Marc, 156.
Bloch (in *Le Temps retrouvé*), 6.
Blum, Léon, 80, 117, 150.
Boak, Denis, 95n.
Bocca, Geoffrey, 294.
Bodard, Lucien, 253-254.
Boisdeffre, Pierre de, 162.
Böll, Heinrich, 46.
Bollardière, General Paris de la, 272.
«Bonheur de Bolinka, Le» (Gascar), 212-213.
Bonnard, Abel, 155.
Bonnetain, Paul, 13.
Bonneville, Georges, 152.
Bontemps (in *Le Temps retrouvé*), 5.
Borde, Alain, 158.
Bordeaux, Henry, 83, 155.
Bory, Jean-Louis, 137, 151, 275.
Bosch, Hieronymus, 202.
Bose, Jagadis, 73.
Bose, Subhas, 73.
Bost, Pierre, 158.
Boulanger, General Georges, 12, 14.
Boupacha, Djamila, 279.
Bouthoul, Gaston, 43, 136n.
Brackner (in *Les Forêts de la nuit*), 168, 169, 170, 171, 174, 179.
Brando, Marlon, 168.
Brasillach, Robert, 153, 161.
Brecht, Bertolt, 46.
Brichot (in *Le Temps retrouvé*), 6.
Bricoule, Alban de (in *Le Songe*), 32-35, 238, 271.

Brodin, Pierre, 114.
Brogan, Denis W., 113n.
Brooke, Rupert, 40.
Brossolette, Pierre, 53n.
Broussards d'Indochine (Descamps), 257, 263.
Brueghel, Pieter, the Younger, 202.
Brune, Jean, 294.
Bucard, Marcel, 149, 190.
Buis, Georges, 294.
Bunau-Varilla, Maurice, 151n.
Burney, Christopher, 203.

C

Caesar, Julius, 217.
Cahier noir, Le (Mauriac), 140.
Caine Mutiny, The (Wouk), 232.
Calligrammes (Apollinaire), 23-25.
Camus, Albert, 70n, 139, 158, 161, 162, 268, 278, 280-282.
Carnets de René Mouchotte, Les (Mouchotte), 232.
Carrière (in *L'Année des vaincus*), 124.
«Caserne haïe» (Drieu la Rochelle), 20.
Cassagnac, Guy de, 1.
Cassou, Jean, 158.
Castries, Colonel Christian de, 255.
Cauchois (in *Les Sept Dernières Plaies*), 135.
Cavalier Miserey, Le (Hermant), 13, 92.
Cayrol, Jean, 158, 197, 202, 205.
Céline, Louis-Ferdinand (pseud. of Louis-Ferdinand Destouches), 47, 70, 88, 152.
Centurions, Les (Lartéguy), 261, 264, 265, 292-293.
Cesbron, Gilbert, 286.
Cette haine qui ressemble à l'amour (Brune), 293-294.
Chaban-Delmas, Jacques, 156.
Chack, Paul, 155.
Chagrin et la Pitié, Le (Ophuls), 149, 184n.
Chamberlain, Neville, 107.

Chamson, André, 117-127, 158.
Chanson de Roland, La, 257n.
Chanson, General, 263.
«Chant de l'honneur» (Apollinaire), 25.
Chants et prières pour les pilotes (Roy), 218.
Char, René, 157.
Chardonne, Jacques, 155.
Charles X, 221.
Charlus, Baron de (in *Le Temps retrouvé*), 5.
Chastenet, Jacques, 1.
Chateaubriand, François-René de, 7.
Châteaubriant, Alphonse de, 79, 123, 154.
Cheval, René, 70n.
Chevallier, Gabriel, 48.
«Chevaux, Les» (Gascar), 198-199.
Chevaux du soleil, Les (Roy), 231.
Chevigné, Pierre de, 257n.
Chevrier in *La Vallée heureuse*, 223, 227-228, 231.
Choltitz, General Dietrich von, 186, 220.
Chronique de la Grande Guerre (Barrès), 64.
Cinq Ans prisonnier des Viets (Richard), 257.
Civilisation (Duhamel), 128, 131-133, 135.
Clanricard (in *Les Hommes de bonne volonté*), 55.
Clarté (Barbusse), 90-91, 92.
Claudel, Paul, 83, 147.
Clausewitz, Karl von, 63, 264, 286.
Clavel, Bernard, 289n.
Clemenceau, Georges, 9, 75-76, 120, 255, 268.
Clerambault (Rolland), 70-71.
Clerambault (in *Clerambault*, 70-71.
Clermont, Émile, 1, 9.
Clifford, Lord (in *Le Temps viendra*), 57.
Clostermann, Jacques, 232.
Clostermann, Pierre, 229, 231-245.
Cogny, General René, 255-256.

Coignard, L'abbé (in *Les Opinions de M. Jérôme Coignard*), 15.
Colette, Gabrielle-Sidonie, 161.
Coligny-Châtillon, Louise de, 24.
Collins, Larry, 186.
Comédie de Charleroi, La (Drieu la Rochelle), 20-21.
Comme un mauvais ange (Roy), 228.
«Comprenne qui voudra» (Éluard), 159n.
«Concert, Un» (Duhamel), 135.
Contre la torture (Simon), 285-286.
Convulsion de la force (Alain), 49-50.
Corday, Michel, 48.
Corneille, Pierre, 37, 172, 285.
Costellot, Jacques (in *Les Forêts de la nuit*), 163, 171-172, 177, 179.
Costellot, Marguerite (in *Les Forêts de la nuit*), 163, 168, 170-171, 174, 179.
Cotta, Michèle, 146n.
Couple France-Allemagne, Le (Romains), 52-53.
Courtade, Pierre, 158, 252.
Courteline, Georges (pseud. of Georges Moinaux), 87.
Crane, Stephen, 33, 93, 193.
Croix de bois, Les (Dorgelès), 51, 90.
Cru, Jean Norton, 86.
Cruel Sea, The (Monsarrat), 232.
Curtis, Jean-Louis, 137, 162-192.

D

Daladier, Édouard, 30, 79, 107, 142.
Daniel (in *Les Thibault*), 97, 102, 106.
Dante Alighieri, 203.
Danse sur le feu et l'eau, La (Faure), 45-46.
Darlan, Admiral François, 150.
Darnand, Joseph, 149.
Darricade, Justin (in *Les Forêts de la nuit*), 163, 164-166, 176, 178, 180-181.

Daudet, Léon, 16, 83.
Daudet, Lucien, 64.
Déat, Marcel, 49, 148-149.
Débâcle, La (Zola), 13, 129.
Debout les vivants (Margue-
ritte), 48.
Debû-Bridel, Jacques, 158.
Decatur, Stephen, 122.
Decour, Jacques (pseud. of
Jacques Decourdemanche), 158.
Défense des lettres (Duhamel),
128.
*De la chute à la libération de
Paris* (D'Astier de la Vigerie),
186.
Delahaye, Cécile (in *Les Forêts
de la nuit*), 163, 168, 173, 174,
178-179.
Delahaye, Gérard (in *Les Forêts
de la nuit*), 163, 173, 176.
«De la situation faite au parti
intellectuel devant les acci-
dents de la gloire temporelle»
(Péguy), 36.
Delestraint, General Charles, 164.
Delvert, Charles, 48.
Demokos (in *La Guerre de Troie
n'aura pas lieu*), 30.
«Dernier, Le» (Duhamel), 135.
Déroulède, Georges-Léon, 51.
Desastres de la guerra, Los (Go-
ya), 263.
Descamps, Georges-Léon, 257, 262.
Descaves, Lucien, 13.
«Déserteur, Le» (Vian), 271.
Desnos, Robert, 158.
Des Pres, Terrence, 197n.
Despuech, Jacques, 254-255.
Devaulx, Noël, 158.
Domenach, Jean-Marie, 158, 248,
274, 283.
Donadieu, François (in *Les Justes
Causes*), 188-189, 190, 191.
Donat, Alexander, 197, 203.
Dongo, Fabrice del (in *La Char-
treuse de Parme*), 101, 238.
Dorgelès, Roland (pseud. of
Roland Léclavelé), 51-52, 90,
161.
Doriot, Jacques, 149, 191.
Dorval, Commandant Jacques (in

Appui-feu sur l'oued Hallaïl),
245.
Dos Passos, John, 92.
Dossier Jean Muller (Muller),
286.
Dostoyevsky, Feodor, 203.
Dreyfus, Alfred, 3, 4, 14, 37.
Drieu la Rochelle, Pierre, 18-22,
152.
Drôle de jeu (Vailland), 165, 182-
183.
Drouot, Paul, 1.
Drumont, Édouard, 171.
Duhamel, Georges, 47, 80, 127-136,
147, 266.
«D'un romanesque concentration-
naire» (Cayrol), 202n.
Duras, Marguerite, 159.
Durtain, Luc (pseud. of André
Nepveu), 47.
Dutourd, Jean, 138n, 147-148, 158.
Duval, Archbishop Léon, 268.

E

Ebrennac, Werner von (in *Le
Silence de la mer*), 168.
Échec de la force (Alain), 49-50.
Eckermann, Johann Peter, 196.
Eichmann, Adolf, 207, 220.
Einstein, Albert, 116.
Einstein, Carl, 176n.
Eisenhower, General Dwight,
157.
Éluard, Paul, 158, 159n.
Emerson, Ralph Waldo, 136.
Emmanuel, Pierre (pseud. of
Noël Mathieu), 147n, 158.
Enchaînements, Les (Barbusse),
92-93.
Engels, Friedrich, 60n.
Enlisement, L' (Bodard), 253.
Ennemis complémentaires, Les
(Tillion), 288.
Enrico, Major (in *La Grotte*),
294.
Entre chiens et loups (Cesbron),
286.
«Entre chiens et loups» (Gascar),
200-201.
Entretiens dans le tumulte
(Duhamel), 134-135.

Épilogue (Martin du Gard), 94, 102-107.
Équarrissage pour tous, L' (Vian), 183.
Équinoxe de septembre, L' (Montherlant), 35.
Erasmus, 122.
Ernst (in *Le Temps des morts*), 211.
Escholier, Raymond, 48.
«Étangs de Fontargente, Les» (Pozner), 288.
Été 1914, L' (Martin du Gard), 94, 95-102.
Etes-vous neutres devant le crime? (Loyson), 65.
Etiemble, René, 148, 152, 160.
«Europe» (Romains), 52.
«Ève» (Péguy), 41.
Exil, L' (Montherlant), 32.

F

Fabre-Luce, Alfred, 155.
Faits divers (Barbusse), 93n.
Fall, Bernard, 247.
Farewell to Arms, A (Hemingway), 129.
Faure, Elie, 20, 45.
Favre, Geneviève, 40.
Femme infidèle, La (Roy), 230.
Femmes, Les (Gascar), 212.
«Femmes, Les» (Gascar), 212-213.
Fénelon, Bertrand de, 3.
Feraoun, Mouloud, 272.
Fer de Dieu, Le (Hardy), 251.
Fernandez, Ramon, 155.
Ferrer, Hélène (in *La Femme infidèle*), 230.
Feu, Le (Barbusse), 81-83, 85-90, 91, 109.
Feux du ciel (Clostermann), 234, 243-244.
Figeac (in *Les Forêts de la nuit*), 180.
Fils de Jerphanion, Le (Romains), 183n.
Fins dernières, Les (De Boisdeffre), 162.
Fin des illusions, La (Guillain), 256n.

Finiels (in *Roux le bandit*), 118, 121.
Fisson, Pierre, 157.
Fleming, Henry (in *The Red Badge of Courage*), 33, 238.
Fleuve rouge, Le (Roy), 259, 265.
Florian-Parmentier, Ernest, 48.
Foch, Marshal Ferdinand, 9.
Foerster, Wilhelm, 66.
Fonck, René, 234, 238.
Fond de cantine (Drieu la Rochelle), 20.
Fontanes, Thibault (in *Les Justes Causes*), 189, 191.
Fontanin, Madame de (in *Les Thibault*), 97.
Force de l'âge, La (De Beauvoir), 142n.
Force des choses, La (De Beauvoir), 278-279, 280.
Forel, Auguste, 68.
Forêts de la nuit, Les (Curtis), 137, 162-181, 183-185, 191-192.
Fouchet, Max-Pol, 158.
Fowler (in *The Quiet American*), 260.
Fragonard, Jean Honoré, 198.
Fraigneau, André, 155.
Français, si vous saviez... (Bernanos), 149n.
France, Anatole (pseud. of Jacques Anatole Thibault), 2, 12-18, 61, 64, 80.
Franco, General Francisco, 125, 280.
Françoise (in *Le Temps retrouvé*), 6.
François-Poncet, André, 267.
Frank, Anne, 203.
Franklin, Benjamin, 126.
Franz, Kurt, 168, 207n.
Franz (in «Entre chiens et loups»), 200-201.
Franz-Ferdinand, Archduke, 95.
Frénaud, André, 158.
Fumet, Stanislas, 158.
Funke Leben, Der (Remarque), 205-206.

G

Galliéni, Marshal Joseph, 9.

Galsworthy, John, 63.
Galtier-Boissière, Jean, 136n, 141, 151.
Gandhi, Mohandas, 73, 74, 77, 78, 285.
Gary, Romain, 193-194.
Gascar, Pierre (pseud. of Pierre Fournier), 193-194, 198-202, 208-213.
Gaspard (Benjamin), 83-85.
Gaspard (in *Gaspard*), 84.
Gaulle, General Charles de, 12, 148, 155, 219, 220, 268, 278, 283-284, 287, 291.
Genet, Jean, 269.
Géniaux, Claire, 48.
Géographie cordiale de l'Europe (Duhamel), 128.
George, Lloyd, 75-76.
Gérard, Georges, 146.
Gérard (in *La Trompette des anges*), 250.
Gerbe des forces, La (De Châteaubriant), 154.
Gerlach, Frantz von (in *Les Séquestrés d'Altona*), 276.
Giap, General Vo nguyen, 247, 249, 254-255.
Gide, André, 2, 7-12, 94, 97, 143n, 169, 190.
Gilbert, Gustave M., 207n.
Giono, Jean, 47, 107-116, 125-126, 154.
Giraudoux, Jean, 26-31, 48, 128.
Giron, Roger, 158.
Godorp, Madame (in *Les Hommes de bonne volonté*), 56.
Goebbels, Joseph, 30.
Goering, Hermann, 168, 238.
Goes, Albrecht, 211.
Goethe, Johann Wolfgang von, 9, 67, 196, 198.
Gorki, Maxim, 68.
Gouzenko, Igor, 78n.
Goya y Lucientes, Francisco de, 263.
Grancher, Marcel, 48.
Grand Cirque, Le (Clostermann), 232-244.
Grand Naufrage, Le (Roy), 219-220.

Grand Troupeau, Le (Giono), 108-111.
Grand Voyage, Le (Semprun), 195n.
Grande Illusion, La (Renoir), 46, 142.
Grands Cimetières sous la lune, Les (Bernanos), 287n.
Grautoff, Otto, 63.
Grauwin, Paul, 257, 266.
Gray, J. Glenn, 23n.
Greene, Graham, 259-260.
Grotte, La (Buis), 294.
Groussard, Serge, 158.
Guedj, Max, 231, 237, 243.
Guéhenno, Jean, 47, 83n, 118, 141, 148, 158.
Guérin, Roland (in *Entre chiens et loups*), 286.
Guerre d'Algérie, La (Roy), 282.
Guerre de Troie n'aura pas lieu, La (Giraudoux), 29-30, 48-49.
Guerre d'Indochine, La (Bodard), 253-254.
Guerre et la paix, La (Proudhon), 43.
Guerre et Littérature (Duhamel), 135.
Guerre n'existe pas, La (Durtain), 47.
Guerre sans visage (Mus), 291-292.
Guesclin, Bernard du, 92.
Guillain, Robert, 256n.
Guillevic, Eugène, 158.
Guilloux, Louis, 48.
Guiraud, Georges-Henri, 252.
Guitry, Sacha, 151.
Gun, Nerin, 194n.
Guynemer, Georges, 238.

H

Halimi, Gisèle, 279.
Hamilton, Alastair, 142n.
Hannibal, 31, 39, 265.
Harcourt, Pierre d', 196, 203.
Hardy, René, 158, 251.
Haughey, Seamus, 32n.
Hauptmann, Gerhart, 67.
Haverkamp (in *Les Hommes de bonne volonté*), 54-55.

20

Hector (in *La Guerre de Troie n'aura pas lieu*), 29, 48-49.
Hécube (in *La Guerre de Troie n'aura pas lieu*), 30.
Héduy, Philippe, 270, 290-291.
Hegel, Georg, 122.
Heine, Heinrich, 59.
Hélène (in *La Guerre de Troie n'aura pas lieu*), 29-30.
Hemingway, Ernest, 129.
Henri IV, 146.
Henriot, Philippe, 150.
Hermant, Abel, 13, 92, 155.
Hérold-Paquis (pseud. of Jean Hérold), 149.
Herr, Lucien, 39.
Hervé, Gustave, 39, 61, 99, 155.
Heydrich, Reinhard, 168.
Hidden Enemy, The (D'Harcourt), 196n.
Hillary, Richard, 229, 241n.
Himmler, Heinrich, 198, 220, 276.
Hiroshima, mon amour (Duras), 159.
Histoire de la captivité des Français en Allemagne, 1939-1945 (Gascar), 210n.
Hitler, Adolf, 29, 44, 136, 142, 150, 154, 198.
Ho Chi Minh, 249, 260, 263.
Hoess, Rudolf, 206-207, 220.
Hoffman, Stanley, 184n.
Homer, 46.
Homme à l'épée, L' (Roy), 32n.
Hommes de bonne volonté, Les (Romains), 54-57.
Horsman, David (in *Les Forêts de la nuit*), 171-172.
Hougron, Jean, 251, 263.
Huddleston, Sisley, 151n.
Huggard, William, 136n.
Hugnet, Georges, 158.
Hugo, Victor, 16, 37, 40, 227, 266.
Humiliation, L' (Bodard), 253.

I

Ikor, Roger, 284-285, 286.
Indy, Vincent d', 64.
Inskip, Donald, 27n.
Interrogation (Drieu la Rochelle), 19-20.

«In the Looking Glass» (Hoffman), 184n.
Invasion 14 (Van der Meersch), 48.
Ionesco, Eugène, 151.
Irving, David, 226n.
Is Paris Burning? (Collins and Lapierre), 186.

J

J'accuse le général Massu (Roy), 220.
Jacques (in *Les Thibault*), 96, 97-102, 103.
Jalicot (in *Lectures pour une ombre*), 28.
Jallez (in *Les Hommes de bonne volonté*), 55, 56.
Jarry, Alfred, 25n.
Jaurès, Jean, 18, 39, 71, 99, 100n.
Jean-Christophe (Rolland), 58-60, 63, 70.
Jean-Christophe (in *Jean-Christophe*), 59-60, 61, 78.
Jean le Bleu (Giono), 111.
Jeanson, Colette, 274.
Jeanson, Francis, 248, 274.
Jenny (in *Les Thibault*), 97, 103.
Jérôme (in *Les Thibault*), 96.
Jerphanion, Jean (in *Les Hommes de bonne volonté*), 55, 56.
Jerphanion, Jean-Pierre (in *Le Fils Jerphanion*), 183n.
Jessup, Everett, 45n.
Jésus (Barbusse), 81.
J'étais médecin à Dien-Bien-Phu (Grauwin), 257.
Joffre, Marshal Joseph, 9, 120, 136.
Joinville, Jean sire de, 20, 37.
Jolinon, Joseph, 48.
Jouhandeau, Marcel, 155.
Jourdain, Francis, 107.
Journal des années de guerre 1914-1919 (Rolland), 64n, 65n, 67n.
Journal des années noires (Guéhenno), 47n, 141.
Journal d'un combattant Viet-Minh (Ngo-Van-Chiêu), 262.
Journal 1955-1962 (Feraoun), 272n.

Journal (1913-1922) (Gide), 8-11.
Journal (1942-1949) (Gide), 9n.
Jours sanglants (Chastenet), 1.
Jouve, Pierre-Jean, 47-48, 79.
Juin, General Alphonse, 291.
Jünger, Ernst, 46, 143, 169n.
Justes Causes, Les (Curtis), 185-192.
«Justice pour les collabos» (Etiemble), 152.

K

Kafka, Franz, 198, 285.
Kant, Immanuel, 44, 63.
Karr, Alphonse, 180.
Kennedy, John F., 269.
Kessel, Joseph, 150, 181 182.
Kipling, Rudyard, 19, 46, 63, 264.
Kleist, Siegfried von (in *Siegfried* and in *Siegfried le Limousin*), 19.
Koestler, Arthur, 143, 189-190.
Kogon, Eugen, 203.
Kuragin, Anatol (in *War and Peace*), 130.

L

La Bruyère, Jean de, 46.
Lacoste, Robert, 272, 283.
Lacretelle, Jacques de, 155.
Lafon, André, 1.
La Gorce, Paul-Marie de, 257n.
Lajpat Rai, 73.
Lallemand, Marcel, 95.
Lalou, Étienne, 158.
Lamartine, Alphonse de, 53.
Lang, Rudolf (in *La Mort est mon métier*), 206-207.
Langevin, Paul, 107.
Lanzmann, Claude, 275.
Lapierre, Dominique, 186.
Laporte, René, 158.
La Praye, Laurent, 250, 264, 265.
Lardenne, Victor (in *Les Forêts de la nuit*), 163, 171, 179.
Larsanne, Commandant Jean de (in *Portrait d'un officier*), 285.
Lartéguy, Jean, 158, 261, 262, 264, 265, 292-293.

Lattre de Tassigny, Lieutenant Bernard de, 257.
Lattre de Tassigny, Marshal Jean de, 126, 253-254, 260.
Latzko, Andreas, 68, 92.
Laulerque (in *Les Hommes de bonne volonté*), 55.
Laurent, Jacques, 158.
Laurentie, Lucienne, 158.
Laval, Pierre, 148n, 150, 159.
La Varende, Jean de, 155.
Lavedan, Henri, 56.
Lavoncourt, Jean de (in *Les Forêts de la nuit*), 163, 177.
Lawrence, T. E., 266.
Lazareff, Pierre, 274.
Léautaud, Paul, 130.
Lebrun, Albert, 108.
Leclerc, General Charles, 263
Leclerc, Lieutenant, 257.
Lectures pour une ombre (Giraudoux), 27-28.
Lefebvre, Raymond, 48, 80.
Légende des siècles, La (Hugo), 227.
Le Goff, Marcel, 17.
Leiris, Michel, 158, 248.
Lenin, Vladimir, 78.
Lépreuses, Les (Montherlant), 31.
Lescure, Jean, 158.
Lescure, Pierre de, 158.
Lettre aux directeurs de la Résistance (Paulhan), 162.
Lettre aux paysans sur la pauvreté et la paix (Giono), 108, 113-114.
«Lettre ouverte à Gerhart Hauptmann» (Rolland), 67.
Lettres de Guillaume Apollinaire, (Apollinaire), 25n.
Lettres et entretiens (Péguy), 40.
Lévi-Strauss, Claude, 275.
Lewis, Cecil, 241.
Leyris, Pierre, 158.
Lieu du supplice, Le (Pozner), 288.
Lieutenant en Algérie (Servan-Schreiber), 290.
Liluli (Rolland), 69-70.
Liluli (in *Liluli*), 69.
Llôp'ich (in *Liluli*), 69.

Loti, Pierre, 13.
Louis XIV, 146, 275.
Louis XVIII, 221.
Loyson, Paul-Hyacinthe, 65-66.
Luce (in *Pierre et Luce*), 72.
Luchaire, Jean, 149.
Lucifer (in *La Révolte des anges*), 14.

M

MacGregor, G. H. C., 120n.
Mac Orlan, Pierre, 155.
Macquart, Jean (in *La Débâcle*), 111.
Maeterlinck, Maurice, 63-64.
Mahatma Gandhi (Rolland), 73.
Maistre, Joseph de, 44, 122.
Maître-Dieu (in *Liluli*), 69.
Major, Jean-Louis, 230n.
Malerbe, Henri, 158.
Mallet-Joris, Françoise, 279.
Malraux, André, 156, 157, 197, 245, 251, 277-278.
Man, Henri de, 53.
Mangin, General Charles, 51.
Mann, Thomas, 63.
Mannock, Edward, 238.
Manuel (in *Les Thibault*), 102.
Mao Tse-tung, 264.
Marat (in *Drôle de jeu*), 165, 182-183.
Marc (in *L'Ame enchantée*), 75, 76-77.
Marceau, Félicien, 147n.
Marcel (in *Le Temps retrouvé*), 3.
Marcenac, Jean, 158.
Margueritte, Victor, 48, 107.
Marin la Meslée, Edmond, 224, 231, 238.
Mars ou la guerre jugée (Alain), 49-50, 103.
Martel, Thierry de, 139.
Martin, Henri, 248-249.
Martin, Marietta, 158.
Martin-Chauffier, Louis, 64n, 158, 195, 269-270, 287.
Martin du Gard, Roger, 94-107, 158, 278.
Marx, Karl, 60n.

Massip, Roger, 158.
Massis, Henri, 65.
Masson, Loys, 158.
Massu, General Jacques, 220, 270, 272.
Maupassant, Guy de, 13.
Maurel, Micheline, 158.
Mauriac, François, 139-142, 147, 150, 158, 160-162, 191, 270, 278, 281, 283-284, 290.
Maurois, André, 2n, 88.
Maurras, Charles, 16, 19, 39, 83, 99n, 152-153, 171, 258.
Maxime (in *Clerambault*), 71.
Maydieu, Jean, 158.
Mazet (in *Les Thibault*), 105.
Mazière, Christian de la, 149.
Mein Kampf (Hitler), 44, 154.
Meister, Joseph, 139.
Melik, Rouben, 158.
Mellor, Alex, 277.
Melville, Herman, 46.
Mémoires d'outre-tombe (Chateaubriand), 7.
Mémoires politiques (Mauriac), 140.
Mémorial de la guerre blanche (Duhamel), 128.
Mendès-France, Pierre, 231.
Men in War (Latzko), 92.
Mère et fils (Rolland), 75-76.
Merglen, Albert, 248n.
Merkel (in *Les Forêts de la nuit*), 174-175.
Merle, Robert, 205-208.
Merleau-Ponty, Maurice, 158, 272.
Mesure de la France (Drieu la Rochelle), 21.
Métier des armes, Le (Roy), 218-221.
Meynestrel (in *Les Thibault*), 98-99, 100.
Michelet, Edmond, 158, 203.
Michelet, Jules, 37.
Millet, Raymond, 158.
Mirabeau, Honoré de, 139.
Mirbeau, Octave, 61.
Missions inutiles à Saïgon (Despuech), 255.
Mithoerg (in *Les Thibault*), 98.
Mitterrand, François, 269.

«M. Leconte de Lisle à l'Académie Française» (France), 13.
Mollet, Guy, 283.
Mon Journal pendant l'Occupation (Galtier-Boissière), 141.
Monsarrat, Nicholas (pseud. of John Turney), 232.
Montaigne, Michel de, 275.
Montesquieu, Charles de Secondat de, 275.
Montherlant, Henry de, 31-36, 154, 271.
Montluc, Blaise de, 20, 217.
Mon Village à l'heure allemande (Bory), 137, 151.
Morand, Paul, 27, 155.
Morel, E. D., 68.
Morel, Robert, 158.
Morgan, Claude, 158.
Mort en fraude, La (Hougron), 251.
Mort est mon métier, La (Merle), 206-208.
Mortier, Jane, 25.
Mottram, Ralph, 88.
Mouchotte, René, 231, 232, 233, 238.
Moulin, Jean, 156, 164.
Mounier, Emmanuel, 158.
Mounin, Georges, 158.
Moussinac, Léon, 158.
Mozart, Wolfgang Amadeus, 144n.
Muller, Charles, 1.
Muller, Jean, 286.
Murmures de la guerre, Les (Ikor), 284-285.
Mus, Émile, 291.
Mus, Paul, 291-292.
Mussolini, Benito, 179, 283.

N

Naegelen, René, 48.
Naissance des mercenaires, La (Merglen), 248n.
Napoleon I, 19, 44, 62, 136, 221, 258.
Naufragés de l'occident, Les (Barkan), 252.
Navarre, General Henri de, 255, 256.

Navigateur, Le (Roy), 230.
Nehru, Jawaharlal, 73.
Ngo-Van-Chiêu, 262.
Nicolaï, G.-F., 68.
Niess, Robert J., 47n.
Nietzsche, Friedrich, 5, 19, 31, 34, 142.
Nivelle, General Robert, 80-81.
Non (Margueritte), 48.
«Non, je ne regrette rien» (Piaf), xiii.
Nordling, Raoul, 186.
Norpois, Marquis de (in *Le Temps retrouvé*), 6.
«Notre Patrie» (Péguy), 40.
«Notre Père» (Gérard), 146.
Nourritures terrestres, Les (Gide), 97.
Nous avons pacifié Tazalt (Alquier), 292.
Nous étions à Dien-Bien-Phu (Pouget), 256-257.
Nous nous aimerons demain (Stil), 288-289.
Nouveau Bloc-Notes: 1958-1960, Le (Mauriac), 270.
Novotny, Walter, 242.
Noyes, Alfred, 63.
Nuit, La (Wiesel), 204.
Nuit indochinoise, La (Hougron), 251-252.
Nungesser, Charles, 238.

O

«Ode génois» (Romains), 52.
Olivier (in *Jean-Christophe*), 60, 61.
Olivier (in *Le Grand Troupeau*), 109.
Opération gâchis (De Pirey), 259.
Ophuls, Marcel, 149, 184n.
Opinions de M. Jérôme Coignard, Les (France), 14-16.
Oraisons funèbres (Malraux), 156.
Oscar (in *Les Thibault*), 96.
Owen, Wilfred, 88, 91.
Oyarzun, Roland (in *Les Justes Causes*), 189-190, 191.

P

Pagès, Madeleine, 94.

Pages de journal, 1939-1942 (Gide), 11-12.

Pain des temps maudits, Le (Tillard), 211n.

Paravents, Les (Genet), 269.

«Paris sous l'Occupation» (Sartre), 145.

«Paroles au Maréchal» (Claudel), 147.

Parrot, Louis, 158.

Passion de Saint-Exupéry (Roy), 228-229.

Pasteur, Louis, 139.

Paths of Glory, 46.

Patrie humaine, La (Margueritte), 48.

Patton, General George, 44.

Paulhan, Jean, 158, 161.

Paulin, Simon (in *Clarté*), 90, 91.

Pauvre Bitos (Anouilh), 162.

Paxton, Robert, 145n.

«Peace» (Brooke), 40.

Peer (in «Les Chevaux»), 198-199.

Péguy, Charles, 1, 2, 9, 19, 36-41, 79, 146n, 172, 257, 285.

Péguy, Marcel, 146n.

Pellepoix, Darquier de (pseud. of Louis Darquier), 149.

Pergaud, Louis, 1.

Péri, Gabriel, 164, 165.

Pericles, 44.

Permission, La (Anselme), 273.

Perret, Jacques, 157.

Peste, La (Camus), 139.

Pétain, Marshal Henri Philippe, 9, 11, 120, 145-148, 155n, 159, 166, 172, 173, 219.

Peyrefitte, Roger, 155.

Philip (in *Les Thibault*), 106-107.

Piaf, Edith, xiii.

Picasso, Pablo, 279.

Pierre (in *Pierre et Luce*), 72.

Pierre et Luce (Rolland), 71-73.

Pierre-Quint, Léon, 7.

Pilote de guerre (Saint-Exupéry), 216-217.

Pioch, Georges, 107.

Pirey, Phillippe de, 259, 260-261, 263.

«Plein ciel» (Hugo), 227.

Plievier, Theodor, 266.

Plumyène, Jean, 146n.

Poids du ciel, Le (Giono), 108.

Poissonard, Charles-Hubert (in *Au Bon Beurre*), 138n.

Poissonard, Julie (in *Au Bon Beurre*), 138n.

Polichinelle (in *Liluli*), 69.

Politzer, Georges, 158.

Polonius (in *Liluli*), 69.

Ponchardier, Dominique, 158.

Ponge, Francis, 158.

Pons, Maurice, 275.

Pontecorvo, Gillo, 271n.

«Porte de l'enfer, La» (Rodin), 205.

Portrait d'un officier (Simon), 285.

Possession du monde, La (Duhamel), 133-134.

Pouget, Jean, 256-257.

Poulaille, Henry, 48.

Pourrat, Henri, 123.

Pozner, Vladimir, 288.

Préau, Lieutenant, 257.

Précisions (Giono), 108, 115.

Précurseurs, Les (Rolland), 68-69, 70.

Prélude à Verdun (Romains), 54-57.

Prévert, Jacques, 248.

Prévost, Jean, 157.

Prinet, Stanislas (in *Le Songe*), 33, 34, 35.

Promesse de l'aube, La (Gary), 194n.

Proudhon, Pierre-Joseph, 32, 43, 44.

Proust, Marcel, 2-7.

Psichari, Ernest, 1, 9, 217, 220-221, 257.

Pupion (in *Lectures pour une ombre*), 28.

Pyle, Alden (in *The Quiet American*), 259-260.

Q

Quatre mois (Chamson), 126.

Queneau, Raymond, 158.

«Qu'est-ce qu'un collaborateur?» (Sartre), 151.

Question, La (Alleg), 289-290.

Quiet American, The (Greene), 259-260.
Quinze Ans de combat (Rolland), 60n, 74, 78.
Quisling, Vidkun, 148n.

R

Rabelais, François, 46.
Raspéguy, Colonel (in *Les Centurions*), 293.
Rebatet, Lucien, 149.
Reboux, Paul, 48.
Red Badge of Courage, The (Crane), 33.
Redfern, W. D., 114n.
Refus d'obéissance (Giono), 108.
Reitlinger, Gerald, 197n.
Remarque, Erich Maria, 44, 88, 90-91, 93, 193, 205-206, 264.
Rémy, Colonel (pseud. of Gilbert Renault), 156.
Renan, Ernest, 220.
Renn, Ludwig, 193.
Renoir, Jean, 142.
République et son armée, La (De La Gorce), 257n.
Retour de l'enfer (Roy), 223-228.
Retour d'Espagne (Chamson), 125.
«Retour du soldat, Le» (Drieu la Rochelle), 21.
Réveil des morts, Le (Dorgelès), 51-52.
Révolte des anges, La (France), 14.
Révolution de dix-neuf, La (Chamson), 117.
Rhinocéros (Ionesco), 151.
Ribbentrop, Joachim von, 53.
Richard, Pierre, 257.
Richepin, Jean, 56.
Richthofen, Baron Manfred von, 234, 238.
Rilke, Rainer Maria, 198.
Rinaldi (in *A Farewell to Arms*), 129.
Rivière (in *Vol de nuit*), 231.
Rivière noire, La (Courtade), 252.
Robbe-Grillet, Alain, 275.
Rodin, Auguste, 205.

Roland (in *La Chanson de Roland*), 257n.
Rolland, Marie Romain, 64n.
Rolland, Romain, 5, 16, 57-79, 80, 87, 94, 107, 117, 127.
Romain Rolland contre la France (Massis), 65.
Romain Rolland vivant, 1914-1919 (Jouve), 48.
Romains, Jules (pseud. of Louis Farigoule), 52-57.
Roman d'un spahi, Le (Loti), 13.
Romeo and Juliet (Shakespeare), 196.
Rommel, Marshal Erwin, 44.
Rops, Daniel, 161.
Rouge et le Noir, Le (Stendhal), 9n.
Rousseaux, André, 158.
Rousselot, Jean, 158.
Rousset, David, 203.
Roux (in *Roux le bandit*), 118-121.
Roux le bandit (Chamson), 118-121, 125-126.
Roy, Claude, 158, 275.
Roy, Jules, 32n, 193, 217-231, 237, 255-256, 257, 259, 263, 264, 265, 266, 279, 282, 283.
Rumelles (in *Les Thibault*), 105, 106.
Russell, Bertrand, 126.
Rustiger, Lieutenant Friedrich (in *Les Forêts de la nuit*), 168-169, 173.

S

Sadoul, Georges, 158.
Sagan, Françoise, 275, 279.
Saint Aignan, 37.
Saint Augustine, 119.
Saint Bernard, 37.
Sainte Geneviève, 37.
Saint-Exupéry, Antoine de, 215-217, 228-229, 230, 237, 239n, 240, 245.
Saint Louis, 37.
Saint Loup, 37.
Saint-Loup, Robert de (in *Le Temps retrouvé*), 5-6.

Saint Martin, 37.
Saint-Pierre, Bernardin de, 72.
Saint-Saëns, 64.
Salan, Georges, 277n.
Salan, General Raoul, 268, 277n.
Salomé, Coryse (in *Les Forêts de la nuit*), 167, 178.
Salvaing, Louis (in *Les Étangs de Fontargente*), 288.
Sarraute, Nathalie, 275.
Sartre, Jean-Paul, 144-145, 148n, 151, 157, 166, 169, 248, 276-277, 278, 279.
Sassoon, Siegfried, 88.
Sauckel, Fritz, 144.
Saxe, Marshal Maurice de, 272.
Scheler, Lucien, 158.
Schiller, Friedrich von, 6.
Schlumberger, Jean, 161.
Schnitzler, Arthur, 132n.
Schoendoerffer, Pierre, 249-250, 263.
Schubert, Franz, 198.
Schumann, Robert, 5.
Schwarz-Bart, André, 158.
Schwob, André, 156n.
Scipio Africanus, 31.
Seghers, Pierre, 158.
Semprún, Jorge, 195n.
Sentiments, Passions et Signes (Alain), 24n.
Sept Dernières Plaies, Les (Duhamel), 135.
Sept Mystères du destin de l'Europe (Romains), 53-54.
Séquestrés l'Altona, Les (Sartre), 276-277.
Sernet, Claude, 158.
Servan-Schreiber, Jacques, 290.
Servitude et grandeur militaires (Vigny), 44, 220-222.
Shaw, George Bernard, 63.
Siegfried (Giraudoux), 29.
Siegfried et le Limousin (Giraudoux), 29.
Signoret, Simone, 275.
Silence de la mer, Le (Vercors), 158, 168.
Silence des armes, Le (Clavel), 298n.
Simon, Claude, 275.

Simon, Pierre-Henri, 285-286.
Soirées de Médan, Les (Zola), 13.
Soleil au ventre (Hougron), 251.
Solstice de juin (Montherlant), 36.
Sommer, Master Sergeant, 211.
Songe, Le (Montherlant), 32-35.
Soubrier, Dominique (in *Le Songe*), 34.
Souday, Paul, 65.
Sous-offs (Descaves), 13.
Spellman, Cardinal Francis, 122.
Stangl, Franz, 196.
Steegmuller, Francis, 144n.
Steiner, Georges, 198, 276.
Steiner, Jean-François, 206n, 208n, 209n.
Stendhal (pseud. of Henri Beyle), 46, 101.
Stéphane, Roger, 158, 281.
Stil, André, 288-289.
Stroheim, Erich von, 142.
Stülpnagel, General Karl Heinrich von, 143.
Suffert, Georges, 274.
Sulphart (in *Les Croix de bois*), 90.
Sunday, Billy, 68.
Sur la voie glorieuse (France), 16.
«Sur l'eau» (Maupassant), 13.
Suzanne et le Pacifique (Giraudoux), 27.

T

Tagore, Rabindranath, 73.
Tardieu, Jean, 158.
Tauriac, Michel, 251, 264, 265.
Tavernier, René, 158.
Taxis de la Marne, Les (Dutourd), 147.
Témoins (Cru), 86n.
Temps des morts, Le (Gascar), 193, 201-202, 208-212, 213.
Temps retrouvé, Le (Proust), 3-7.
Temps viendra, Le (Rolland), 57-58.
Thérive, André, 48.

Thibault, Les (Martin du Gard), 94, 95-107.
Thierry, Albert, 1.
Thiry, Marcel, 158.
Thody, Philip, 281.
Thomas, Edith, 158.
Three Soldiers (Dos Passos), 92.
Tillard, Paul, 158, 211n.
Tillion, Germaine, 287-288.
Tolstoy, Count Lev, 46, 56, 78, 93, 130, 217.
Torture, La (Mellor), 277.
Torture: Cancer of Democracy (Vidal-Naquet), 279.
Trachel, Clément (in *Les Enchaînements*), 92.
Trafic des piastres, Le (Despuech), 255.
Treblinka (J.-F. Steiner), 206n, 208n, 209n.
Triolet, Elsa, 158.
Triomphe de la vie (Giono), 116.
317e Section, La (Schoendoerffer), 249-250.
Trompette des anges, La (La Praye), 250, 265.
Trou, Le (Tauriac), 251.
Tu récolteras la tempête (Hougron), 251.
Turenne, Vicomte Henri de, 92.
Turpin (in *La Chanson de Roland*), 122.
Tzara, Tristan, 158.

U

Ubu Roi (Jarry), 25n.
Unruhige Nacht (Goes), 211.
Unsdorfer, S. B., 196, 203.
Uranus (Aymé), 178.

V

Vailland, Roger, 158, 165, 182-183.
Vaillant-Couturier, Paul, 48, 80.
Valéry, Paul, 7, 144n, 147, 161.
Valion (in *Le Fleuve rouge*), 259.
Vallée heureuse, La (Roy), 223-228.
Van der Meersch, Maxence, 48.
Vaudal, Jean, 158.

Vauvenargues, Luc de Clapiers, Marquis de, 126.
Véchard, Denise (in *Mon Village à l'heure allemande*), 151.
Vercors (pseud. of Jean Bruller), 158, 168, 248, 275.
Verdun (Romains), 54-57.
Verdurin, Madame (in *Le Temps retrouvé*), 4-5.
Vergniaud (in *Lectures pour une ombre*), 28.
Vernet, François, 158.
Vian, Boris, 183, 271.
Vidal-Naquet, Pierre, 279.
Vie des martyrs (Duhamel), 128-131, 133, 135.
Viet-Minh, Le (Fall), 260n.
Vigny, Alfred de, 12, 44, 136, 220-222, 271.
Vildrac, Charles, 60n, 158.
Villain, Raoul, 99.
Villon, François, 22.
Viollis, André, 118.
Voltaire, François Marie Arouet de, 46.
Vomécourt, Philippe de, 156.
Vonnegut, Jr., Kurt, 126, 226.
Voyage au bout de la nuit (Céline), 47.
«Voyage des amants, Le» (Romains), 52.
Vraies Richesses, Les (Giono), 108, 111-112.

W

Wagner, Richard, 5.
Watteau, Jean Antoine, 198.
Wazemmes (in *Les Hommes de bonne volonté*), 56.
Wellington, Duke of (Arthur Wellesley), 44.
Wells, H. G., 63, 67n.
Werner (in *Les Forêts de la nuit*), 169, 176, 180.
Werth, Alexander, 147, 258.
Werth, Léon, 48.
Weygand, General Maxime, 142.
Whitman, Walt, 130.
Wiechert, Ernst, 203.
Wiesel, Elie, 197, 200, 203-204, 213.

Wiesenthal, Simon, 207n, 213.
Wilhelm I, Kaiser, 142.
Wilhelm II, Kaiser, 5, 38.
Wilson Woodrow, 105.
Wouk, Herman, 232.

Y

Yacef, Saadi, 288.
Young Lions, The (Dmytryk), 168.

Yussef, Sidi Mohammed Ben, 234.

Z

Zarathustra (Nietzsche), 19.
Zimmer, Bernard, 158.
Zola, Émile, 13, 111, 129, 266.
Zweig, Stefan, 68.

SE TERMINÓ DE IMPRIMIR EN
LA CIUDAD DE MADRID EL DÍA
1 DE NOVIEMBRE DE 1978.

stuдia humanitatis

Louis Marcello La Favia, *Benvenuto Rambaldi da Imola: Dantista.* XII-188 pp. US $9.25.

John O'Connor, *Balzac's Soluble Fish.* XII-252 pp. US $14.25.

Carlos García, *La desordenada codicia,* edición crítica de Giulio Massano. XII-220 pp. US $11.50.

Everett W. Hesse, *Interpretando la Comedia.* XII-184 pp. US $10.00.

Lewis Kamm, *The Object in Zola's* Rougon-Macquart. XII-160 pp. US $9.25.

Ann Bugliani, *Women and the Feminine Principle in the Works of Paul Claudel.* XII-144 pp. US $9.25.

Charlotte Frankel Gerrard, *Montherlant and Suicide.* XVI-72 pp. US $5.00.

The Two Hesperias. Literary Studies in Honor of Joseph G. Fucilla. Edited by Americo Bugliani. XX-372 pp. US $30.00.

Jean J. Smoot, *A Comparison of Plays by John M. Synge and Federico García Lorca: The Poets and Time.* XII-220 pp. US $13.00.

Laclos. Critical Approaches to Les Liaisons dangereuses. Ed. Lloyd R. Free. XII-300 pp. US $17.00.

Julia Conaway Bondanella, *Petrarch's Visions and their Renaissance Analogues.* XII-120 pp. US $7.00.

Vincenzo Tripodi, *Studi su Foscolo e Stern.* XII-216 pp. US $13.00.

Lope de Vega, *El Amor enamorado,* critical edition of John B. Wooldridge, Jr. XII-236 pp. US $13.00.

Nancy Dersofi, *Arcadia and the Stage: A Study of the Theater of Angelo Beolco* (called *Ruzante*). XII-180 pp. US $10.00.

JOHN A. FREY, *The Aesthetics of the* ROUGON-MACQUART. XVI-356 pp. US $20.00.

CHESTER W. OBUCHOWSKI, *Mars on Trial: War as Seen by French Writers of the Twentieth Century.* XVI-320 pp. US $20.00.

FORTHCOMING PUBLICATIONS

El cancionero del Bachiller Jhoan Lopez, edición crítica de Rosalind Gabin.

Studies in Honor of Gerald E. Wade, edited by Sylvia Bowman, Bruno M. Damiani, Janet W. Díaz, E. Michael Gerli, Everett Hesse, John E. Keller, Luis Leal and Russell Sebold.

HELMUT HATZFELD, *Essais sur la littérature flamboyante.*

MARIO ASTE, *La narrativa di Luigi Pirandello: Dalle novelle al romanzo «Uno, Nessuno, e Centomila».*

JOSEPH BARBARINO, *The Latin Intervocalic Stops: A Quantitative and Comparative Study.*

NANCY D'ANTUONO, *Boccaccio's novelle in Lope's theatre.*

ANTONIO PLANELLS, *Cortázar: Metafísica y erotismo.*

Novelistas femeninas de la postguerra española, ed. Janet W. Díaz.

MECHTHILD CRANSTON, *Orion Resurgent: René Char, Poet of Presence.*

La Discontenta and La Pythia, edition with introduction and notes by Nicholas A. De Mara.

PERO LÓPEZ DE AYALA, *Crónica del Rey Don Pedro I,* edición crítica de Heanon and Constance Wilkins.

ALBERT H. LE MAY, *The Experimental Verse Theater of Valle-Inclán.*

JEREMY T. MEDINA, *Spanish Realism: Theory and Practice of a Concept in the Nineteenth Century.*

Robert H. Miller, ed. *Sir John Harington: A Supplie or Addicion to the «Catalogue of Bishops» to the Yeare 1608.*

María Elisa Ciavarelli, *La fuerza de la sangre en la literatura del Siglo de Oro.*

Mary Lee Bretz, *La evolución novelística de Pío Baroja.*

Dennis M. Kratz, *Mocking Epic.*